W9-DFQ-347

CARROLL COUNTY, GEORGIA

Pioneers

By Myron House Designer: Ozzie Binion

Best wishes,
Myron W House

CARROLL COUNTY, GEORGIA
Pioneers

SKETCHES OF EARLY SETTLERS
OF CARROLL COUNTY, GEORGIA
AND THEIR DESCENDANTS
SELECTED FROM NINETEENTH-
CENTURY BIOGRAPHICAL
SOURCES

Compiled By Myron Wade House

Published by Myron Wade House - 2009

SKETCHES OF
EARLY
SETTLERS
OF CARROLL
COUNTY,
GEORGIA
AND THEIR
DESCENDANTS
SELECTED FROM
NINETEENTH-
CENTURY
BIOGRAPHICAL
SOURCES

CARROLL COUNTY,
GEORGIA
PIONEERS

COMPILED BY
MYRON WADE HOUSE

DESIGNED BY
OZZIE BINION
2009

Published by the author

Printing by
GATEWAY PRINTING
925 Pacific Avenue
Bremen, GA 30110

Binding by
**NATIONAL LIBRARY
BINDERY of GEORGIA**
100 Hembree Park Drive
Roswell, GA 30076-3873

ISBN
9780982558300

First printing____63____ of 200

DEDICATION

To my mother-in-law Mary Martha Fox who upon my retirement made the first contribution to a publications fund

PREFACE

When the author retired from the University of West Georgia in 2006, he began work on a projected series of histories dealing with Carroll County and its early settlers. As one of the tasks in preparation for this undertaking, he commenced the collection of biographies of Carroll Countians and their descendants published in the multitude of biographical sources prolific in the last two decades of the nineteenth century.

This collection of biographical sketches continued until it became this present work. It is published by the author as a separate work standing on its own merits because rather than extract from the sketches herein presented only those portions of use to him in writing the history of Carroll County, the complete sketches are so interesting that he deemed it profitable to maintain them in their entirety, even though great portions of the sketches deal with other localities.

The author wishes to warn the reader of some caveats. First, the author does not claim to have consulted every biographical compilation published in the nineteenth century. A list of those sources consulted by the author follows this preface. The author tried to cover the Southeast well and the Western states to a lesser extent. Second, the author cannot claim to know every person who passed at one time or another through Carroll County and he may possibly have missed some sketches in these volumes he should have included. On the other hand, the author does have a great familiarity with the early families of the county and the reader will notice that many sketches included in this volume make no reference to Carroll County at all, their inclusion coming because the author recognized someone in the sketch as a former resident of Carroll County. A note at the end of these sketches will indicate why the author included those particular biographies.

In four or five instances, where lengthy original sketches had no paragraphing, the author created paragraphs for ease of reading.

Those individuals and institutions due thanks are many. My wife has supported me throughout the past year of gathering and typing. When I retired my mother-in-law made the first contribution to a publications fund and enough has been added to it to pay printing and binding this present volume. I want to thank individuals, especially Jan Ruskell and Dr. Keith Bohannon of the University of West Georgia, for suggesting sources I had not considered. I also want to thank Penny Enlund and all of those individuals who by their interest and inquiries as to how things were going with my research proved to be great encouragers and also made me hopeful that the results of the research would not go unappreciated. Ozzie Binion did the layout for this volume and I owe him a great debt of gratitude.

The author has visited numerous libraries including the Irvine Sullivan Ingram Library of the University of West Georgia, the Main Library at the University of Georgia, the Georgia Department of Archives and History, the Birmingham, Alabama, Public Library, the Chattanooga-Hamilton County Bicentennial Library, Chattanooga, Tennessee, the Washington Memorial Library (Macon, Georgia), the Simon Schwob Memorial Library of Columbus State University, the Main Branch of the Cobb County Public Libraries, Marietta, Georgia, the Central Library of the Atlanta-Fulton Public Library System, the J. D. Williams Library at the University of Mississippi, the Lafayette County-Oxford Public Library, Oxford, Mississippi, the Ladson Genealogical Library of the Vidalia-Toombs County Library of the Ohoopee Regional Library System, and the West Georgia Regional Library, Carrollton, Georgia. Finally this work could not have been completed without the interlibrary loan privileges extended by the University of West Georgia and the capable help of Angela Mehaffey of the Interlibrary Loan Department, Irvine Sullivan Ingram Library.

SOURCES

SOURCES CONSULTED IN COMPILING THIS WORK

GENERAL WORKS

Cathcart, William, ed. *The Baptist Encyclopedia.* 2 vols. Philadelphia: Louis H. Everts, 1881.

Evans, Clement A., ed. *Confederate Military History.* 12 vols. Atlanta: Confedrate Publishing Company, 1872.

The Encyclopedia of the New West, Containing Fully Authenticated Information of the Agricultural, Mercantile, Commercial, Manufacturing, Mining and Grazing Industries, and Representing the Character Development, Resources and Present Condition of Texas, Arkansas, Colorado, New Mexico and Indian Territory. Also Biographical Sketches of Their Representative Men and Women. Marshall, Texas: The United States Biographical Publishing Company, 1881.

ALABAMA

Brewer, W. *Alabama: Her History, Resources, War Record, and Public Men. From 1540 to 1872,* 1872.

Memorial Record of Alabama: A Concise Account of the Political, Military, Professional and Industrial Progress, Together With the Personal Memoirs of Many of Its People. 2 vols. Madison, Wis.: Brant & Fuller, 1893.

Northern Alabama Historical and Biographical. Birmingham, Ala.: Smith & DeLand, 1888.

Garrett, William. *Reminiscences of Public Men in Alabama, for Thirty Years.* Atlanta: Plantation Publishing Company's Press, 1872.

ARIZONA

A Historical and Biographical Record of the Territory of Arizona. Chicago: McFarland & Poole, 1896.

ARKANSAS

Biographical and Historical Memoirs of Benton, Washington, Carroll, Madison, Crawford, Franklin, and Sebastian Counties, Arkansas. Chicago: Goodspeed, 1899. Also known as *Biographical and Historical Memoirs of Northwest Arkansas.*

Biographical and Historical Memoirs of Eastern Arkansas. **Chicago: Goodspeed, 1890.**

Biographical and Historical Memoirs of Northeast Arkansas. **Chicago: Goodspeed, 1899.**

Biographical and Historical Memoirs of Pulaski, Jefferson, Lonoke, Faulkner, Grant, Saline, Perry, Garland and Hot Spring Counties, Arkansas. **Chicago: Goodspeed, 1889. Also known as** *Biographical and Historical Memoirs of Central Arkansas.*

Biographical and Historical Memoirs of Southern Arkansas. **Chicago: Goodspeed, 1890.**

Biographical and Historical Memoirs of Western Arkansas. **Chicago: Goodspeed, 1891.**

Hempstead, Fay. *A Pictorial History of Arkansas From Earliest Times to the Year 1890.* **St. Louis: N. D. Thompson Publishing Co.,1890.**

A Reminiscent History of the Ozark Region Comprising a Condensed General History, a Brief Descriptive History of Each County, and Numerous Biographical Sketches of Prominent Citizens of Such Counties. **Chicago: Goodspeed, 1894.**

CALIFORNIA

The Bay of San Francisco, the Metropolis of the Pacific Coast and its Suburban Cities: A History. **Volume 2. Biographical Sketches. Chicago: Lewis Publishing Company,1892.**

An Illustrated History of Southern California. **Chicago: Lewis Publishing Co., 1890.**

A Memorial and Biographical History of Northern California. **Chicago: Lewis Publishing Co., 1891.**

Memorial and Biographical History of the Coast Counties of Central California. **Chicago: Lewis Publishing Company. 1893.**

Memorial and Biographical History of the Counties of Fresno, Tulare, and Kern, California. **Chicago: Lewis Publishing Company, 1892.**

A Memorial and Biographical History of the Counties of Merced, Stanislaus, Calaveras, Tuolumne and Mariposa, California. **Chicago: Lewis Publishing Company, 1892.**

COLORADO

Legislative, Historical and Biographical Compendium of Colorado.

SOURCES

Denver: C. F. Coleman's Publishing House, 1887.

Portrait and Biographical Record of the State of Colorado Containing Portraits and Biographies of Many Well Known Citizens of the Past and Present. **Chicago: Chapman Publishing Company, 1899.**

FLORIDA

Biographical Souvenir of the States of Georgia and Florida, Containing Biographical Sketches of the Representative Public, and Many Early Settled Families in These States. **Chicago: F. A. Battey & Company, 1889.**

GEORGIA

Biographical Souvenir of the States of Georgia and Florida, Containing Biographical Sketches of the Representative Public, and Many Early Settled Families in These States. **Chicago: F. A. Battey & Company, 1889.**

Campbell, J. H. *Georgia Baptists: Historical and Biographical.* **Macon, Ga.: J. W. Burke & Co., 1874.**

History of the Baptist Denomination in Georgia: With Biographical Compendium and Portrait Gallery of Baptist Ministers and Other Georgia Baptists. **Atlanta: James P. Harrison & Co., 1881.**

Memoirs of Georgia. **2 vols. Atlanta: Southern Historical Association, 1895.**

IDAHO

An Illustrated History of the State of Idaho. **Chicago: Lewis Publishing Company, 1899.**

LOUISIANA

Biographical and Historical Memoirs of Louisiana. **2 vols. Chicago: Goodspeed, 1892.**

Biographical and Historical Memoirs of Northwest Louisiana. **Nashville: Southern Publishing Company, 1890.**

Perrin, William Henry, ed. *Southwest Louisiana Biographical and Historical.* **New Orleans: Gulf Publishing Company, 1891.**

MISSISSIPPI

Biographical and Historical Memoirs of Mississippi. 2 vols. Chicago: Goodspeed, 1891.

MISSOURI

A Reminiscent History of the Ozark Region Comprising a Condensed General History, a Brief Descriptive History of Each County, and Numerous Biographical Sketches of Prominent Citizens of Such Counties. Chicago: Goodspeed, 1894.

OREGON

Hines, H. K. *An Illustrated History of the State of Oregon.* Chicago: Lewis Publishing Company, 1893.

TEXAS

Biographical Souvenir of the State of Texas. Chicago: F. A. Battey & Company, 1889.

Brown, John Henry. *Indian Wars and Pioneers of Texas.* Austin, Texas: L. E. Daniell, 1890.

Memorial and Biographical History of Dallas County, Texas. Chicago: Lewis Publishing Company, 1892.

Memorial and Genealogical Record of Southwest Texas. Chicago: Goodspeed Brothers, 1894.

Memorial and Genealogical Record of Texas (East). Chicago: Goodspeed Brothers, 1895.

Z. T. ADAMS

Z. T. Adams, farmer, Temple, Carroll Co., Ga., son of Absalom and Elizabeth (Reid) Adams, was born in Carroll county in 1845. His grandparents, Adams, were Virginians, and moved thence to Tennessee, whence they subsequently came to Carroll county, where they died. Mr. Adams' father came from Tennessee to Georgia and settled in Carroll county in 1829, where he cleared a farm. He was a soldier in the Indian war of 1838. His great-grandfather on his mother's side, Reid, was a soldier in the war of 1812, during which he was shot in the stomach, the ball passing through the body. A silk handkerchief was drawn through the orifice afterward and he recovered and lived many years. His maternal grandparents, Reid, were early settlers in this part of the state. Mr. Adams was reared on the farm and received a common country school education. Being too young to enter the Confederate service he enlisted in 1863, in Company F (Capt. Long), Georgia regiment, state troops. Mr. Adams was married in 1864 to Miss Rebecca C. Coleman, daughter of W. A. and Sarah Ann (Barnes) Coleman, old settlers of this part of the state. When he was married he had nothing – was very poor. He has always been a plain farmer; has now a nice improved farm of nearly 200 acres with a comfortable house on it, within the corporate limits of Temple. Mr. and Mrs. Adams have had six children born to them: William M., born Nov. 14, 1865; Henry T., born Jan. 16, 1868, a teacher in Texas; David N., born July 11, 1869; Gilbert E., born Oct. 30, 1872; Z. T., born Nov. 22, 1876; and Bessie, born Feb. 10, 1884. Himself and wife are devoted and exemplary members of the Missionary Baptist church.

Source: *Memoirs of Georgia*, 1895. Volume 1.

GEORGE M. ADAMSON

Dr. George M. Adamson, farmer and physician of Lafayette Township, was born October 14, 1830, in Henry County, Ga., a son of William C. and Elizabeth (Crawly) Adamson, natives of Georgia. William C. Adamson was born in 1797, a son of Greenbury Adamson and ———— (Coats) Adamson, natives of Maryland and Georgia, respectively. Greenbury Adamson was born near Rockford, Md., a son of Seabron Adamson. Sebron Adamson was born in England, in Amsterdam City, of Scottish descent, and with Frederick Adamson came to the United States before the Revolutionary War (in which they both served), settling in Maryland. The paternal grandmother was of Scotch descent. William C. Adamson, father of our subject, was a large planter of Georgia, owning about 1,000 acres of land, and from fifteen to twenty slaves. He died July 13, 1879. Elizabeth (Crawly) Adamson was a daughter of Charles Crawly, who was born in Virginia about 1750, and died in 1850. She died December 25, 1865. She was the mother of ten children, seven of whom are still living, viz.: Charles Quincy (a merchant of Atlanta, Ga.), William L. (a farmer and merchant of Carroll County, Ga.), Nancy C. (now Mrs. Milton Dorough, of Bowdon, Ga.), George M. (the subject of this sketch), Simon Frederick (a farmer of Alabama), Samuel M. (a farmer and Baptist minister of Alabama), and James Greenbury (a farmer of Carroll County, Ga.). Those deceased are Augustus M. (died in Henry County, Ga.), Nathaniel T. (died while in the Confederate army), and John W. who died in Bowdon, Ga.). John W. Adamson moved to the locality where Bowdon was afterward established, in 1854, and was one of the founders of that place. He had a family of nine children, all of whom received a good education, two becoming prominent lawyers and well-known men. Dr. G. M. Adamson, our subject, was educated at Bowdon, Ga. He studied medicine in an office in Randolph County, Ala., and then attended the medical college at Augusta, Ga. In 1859 he came to Arkansas, locating in Lafayette County, where he commenced to practice medicine. In 1863 he went to Columbia County, where he remained until 1867, when he returned to this county, locating on his present farm, and has since been engaged in the practice of his profession and farming. He has always enjoyed a good practice, and has been equally as successful in farming, owning 360 acres of land, 240 acres where he lives, and 120 acres of timber land, and has over 100 acres under cultivation, raising cotton principally. Dr. Adamson was married January 1, 1861, to Miss Martha C. Butler, born in South Carolina (Orangeburg District), June 28, 1830, a daughter of Thomas and Rachel Butler, natives of South Carolina, and the fruits of this union have been five children, three of whom are still living, viz.: Elizabeth Elenor (was born in Columbia County, June 15, 1864, and was married to John W. Wilson, December 31, 1884, is now the mother of three children, viz.: George Robert, Martha Madieleine and Elizabeth Hattie Dee; she is now living in this township), Martha Lee (was born in Columbia County, September 10, 1865, was married to

GEORGE M. ADAMSON

Daniel Green Jeffus, September 16, 1886, and is now the mother of two children, only one living, viz., Martha Cathrine, now living in this township), Madieleine Nancy (was born in Ouachita County, December 23, 1870, still at home with her parents). Dr. Adamson, Mrs. Adamson and three children are members of the Methodist Protestant Church. The Doctor is a member of the Masonic order, and of the County Wheel. His wife and three daughters are members of the O. E. S. He is a leading Democrat, and one of the best known men in the county, and takes an active interest in all laudable public enterprises.

Source: *Biographical and Historical Memoirs of Southern Arkansas,* **1890.**

GEORGE R. ADAMSON

G. R. Adamson, merchant, Bowdon, Carroll Co., Ga., son of John W. and Mary Ann (McDaniel) Adamson, was born in Henry county, Ga., in 1842. His paternal grandparents were William C. and Elizabeth (Crawley) Adamson. He was born in Wilkes county, Ga., and she was a native of Morgan, where they were married. Mr. Adamson's father was born in Morgan county in 1822, where he was reared and educated. About the time he reached his majority he went to Henry county, settled in the woods and cleared a farm. In 1852 he loaded his ox carts and moved to Carroll county, and again settled in the woods and cleared another farm. A few years after this he went over into Chambers county, Ala., settled in the woods and cleared a third farm. But he liked Georgia too well to be satisfied, so he returned to Carroll county, and for the fourth time settled in the woods and cleared a farm – the subject of this sketch helping him in all, particularly the last three. In 1860 he began the mercantile business in Bowdon, but the war coming on the business collapsed, and everything was lost. In 1862 his father enlisted in Capt. Estes' company, Twenty-sixth Georgia battalion; served through the war – and was at Columbus about the time of the surrender, but escaped being captured. After the war he went into business again at Bowdon, and continued it until he died in 1888.

In 1861 Mr. Adamson enlisted in Company B (Capt. Charles A. McDaniel), Cobb's legion, infantry. Capt. McDaniel was president of the college at Bowdon, and his company was mostly comprised of his pupils, of whom Mr. Adamson was one. He was an active participant n many battles, among them – Dam No. 1, Yorktown, Malvern hill,n many battles, among them – Dam No. 1, Yorktown, Malvern hill, i and South mountain, where he was severely wounded and captured, but was released. As a result of this wound he was disabled, but as soon as he recovered he returned to the army, in Tennessee. Thence he went to Virginia and was at the battle of the Wilderness. While his command was on duty on James river he was released on account of his old wound and returned home. While at Bowdon he was captured a second time, but it happened to be after the surrender. The close of the war left him comparatively destitute. Thus father and son, by their bravery and long continued faithful service, made a record of which they rightly felt proud.

After the war he engaged with his father in business; but when he married, he went to another point, where he remained until his father's death, in 1888; when he returned in 1889 to Bowdon, took charge of and continued his father's business, and is now a leading merchant there. Everything, immediate family connections, natural and by marriage, war record, and splendid business capacity, contributed to this result. Mr. Adamson was married in 1868 to Miss Fannie M. Yarbrough – born in Floyd county, Ga., in 1851 – daughter of Nathan and Margaret (Lampkin) Yarbrough. Her father was born and reared in Franklin county, Ga., and went to DeKalb county, and clerked in a store in Decatur. In 1835 he went to Floyd county, and was one of the pioneers, if not one of the founders, and wrote the first charter of the now flourishing city of Rome. Years afterward he migrated to Texas, and is now living – 85 years of age – in Comanche county. To Mr. and Mrs. Adamson ten children have been born: Edith, John, Herbert, Ralph, Norma (dead), Claris, Mattie, Ethel, Robert and Nathan. Mr. Adamson is a master and royal arch Mason, and himself and wife are members of the Methodist Protestant church.

Source: *Memoirs of Georgia*, 1895. Volume 1.

WILLIAM CHARLES ADAMSON

William Charles Adamson, Judge of the City Court of Carrollton, Ga., was born in Bowdon, Carroll County, Ga., August 13, 1854, and is a son of John W. and Mary A. (McDaniel) Adamson, the former a merchant in Georgia, and the latter a daughter of John McDaniel of Georgia. William Charles is one of nine children born to his parents, six of whom are living. He received his education in

WILLIAM CHARLES ADAMSON

Bowdon College, Ga., graduating with the degree of A. B. in 1874, and then for a time assisting his father in the mercantile business until he began to read law with Judge S. W. Harris. He was admitted to the bar in October, 1876, and practiced with good success in Carrollton, Ga., until he was appointed to his present office in December, 1884. In 1885 he received from the same college the degree of A. M. Judge Adamson also practices outside his own court and stands among the foremost of his profession. He married Miss Minna Reese, daughter of Rev. A. C. Reese, of Georgia, January 29, 1885, and has had born to him two children – Charles and Reese. He is a Master Mason, a member of the I. O. O. F., also holds membership in the Royal Arcanum, and with his wife is a consistent member of the Methodist Protestant Church.

Source: *Biographical Souvenir of the States of Georgia and Florida*, 1889.

WILLIAM J. ALEXANDER

William J. Alexander was born in Calhoun County, Ala., in May, 1842, and is a son of Arthur T. and Rebecca (Borden) Alexander.

The senior Mr. Alexander was born in North Carolina, and when a child taken by his parents to Habersham County, and thence to Carroll County, Ga. He came to Calhoun County, this State, in 1832, and settled eight miles east of Cross Plains (now in Cleburne County), where his father entered lands and improved them. He died in 1851, and a few months later his wife followed him. They left two sons and four daughters, all of whom lived to maturity. The Alexanders and Bordens are of English ancestry.

The subject of this sketch was reared on a farm, received a common-school education, and at the age of seventeen years began life as a farmer, which he has continued ever since.

In July, 1861, he enlisted in Company I, Twenty-fifth Alabama Infantry, and was in the first battle of Farmersville, Tenn., south of Shiloh. He participated in the Kentucky invasion, was taken prisoner at Glasgow, Ky., and was exchanged about two months later. He joined his regiment again at Shelbyville, Tenn., and was in the battles of Chickamauga, Missionary Ridge, in all the fights from Chattanooga to Atlanta and New Hope Church to Atlanta. When Hood made his raid into Tennessee our subject joined Wheeler's cavalry, with which command he remained until the surrender.

At the close of the war he resumed farming. In 1871 he was appointed sheriff of Cleburne County, and in 1874 was elected to that office. He served in this capacity about six years. In 1878 he was elected to the Lower House of the Legislature, reelected in 1882, and in 1884 was elected to the Senate from his district, which office he holds at the present writing (1888). Mr. Alexander was married in August, 1866, to Sarah Cornelia, daughter of Henry A. Smith, of Floyd County, Ga. This union has been blessed with two children, William H. and Bessie E.

Mr. Alexander and wife are members of the Christian Church.
Source: *Northern Alabama Historical and Biographical*, 1888.

C. G. ALMAND

C. G. Almand, a most worthy citizen of Talladega, was born in Atlanta, Ga., in 1847. He was a son of Azman R. and Jane (Hayes) Almand, the former of whom was a Baptist minister for twenty-five years of his life, and managed a large plantation in connection therewith. C. G. Almand was reared on the farm, and had but limited educational advantages, because of the breaking out of the war when he was only fourteen years of age. In 1863 he enlisted in company I, Second Georgia state troops, and served until Lee's surrender. He had fought in some very severe engagements, being with Gen. Johnston on his great retreat, fighting at Kennesaw Mountain and at Marietta, and in the skirmishing down to Atlanta. At Atlanta he was taken sick and furloughed home. While he was in the severe battles mentioned and others, beside many skirmishes, he was wounded only once, and then but slightly, and had his clothing shot through on several occasions. After the war he returned to Georgia, and began life as a farmer. In 1871 he married Mrs. Ada C. (Rainey) Cox, daughter of Etheldredge and Elizabeth (Johnson) Rainey, both of whom were natives of Georgia. To this marriage of C. G. Almand there were born three children, viz.: Albert R., Estelle and Harry. The mother of these children was raised in Georgia. Both Mr. and Mrs. Almand are members of the Baptist church. He is a member of the Knights of Pythias, Knights of Honor and Odd Fellows. In 1881 he removed to

C. G. ALMAND

Talladega and established himself in the lumber business. He manufactures his own lumber, having a large saw mill, and employing twelve men. Mr. Almand is one of Talladega's best citizens, throughly honest and reliable in every way.

Source: *Memorial Record of Alabama*, 1893. Volume 2.

Note: C. G. Almand was residing with his parents in Carroll County, Georgia in 1860 in the Bowdon District. Both of his parents are buried in the Bowdon Methodist Church cemetery. His father died in 1860 and his mother died in 1867.

JAMES W. ANDERSON

Capt. James W. Anderson, son of William U. and Mary Ann (Potts) Anderson, was born in Coweta county, Ga., in March, 1835. His father was born in Coweta county in 1808. He was reared on a farm, and had but little education. During his life he kept a record of the noted historical events which affected Coweta county, and in 1880 had them published in book form, which is interesting and very reliable as to dates. He was an uncompromising democrat and a great worker for the party, but would never accept office except once, when he was assistant warden of the penitentiary under Gov. Johnson. He was one of the thirteen original members of the Baptist church at Newnan. His father, the grandfather of Capt. J. W. Anderson, was a soldier both in the revolutionary war and the war of 1812. Mrs. Anderson, the mother of J. W. Anderson, was a daughter of James Potts, who was a soldier in the revolutionary war, and was one of the pioneer settlers of Coweta county, Ga. James W. Anderson, the subject of this sketch, was reared in Coweta county, and received but a very limited education. In April, 1861, he enlisted in Company A, First Georgia regiment, and was present in the first battle in which his company was engaged, and was with it until the close of the war. He was with his company at the retreat of Laurel hill and Greenbrier river under Gen. Jackson. After the battle of Cheat mountain, their time being out, the entire company was discharged; but after being home one month Mr. Anderson enlisted in a company known as the Newnan guards, Twelfth Georgia battalion of artillery, with which he remained through the war. He was adjutant of the first company he was in, and in 1863 was elected captain. He went out in the Twelfth Georgia battalion, though, as first lieutenant. His company, after its reorganization, was ordered to go to Gen, Bragg with the artillery, and went through Kentucky, after which it was transferred to the infantry, but still drew pay as artillery. They then went through the country as far as Charleston, S. C., and served there during the whole siege. In 1864 he was wounded at Winchester, Va., being shot through the thighs, which rendered him unfit for further service. After the war he returned to Coweta county, and began at first as a contractor and builder, working at this several years. He finally saved up a sufficient amount of money to purchase a farm, where he remained until he moved to Newnan. In 1875 he was elected sheriff of Coweta county, serving six years. In 1866 he was married to Miss Sarah, daughter of Joseph and Elizabeth (Rollen) Brown; this lady died in a very short time, and in 1879 he married Elizabeth Blankenship, daughter of Francis and Sarah (Curtis) Blankenship, the former of whom was a native of Tennessee and came to Georgia in 1847. Mrs. Anderson was born and reared in Georgia, and is a member of the M. E. church, while her husband is a member of the Presbyterian. Mr. Anderson is a member of the masonic fraternity and is one of the leading citizens of the town.

Source: *Memoirs of Georgia*, 1895. Volume 1.

Note: In 1860 James W. Anderson was residing in Carrollton, Georgia. His occupation was listed as printer. In fact James W. Anderson was printing *The Carrollton Advocate*, Carrollton's first newspaper. The Civil War and military service brought an end to the newspaper. On December 9, 1866 Anderson married Sarah M. Brown in Coweta County, Georgia. The 1870 Census shows James and his wife in Carroll County again, his occupation being that of cabinet workman. The couple returned to Coweta County and both are buried there in Oak Hill Cemetery in Newnan.

HENRY CLAY ARNALL

Henry Clay Arnall, a successful merchant of Newnan, Ga., was born in Coweta County, Ga., May 17, 1850. His father, John G., a native of Putnam County, Ga., and a planter by occupation, died in 1873, at the age of sixty-three years. He was a son of Golston Arnall, who was born in Philadelphia, Pa. John G. Arnall married Miss Ann Gibbs, a native of Walton County, Ga., who died in 1873. She bore

HENRY CLAY ARNALL

her husband ten children, viz.: Elizabeth, James M., William T., John G., Martha C., Louisa, Almeda, Henry Clay, Joshua F., and Francis M. Henry C. Arnall was educated in the common schools of Coweta County. He opened a general store in Newnan when but twenty years of age, and this enterprise has steadily grown and prospered since. Mr. Arnall is one of the energetic citizens of Newnan, and is held in high esteem in that place. He was a member of the city council for two terms. In 1874 he married Miss Sallie K. Wynn, daughter of G. O. and A. P. (Lumpkin) Wynn, of Coweta County, Ga. To their marriage has been born six children: Anna P., Henry C., Jr., Alton W., Joseph G., Frank and Katie. Mr. Arnall is a member of the I. O. O. F. and the Baptist Church.

Source: *Biographical Souvenir of the States of Georgia and Florida*, 1889.

Note: Henry Clay Arnall's brother, John Gibbs Arnall, was a resident of Villa Rica District in 1870. John Gibbs Arnall was a physician.

MERRILL C. AWTREY

Merrill C. Awtrey was born in what is now Walton County, Ga., July 18, 1816. His father (Jacob) was born in Greene County, Ga., April 22, 1789. He moved to Carroll County, Ga., in the early part of this century where he died. He was by occupation a farmer and was a son of Absalom Awtrey, a native of South Carolina, who had ten children. Jacob was the eighth child, and was married in 1809 to Miss Nancy, daughter of John and Anaomi (Camp) Hill, natives of North Carolina. The fruit of this union was nine children who lived to maturity. The subject of this sketch was the second child born to them. He was reared on the farm and educated in the common schools. In 1835 he commenced the mercantile business in Carroll County and continued the same there until 1851, when he removed to Acworth, Ga., where he has been in business ever since with the exception of the period of the late war. The firm is now known as M. C. & O. Awtrey. September 5, 1842, he was united in marriage with Sarah, daughter of Sarah (Moody) and Joseph Chambers, of Carroll County, Ga., but originally from North Carolina. Mr. Awtrey is a member of the primitive Baptist Church, and in politics is a Democrat.

Source: *Biographical Souvenir of the States of Georgia and Florida*, 1889.

Noel P. Baker is the present efficient justice of the peace in Ward 3, De Soto Parish, La., and is also engaged in tilling the soil, his plantation, which is seven miles southwest of Mansfield consisting of 160 acres, all of which he has obtained by his own unaided efforts. He was born in Coosa County, Ala., in 1848, and is a son of Joseph Cannon and Rebecca (Knight) Baker, who were born in South Carolina in 1804 and 1807, respectively, their marriage taking place in 1825. They first removed from their native State to Georgia and thence to Alabama, thence, in 1866, to De Soto Parish, La. Mr. Baker died here the following year, having been a member of the Methodist Church, and his widow, who survives him, is also a member. He was a wheelwright and blacksmith and socially was a member of the A. F. & A. M. His father, William Baker, the grandfather of Noel P., was born in England and died in South Carolina. Enoch Knight, the mother's father, spent his life in Georgia and died in Alabama. Noel P. Baker is the tenth of eleven children, four sons and two daughters living, and was reared on a farm, receiving a common-school education. He came with his parents to De Soto Parish, and was here married in 1873 to Miss Martha B., daughter of Thomas and Dorinda Lawrence, the former of whom was born in South Carolina and the latter in Alabama. About the year 1857 they came to De Soto Parish, and here Mr. Lawrence passed from life in 1872, his widow dying in 1889, she being an earnest member of the Presbyterian Church. He was a soldier in the Confederate army for four years. Mrs. Baker was born in Alabama in 1856 and her marriage with Mr. Baker has resulted in the birth of five children, two sons and two daughters living. They have resided on their present farm since 1874. Mr. Baker held the office of constable from 1879 to 1883, and since 1883 he has been justice of the peace; is also road and bridge commissioner and was one of the census enumerators of De Soto Parish, La., for the United States in June, 1890. He is a Methodist and his wife is a Cumberland Presbyterian.

Source: *Biographical and Historical Memoirs of Northwest Louisiana,* 1890.

Note: Joseph C. Baker and family were residents of District 713 in Carroll County in 1840.

B. F. BALLARD

B. F. Ballard, conceded to be among the prosperous farmers of Hot Springs Township, Garland County, Ark., was the oldest in a family of ten children born to Eli Ballard and Sethenia (McVen) Ballard, natives of Georgia. His birth occurred in Georgia in 1837. His father, who was reared on a farm, received a limited education in youth, and was married in 1836, rearing a family which consisted of four boys and six girls: B. F. (the subject of this biography), Robert M. (deceased), W. B., Joshua, Cassandra, Elizabeth, Rachel, Martha J., Maria and Catharine. Mrs. Ballard died in 1883, as a member of the Methodist Episcopal Church. Mr. Ballard is a stanch Democrat. B. F. Ballard was educated in the common schools of Georgia, and began farming for himself in 1855. The following year he married Eliza Strickler, daughter of Roswell Strickler, of Georgia. Subsequently the affairs of ordinary life were interrupted by war troubles, and, in 1862, Mr. Ballard enlisted in the Fifty-sixth Regiment Arkansas Infantry, Company A, under Capt. Brewster, remaining in service until the surrender, in 1865, at Greensboro, in North Carolina. He participated in nearly all of the principal engagements. Mr. and Mrs. Ballard are the parents of nine children, four of whom are deceased: Julian (deceased), Caria (now Mrs. Bworo), Mary (deceased), Eddie, Russie E., John W., Martha J. (deceased), Eli (deceased) and Alphonso. Mr. Ballard owns 150 acres of fine land, and ranks among the influential and enterprising citizens of the township. He is a Democrat in politics. Mrs. Ballard is a member of the Baptist Church.

Source: *Biographical and Historical Memoirs of Pulaski, Jefferson, Lonoke, Faulkner, Grant, Saline, Perry, Garland and Hot Spring Counties, Arkansas,* 1889.

Note: Eli Ballard and family were residing in the Second District of Carroll County in 1860.

JAMES JETHRO BARNES

James Jethro Barnes, present sheriff of Fulton county, Ga., was born in Fayette county (now known as Clayton) on April 10, 1840. He resided in this locality until nineteen years old, attending school in the adjoining town of Jonesboro. In 1859 he accompanied his parents to Bowdon, Ga., and there entered Bowdon college. In June, 1861, he left the recitation room for the camp and bivouac. At the first approach of war he enlisted as a private in Cobb's legion and served as such in that command throughout the conflict. At South Mountain, Md., Mr. Barnes received a painful gun-shot wound, being shot through the left knee and was captured and held prisoner for three months. On recovering he immediately rejoined the army, but after an examination the leading surgeons pronounced him totally unfit for field service and he was given light duties in a hospital at Richmond, Va. This indolent, inactive, routine life proved of great annoyance to his restless, patriotic spirit. He refused to stay, and eluding the vigilant watch of those in charge availed himself of a favorable opportunity and made his escape, and by much exertion reached his command about one week before the battle of Gettysburg, in which he participated. He then destroyed the discharge he had received before this battle, which granted a furlough on the grounds of physical disability, because of his reluctance to leave the army, and remained with his company until the same was captured at the close of the last campaign. At Cold Harbor, Drewry's Bluff, Petersburg and in many other minor engagements Mr. Barnes conducted himself in a fearless, daring manner that elicited the praise of his comrades. When the surrender betokened peace and union, he was furnished transportation from Newport News to Savannah, and walked from there to Waynesboro, Ga., and there received additional transportation to Augusta, Ga., and on to Atlanta. From this city he returned to Carroll county and found his father bankrupt, having lost everything. Thinking a more encouraging business outlook could be found in Atlanta he came back and worked three months for his board alone, and afterwards secured a position with Peter Lynch, who kept then, as now, a general store at 95 Whitehall street, at seventy-five dollars per month. He worked in this establishment for nine months, and on leaving Mr. Lynch entered into partnership with W. M. Middlebrook, the style of the firm being Middlebrook & Barnes, which continued through the year 1872. Early in 1873 he went into the wholesale produce and commission business. This is still operating in his name. In 1879 Mr. Barnes was elected to the city council and served two years as representative of the First ward. In 1891 he was made deputy sheriff under J. W. Morrow, and during 1893 was placed in the office of sheriff, and re-elected in the fall of 1894. Mr. Barnes was married in 1868to Miss Cordelia V., daughter of John T. Hall of Atlanta. They have a pleasant family,

JAMES JETHRO BARNES

consisting of three sons and one daughter, as follows: William H., Mary H., James J., Jr., and John S. Mr. Barnes is a member of the I. O. O. F. and the encampment. He belongs to the camp of United Confederate Veterans of Fulton county and rejoices in a reunion where, with friends and old messmates, he recounts the glories and hardships and humor of camp-life. Mr. Barnes is a sturdy supporter of right and honor, and believes that only useful, capable and honest men should hold public office.

Source: *Memoirs of Georgia*, 1895. Volume 1.

JAMES BARROW

He first saw the light in Washington county, Georgia, on the 25th of December, 1801. His father, Moses Barrow, died when he was only three days old, and his mother afterwards married Charles Thompson. At ten he lost his mother, whose last words made a salutary impression on his heart. She gave him the excellent advice: "Follow the people of God, and at the end of that race you will find your mother."

Mr. Barrow was married in 1825 to Lucy Bivins, of Baldwin county, and settled in Upson county, where he united with the church at Antioch, on the third Sabbath in April, 1827, being baptized by Rev. Jacob King. He moved to Talbot county in 1833, residing there nine years, laboring as a mechanic, and preaching as he had opportunity. He settled in Carroll county in 1842, and was ordained at the Carrollton church in 1850. For twelve ensuing years he labored as a missionary for the Marion Board, in Western Georgia and Eastern Alabama, doing faithful service in the Master's cause. He then labored for four years as missionary for the Liberty Association, Alabama, and one year for the Arbacoochee Association. Since 1866 he has been traveling as "a volunteer soldier" for Christ, preaching wherever he has an opportunity, and supported by the voluntary contributions of the brethren.

He is instant in season and out of season, ready to comfort the brethren, warn sinners, and persuade the young. His style of preaching is hortatory, and is characterized by and earnest desire to instil the principles of pure and undefiled religion into the minds of all. A prominent trait in him is the desire to win souls for Jesus; and he has by his success in doing so made full proof of his ministry.

His ardent love for the house of God is well known; and to him no place is so sweet as the assembly of the saints. Like David, his heart is "glad when they say, let us go into the house of the Lord." For four years after the death of his wife, who was fatally burned in 1873, he was absent from the house of worship four Sabbaths only.

This venerable servant of God is now seventy nine years old. He has five children — two sons and three daughters — and about fifty grandchildren. He has long been grievously afflicted in his arms and limbs, and is totally unable to walk without crutches. His afflictions and his life of faithful service to the cause of Christ have endeared him to his brethren, appealing strongly and tenderly to their sympathies.

Source: *History of the Baptist Denomination in Georgia,* 1881.

JAMES BARROW

Rev. James Barrow, and aged and decrepit, but zealous and useful minister of Bowdon, Ga., was born in Washington County, Dec. 25, 1801. He connected himself with the church at Antioch, Upson Co., April 3, 1827, and soon began to preach. He settled in Carroll County in 1842, and was ordained at Carrollton church in 1850. For the next twelve years of his life he labored as a missionary of the Domestic Board of the Southern Baptist Convention, in Western Georgia and Eastern Alabama, and then, for the five succeeding years, he was an associational missionary. Since that time rheumatism has laid its hands heavily upon him, disabling him from all active work, and he has simply preached wherever an opportunity has been afforded. His controlling desire is to win souls to Jesus, and to accomplish this he is instant in season and out of season. His has been a life of faithful service in the face of many disadvantages and discouragements.

Source: Cathcart, ed. *The Baptist Encyclopedia,* vol. 1, 83.

WALTER C. BASKIN

Dr. Walter C. Baskin, a well-to-do farmer and prominent physician of Coat's Bend, Etowah county, Ala., was born on the 18th

WALTER C. BASKIN

of October, 1832, in Carroll county, Ga., the son of James and Henrietta (Williams) Baskin. His father was a native of South Carolina, and removed when a young man to Gwinnett county, Ga. He was a well-known minister of the Methodist church. He was for many years a magistrate, and a man of ability and energy, and died in 1882, aged eighty-eight. Four of his children, out of a family of ten, are living: James L., of Carroll county, Ga.; Mary A., widow of Dr. J. D. Thompson, East Point, Ga.; W. C., and Clark W. of Carroll county, Ga. The mother died in 1872. The great-grandfather, William Baskin, was a native of Ireland, and came to America and settled in South Carolina before the Revolutionary war. Dr. Baskin's mother was born and brought up in Columbia, S. C. At the age of twenty-four years, Dr. Baskin commenced the study of medicine with Dr. M. W. Gray, of Carroll county, and attended lectures at Macon, Ga., where he graduated in 1858 and came to Turkeytown, Etowah county, and engaged in the practice of medicine and farming. He married December 6, 1859, in Etowah county, Martha J. Prater, daughter of A. J. Prater, and they have one child – Herschel V. During the war the doctor served first as surgeon, and after the fall of Fort Donelson was made assistant surgeon. He has made a good success of life, owning a beautiful home in the valley of the Coosa river, and a farm of three hundred acres. He enjoys a large practice. Politically he is a peoples party man, a royal arch Mason, and a member of the Methodist Episcopal church.

Source: *Memorial Record of Alabama*, 1893. Volume 1.

M. M. BAXTER

M. M. Baxter is a son of Nathan Baxter, who was born in Georgia, November 15, 1802, a farmer and miller by occupation, and he was also born there, his birth occurring on March 15, 1834. His native State continued to be his home until 1864, at which time he removed to Indiana, but in 1869 came to his present location in Arkansas. He started out to fight his own way in the world at the age of eighteen years, in Pauline [sic.] County, Ga., and for many years has had the reputation of being an exceptionally fine cabinet-maker and millwright. He has owned his present farm of 290 acres since 1874, and as a tiller of the soil holds a prominent place among the agriculturalists of this section. His land averages one bale of cotton to every three acres, but he has frequently raised one bale to the acre. The average yield of corn is twenty bushels to the acre, but forty bushels are often raised, and he also has abundant harvests of the smaller grains. He was married on January 6, 1856, to a daughter of William Watson, of Georgia, who is now engaged in farming in Arkansas, having come to this State in 1868. Mr. Baxter and his wife are the parents of the following children: Wesley H., Emily Elizabeth (wife of Cornelius Brown), John Marion, Eliza Dora (wife of William Asbury), Martha Ellen (wife of W. A. Mauldin), Mary Missouri, Millie L. (deceased), Margaret Alice (wife of William H. Turner), Robert Lee, Delana Adaline, Emma Ada, Sanford Richard, Thomas Jackson and William Mitchell. Mr. Baxter is a Democrat, and he and wife are members of the Missionary Baptist Church. His paternal grandfather was born in North Carolina, an Englishman by descent, his father having been born in that country, and come to America with Sir Walter Raleigh.

Source: *Biographical and Historical Memoirs of Southern Arkansas,* 1890.

Note: Nathan [Nathaniel] Baxter was a resident of Carroll County, Georgia in 1840. See 1840 Census. Nathan's wife was Elizabeth Bone. They were married in Madison County, Georgia July 23, 1829.

MOSES J. BAXTER

Moses J. Baxter, farmer, Temple, Carroll Co., Ga., son of John and Elizabeth (Stripling) Baxter, was born in Monroe county, Ga., in 1828. His paternal grandparents were John and Nancy (Dowdy) Baxter. His grandfather was born in England, and came to this country after the revolutionary war. He settled first in Virginia, afterward moved to North Carolina, and finally came all the way from North Carolina to Georgia in an ox cart, and settled in the woods in Monroe county — among the pioneers. He followed farming all his life. He was a soldier of the war of 1812, and during his service had a remarkable experience with a wound. The ball went entirely through his body, and a silk handkerchief was drawn through the orifice, yet he recovered and lived many years in excellent health afterward. Mr. Baxter's father was born in 1807, and came to Georgia when a small boy with his father, who came to Carroll county in 1828; the subject of this sketch was an

MOSES J. BAXTER

infant at the time, and the unconscious subject of a thrilling incident. The trip had been made in ox-carts, and when they reached the Chattahoochee river a negro nurse insisted on taking the baby in her arms. When the boat reached the opposite bank, the steers became scared and backed, and the negro jumped overboard with our subject in her arms. When she arose to the surface his father caught and drew them out. His father was a soldier in the Indian war of 1836; and, also, was a member of the Methodist church. His maternal grandparents, John and Mary Stripling, were among the early settlers of Monroe county. Mr. Baxter was reared on the farm in Carroll county, and the very limited education he received was the old time dirt floor log house, with its unsatisfactory accompaniments. In 1862 he enlisted in Company F, Cobb's legion, and went to the front. But he was soon taken sick and was sent to Richmond, where he remained many months, and when he had apparently recovered he returned to the army. It was not long before he was again prostrated, and, this time, came home on a furlough – he was at home at the time of the surrender. Like thousands of others, the war left him stripped of everything; but like them, he went bravely to work, impaired in health as he was, to build up. By dint of hard work and close management he has a fine, large farm, well improved, with nice dwelling and substantial out buildings, half a mile from Temple; and commands the respect of all who know him. Mr. Baxter was married in 1852 to Miss Sarah J., daughter of James and Elizabeth (Baskin) Stripling, early settlers, by whom he has had eight children: William A., N. N., James D., Robert A., John M., Geo., Ann Florence, Frances, and Martha. Mr. Baxter is a master Mason and himself and wife are members of the Methodist church.

Source: *Memoirs of Georgia*, 1895. Volume 1.

BROOK BEALL

Brook Beall was born in Holmes county, Mississippi, August 16, 1830. His father, Josiah Beall, was a native of Cobb county, Georgia, was born in 1805, and when a small boy was taken by his parents to Mississippi, where he remained until his death, which occurred in 1867. He was a farmer and never gave his attention to public affairs. His wife, who bore the maiden name of Nancy Dent, a daughter of Thomas Dent, was born in Carroll county, Georgia, and died in 1877.

BROOK BEALL

Brook Beall, the subject of this brief memoir, received his early training at the district school near his home in Mississippi. He lived in that State until coming to Texas in 1852. He enlisted in 1862 in company C, under Captain Dougherty, DeMoss' regiment, Confederate army, and served two years, when he was discharged, In 1851 he married Miss Angelina, a daughter of Archibald Green. Angelina Green was born January 5, 1837. They now have one child, named Thomas D. Mr. Beall owns 320 acres of land, mostly under cultivation.

Source: *Biographical Souvenir of the State of Texas*, 1889.

FRED BEALL

A prominent lawyer of West Point, Clay county, Miss., is Capt. Fred Beall, who was born July 10, 1837, in Campbell county, Ga. His father, Noble P. Beall, was born in 1799, and was a son of Gen. Frederick Beall, for many years a leader in the military and public affairs of Georgia. Gen. Frederick Beall was a native of Virginia, but came with his parents at an early day to South Carolina, and thence he moved to Georgia, and after an active and successful life of sixty years or more died in Campbell county, respected and loved by all who knew him, for he had been the friend of all, the poor and oppressed as well as the rich and high-born. The mother of Capt. Fred Beall was Justianna D., daughter of Capt. Matthew Hooper. She was born in 1801 in Anderson district, S. C. Her father was an intelligent merchant, of broad and extensive culture. He was a fine classical scholar, and in his old age found great pleasure in reading Virgil and Horace and other like authors. Noble P. Beall and Justianna D. Hooper were married when they were respectively nineteen and seventeen years of age, and lived happily together for sixty years, each attaining the advanced age of seventy-nine. Noble P. Beall was twice completely broken up, and all his property swept from him on account of security debts, incurred by him for the benefit of relatives, but with that indomitable energy which he possessed, he never surrendered to misfortune, but renewed his efforts at every adversity, and with the help and encouragement which his noble wife ever gave him, he bravely encountered, and successfully overcame every obstacle and difficulty in life. In 1839 he, with his brother-in-law, Col. James D. Wood, moved with their families to Tishomingo county, Miss., and bought large bodies of land near

FRED BEALL

Eastport, on the Tennessee river. This was then a wild and unsettled part of the state; there was not even a cornmill in the county; they ground their corn on handmills, like the old-fashioned coffeemill. In this new and untried land Noble P. Beall began life anew. He opened up a fine plantation, which he successfully operated until he was again broken up by the devastations of the Federal army, which invaded that part of the state in 1862, and carried off all his slaves, horses, mules and cattle and destroyed everything else he had except his lands. Having lost all he had by the war, and all his children having married and scattered through Mississippi, Alabama, Tennessee and Georgia, he and wife moved back to Georgia in 1872, and settled in Cartersville, Bartow county, where they had three daughters then living. Noble P. Beall was never a politician or office seeker, but always took an active interest in public affairs, and was all his life a consistent democrat, and never cast other than a democratic vote. He and his wife were active members of the Baptist church, and were always found on the moral side of every question. They were the friends and strong supporters of the cause of education, and at great expense educated their children far beyond what other parents in that part of the state usually did. Capt. Fred Beall when in his seventeenth year was sent to Union university, at Murfreesboro, Tenn., and in two and one-half years completed the full A. M. course of that excellent institution, and at once, as a stepping stone to his chosen profession, the law, began to teach school. At the age of nineteen he was elected principal of a male and female academy upon a salary of $1,200 per year. Two years later he was elected the successor of president W. S. Webb, principal of the Starkville female institute, at Starkville, Miss. While teaching he devoted all his spare time to the study of history and law. When the war between the states broke out, he gave up his school and enlisted as a private soldier in the cavalry service, and continued actively in the Confederate army until its close. Though in an extremely low state of health when he went into the army, so much so that his physicians advised him not to enlist, and warned him that he could not stand the service, and that to attempt to do so would be his early death, yet he never had a furlough on account of sickness, nor was he ever sent to a hospital. He was never absent from duty, and no man was ever truer or more faithful to the Southern cause than he. His first promotion was made on the battlefield, from the position of a private to that of orderly-sergeant. At the battle of Iuka he rendered a very valuable service to General Price, and saved from capture a part of his forces that had been cut off, and were about to be surrendered. Through a perfect hailstorm of bullets, he sped his horse a full mile to where the forces were fighting, and under his direction they were led safely out, for which service he was complimented by General Price. Capt, Beall was a great favorite of General Forrest, under whom he served about one year. The command to which he was attached at the close of the war was under General Wheeler.

When the war closed Capt. Beall located at West Point, and for a few months taught school again, until he could get another start in life. In 1859 he had married Miss Emma G. Brame, a daughter of Mrs. N. F. Brame, of the vicinity of West Point, and a young lady of rare beauty and grace and of superior culture, and when he returned to his young wife and two little children on the 17th of May, 1865, there was no sadder heart in all the South than his. The cause for which he with his countrymen had fought, and for the success of which many of the noblest, truest and bravest of his friends had freely and voluntarily given their lives, had gone down forever before the overwhelming and victorious armies of the Northern states. He who had faced death on many a hard-fought battlefield now wept like a child. While his command had formally surrendered at Washington, Ga., he, in keeping with a resolution he had made when he went into the army, that he never would be made a prisoner alive, refused to surrender, and with a young friend started to join Gen. Dick Taylor, then in command near Mobile, but when they reached the Coosa river, they met some of General Taylor's command who informed them that he had surrendered and also that the Trans-Mississippi army had surrendered. Nothing was then left them but to go on home, which they did, and neither he nor his young friend ever surrendered.

Reared in the school of state rights democracy, the overthrow of the Southern Confederacy was to Captain Beall the overthrow of a great and fundamental principle, upon which the Federal union had been established. However, he did not, at this juncture, have time to stop and mourn over the downfall of the Confederacy; the result must be accepted, and, as far as possible, something must be done for the support of wife and children. He not only had absolutely nothing, but owed about $1,000 in debts incurred in 1861 and 1862, which he was not permitted to pay in Confederate money as they became due. For a few months he taught school, and in the meantime revived his law studies, and in 1866 he began the practice of law, and at once went into a very lucrative practice, which he has retained ever since. At the time he was admitted to the bar West Point was a way station on the Mobile & Ohio railroad in the western part of Lowndes county, and eighteen miles from Columbus, the county seat. He at once began to agitate the question of the formation of a new county, with West Point as the county seat, which was accomplished in 1870, though the county was not organized until 1872. To the efforts of Captain Beall, in this behalf, more than any one else, is due the formation of Clay county. He has always taken an active interest in the cause of education, and was very largely instrumental in the building of the fine public school building, in which is now conducted one of the best graded schools in the state. He has for many years been the chairman of the board of trustees of the city schools. He is an active working member of the state bar association, and has served several years as chairman on the committee of legal education and admission to the bar. He is now, and has been for many years, president of the West Point law and library association. No one in Clay county is more familiar with its general affairs, and no one has done more toward its general improvement and advancement than he. He has always taken an active interest in politics, and to the full extent of his ability and means he contributed to the overthrow of carpet-bag rule in Mississippi in 1875, and to the maintenance of democratic rule in the state since. Unyielding and uncompromising in his devotion to the principles of democracy, he always refused to go into any kind of fusion of parties, and when, in 1873, the democracy of the state met in convention at Meridian, and the majority resolved to disband the party, and unite with what was known then as the conservative republicans, headed by Senator J. L. Alcorn, and try to overthrow the bitter enders, at that time led by General, then Governor, Ames, Captain Beall, with others who were in the minority, refused to be disbanded, but then and there proceeded to organize another convention, which appointed a new state executive committee, to perpetuate the organization of the democratic party. Captain Beall was made a member of that committee, and aided in the preparation of a stirring address to the true democracy of the state, urging them to stand by the time-honored principles of the party, and to never give up the fight. In 1875 the party was reunited, and made that memorable fight for liberty and home rule, which no Mississippian can ever forget. As soon as radicalism was overthrown in the state, Captain Beall took the position that Mississippi should have a new constitution in place of the one made by negroes and carpet-baggers, and he never ceased to work for this until it was accomplished in 1890, though he stood almost solitary and alone in his position on this question for many years. Though always taking an active interest in politics, Captain Beall has persistently refused political office. He has been a man of fixed principles and determined resolutions, and realizing that political office-holding is a delusion and a snare, he, at an early age, resolved never to be a candidate for any political office, and right well has he kept that resolution, though often urged by his fellow-citizens to accept office. An uncompromising democrat, yet Captain Beall has always been popular with all classes, and possibly no lawyer in his part of the state has had a more liberal share of the best practice from members of the republican party. He has ever been an ardent advocate of the absolute equality of all persons before the law, and would have the theory that all classes are equal before the law made practically so. Though it is now more than a quarter of a century since the war between the states closed, yet Captain Beall's devotion to the cause, to which he gave four of the best years of his young manhood, is unabated, and he takes a deep interest in gathering up the history of those bloody years, and in looking after the poor old Confederate soldiers of the county. His professional services are always given freely, without money and without price, to the widow and orphans of his old comrades. Through him the Clay county camp of Confederate veterans was organized, numbering now about two hundred and fifty old Confederate soldiers. The camp showed their appreciation of the Captain by unanimously electing him their commander, which position he now holds. Captain Beall had the misfortune to lose his first wife after there had been born unto them three children: Fred M., Emma and Willie. Fred M. is now practicing law at West Point, Miss.; Emma is unmarried; Willie married W. P. Pope, of Columbus, Miss., who has since been admitted to the bar, and is practicing with his father-in-law. Captain Beall married, a second time, in 1874, his present wife having been Miss Chattie A. McEachin, daughter of Peter and Mariah McEachin, formerly of

FRED BEALL

North Carolina. The present Mrs. Beall is a lady of the highest culture, an earnest Christian worker, beloved by all who know her. The fruit of the last marriage is one daughter, Zoe, yet a little schoolgirl, in disposition and character much like her mother. Captain Beall, wife and all his children, are members of the West Point Baptist church, except his daughter, Willie, who went with her husband to the Presbyterian church. He is also a member of the board of directors of the Young Men's Christian association of West Point, and of the state executive committee of that organization.

Source: *Biographical and Historical Memoirs of Mississippi*, 1891. Volume 1.

Note: General Frederick Beall is buried in Carroll County, Georgia.

HENRY O. BEALL

Henry O. Beall, clerk of the superior court of Randolph County, is a native of Cuthbert, Ga., and was born November 26, 1842. He is the son of Hon. Otho P. Beall, who was born in Virginia in 1817. He was taken to Georgia when young by his parents who settled in Carroll County, and in 1837 removed to Randolph County. He was a farmer and merchant and always was quite a noted man in his county. He represented Randolph County in the legislature for several years and was afterward elected to the State senate from the Eleventh Senatorial District, and was at an early date elected ordinary of Randolph County. Before the war he was in good financial circumstances, but like many others suffered heavy loss during those troublous times. He died in 1877, a member of the F. & A. M. and the I. O. O. F. and a member of the Methodist Church, South. The mother of our subject was Eliza A. (Curtis) Beall, who was born in Gwinnett County, Ga., in about 1820.

Henry O. lived in Cuthbert until the war. In 1862 he joined the Confederate army as orderly sergeant of Company B, Forty-seventh Georgia volunteers, served with that command until 1864, when the Forty-seventh and First Georgia regulars consolidated, and at the close of the war he was first lieutenant of Company F of the First Georgia. After the struggle was over he became agent for the Southwestern Railroad at Cuthbert for a while, and then served with the same company as conductor until 1869, when he took several bridge contracts on the Savannah, Florida and Western Railroad, then being built between Albany and Thomasville, and continued at that until 1875. In 1877 he was elected clerk of the superior court of Randolph County, which office he now ably fills.

July 23, 1867, he was married to Mrs. Laura Walker, daughter of George W. and Amanda A. (Thompson) Smith, of Randolph County. They are the parents of nine children, viz: Mattie M., Olivia, Emma L., Hal T., Otho P., Maggie, Anna L., Lula and Charley R. Mr. Beall is a member of the Methodist Church, South.

Source: *Biographical Souvenir of the States of Georgia and Florida*, 1889.

JAMES W. BECK

Rev. J. W. Beck. One of the most distinguished educators in the state and a learned and brilliant gentleman, is the Rev. James W. Beck, of Concord, Pike Co., Ga. He was born in Wilkes county, Ga., Oct. 23, 1831, and is the son of Rev. T. J. Beck, a native of Ashland, N. C., and one of the most noted Baptist ministers in the south. Rev. T. J. Beck was born in 1805, and deprived of the advantages of an early education, succeeded by indefatigable efforts in surmounting all obstacles and preparing his talented mind for a work which has not been surpassed in the history of the church. He preached his last sermon at Richmond, Va., in 1862, and died that year. Rev. J. W. Beck, who in his youth accompanied his father when on the round of his ministerial duties, was educated up and down the valleys of Georgia, and attended Mercer university in 1857-8-9. His life has been identified with the cause of education and devoted to the service of the church. He was president of the Bowdon college from 1878 to 1883, and president of Jackson, Butts Co., Ga., institute from 1884 to 1890. He entered the service of the Confederacy at the opening of the war, enlisting in Company B, Second regiment, Georgia volunteers, as a private soldier. He was afterward elected captain of Company K, Forty-fourth Georgia regiment, and was made major of the regiment for meritorious service on the field. He was promoted to the rank of lieutenant-colonel for bravery at the battle of Gettysburg. He then commanded the Forty-fourth Georgia regiment till the end of the war, and was in all the battles around Richmond, at Fredericksburg with the Second Army corps and at Chancellorsville with Jackson. He with 400 men, having 360 muskets, marched 5.641 Union prisoners

JAMES W. BECK

taken at the battle of Chancellorsville, to Richmond, Va., in one week. Rev. Beck is a royal arch Mason and for three years was state lecturer for the Farmers' alliance. He was married in 1853 to Margaret Willis, of Meriwether county, by whom he has three children: Marcus W., the present judge of the Flint circuit court; Lenore Beck, president of the Capital Female college at Atlanta and also president of the Woman's Press association of Georgia, and Walter L., business manager of the Griffin Wheel company, of Chicago. All are graduates of colleges and bright in mental accomplishments.

Source: *Memoirs of Georgia*, 1895. Volume 2.

JAMES H. L. BENFORD

James H. L. Benford, farmer, Victory, Carroll Co., Ga., son of John and Martha (Anders) Benford, was born in Twiggs county, Ga., in 1837. His paternal grandparents, George and Elizabeth Benford, were Virginians, and he was a soldier in the patriot army during the revolutionary war. His father was born in Virginia in 1818, came to Georgia when a young man and settled first in Bibb county; he afterward went to Twiggs county and settled in the woods and cleared a farm. He was a soldier in the Indian war of 1836, and was wounded in the arm. His maternal grandparents, Robin and Elizabeth Anders, were natives of Maryland, but migrated to Georgia, and were among the earliest settlers of Twiggs county. Mr. Benford was reared on the farm in Twiggs county and remained on it until he was eighteen years old, when he removed to Carroll county and settled in the woods on the tract whereon he now lives. There was not a stick amiss on the land, and he cleared the land for his farm by himself. There were four families moved together in ox carts, and all of them occupied an eighteen by eighteen log cabin together, cooking, etc., until they could build. He went to school only one week, and was never taught anything but the alphabet. In 1861 he enlisted in Company B, Cleburne's regiment, known as the "Pattison Rangers." He participated in quite a number of battles – Gatling's farm, Petersburg, Columbia, etc., but was most of the time on scouting duty, and often on special courier service. For nearly a month, at one time, his command was chased by Gen. Kilpatrick, fighting nearly every day. He was captured once in Virginia, and when commanded to surrender his gun he threw it down and broke it; and then put his foot on his saber and broke that, too; he then told his captors to take him if they wanted to. As they were taking him to their lines, after dark, dangerous as the attempt seemed, he succeeded in eluding their vigilance and escaped. For along time he was a courier for Gen. Lee, whose pass he bore permitting him to go where and when he pleased at his discretion. At the time of the surrender he was scouting in the rear of the Union army. He came out of the war with nothing but his land, and when his father died had his family to care for, giving the children a fair education. He owns now 1,500 acres of good land, including a well-improved farm, and has the reputation among his neighbors of being one of the most progressive and one of the best farmers in Carroll county. He certainly ranks among the solidest and most substantial of the county's citizens. In 1865 Mr. Benford was married to Miss Fannie Morris, born in Meriwether county and daughter of William and Sarah (Ayers) Morris. Fifteen children have blessed this union, of whom thirteen are living: Henry, Price, Alice, Lity, Warren, Terrell, Eugenia, Perdue, Anna, Sula, Edell, Artentious, and Pious. Mr. Benford is a master Mason, and himself and wife are members of the Missionary Baptist church.

Source: *Memoirs of Georgia*, 1895. Volume 1.

WYATT HEFLIN BLAKE

Wyatt Heflin Blake, B. S., M. D., physician of Lineville, Ala., is a son of John and Marietta (Heflin) Blake. The Blake family came originally from Hall county, Ga. Thomas Blake, the father of John Blake, left Hall county and removed with his family to Randolph county, Ala., about 1833. He was the first representative in the legislature of Alabama from Randolph county. He reared his family in that county, and was a planter and stock raiser by occupation. John Blake came to maturity in Randolph county, and married in 1852. He lived at what is known as Blake's Ferry. He was a merchant and planter, a man of thrift and energy, and accumulated considerable property. He was not a public man. His family consisted of six children, viz.: Wyatt Heflin; Young, of Roanoke, Ala.; Henry W., of Anniston, Ala.; Stell, of Wedowee, Ala.; Marietta, wife of James B. Steed of Lineville, Ala.; Rogers M., a minor. The mother of this family died in 1876, and the father in 1885.

WYATT HEFLIN BLAKE

Wyatt Heflin Blake was born June 21, 1856, at Blake's Ferry. The old homestead was originally the site of an Indian village, on a reservation owned by a Creek Indian. The doctor has the original Indian deed in his possession at the present time. Dr. Blake was educated at Lineville in early life. In 1874 he went to Newnan, Ga., and there attended an academy one year. In 1875, he went to the A. & M. college at Auburn, Ala., and in 1879 graduated from that institution with the second honors of a class consisting of nineteen young men. He was captain of company A, corps of cadets. While at college he gave considerable attention to oratory, and has since leaving school delivered a number of addresses which have been highly spoken of. He delivered an address before the alumni association of his school in 1891, on the Aborigines of Alabama, and in this address made a strong plea for a school history of the state. This address was highly spoken of by the critics of the day. After graduating he taught at Roanoke during the years 1880 and 1881. He then went to Vanderbilt university, where he graduated in the spring of 1883 in the medical department of that institution. He then secured the appointment of assistant to the chair of chemistry in that institution, and remained there a short time. His father's illness called him home, and for some time he managed his father's mercantile business, and at the same time practiced his profession.

In 1888 Dr. Blake moved to Lineville, Ala., where he still lives. He was married July 26, 1885 at Roanoke, Ala., to Mattie L. Shaffer, daughter of Dr. J. P. Shaffer of Dadeville, Ala., whose sketch appears elsewhere in this work. By this marriage he has three children, viz.: John, Jephtha H. and Margaret E. Politically Dr. Blake is a democrat, and is the Clay county member of the democratic executive committee of the fifth congressional district of Alabama. He is a member of the Chi Phi fraternity of the state medical association, being a counselor in that body of the Clay county medical society, and is one of the censors for the county. He graduated with the degree of bachelor of science at the A. & M. college of Ala., and with the degree of doctor of medicine at Vanderbilt university. He is an excellent physician and a man of considerable merit in literary matters. His address before the alumni association of his college in 1891 has already been referred to. The following extracts from that address are here introduced: "I have recently examined a number of the popular school histories in use throughout our country, and I find that the greatest space devoted to a history of our own state in any of the books examined is ten lines." "Should our children be taught of Salem witchcraft, the Acadians in Nova Scotia, the Pequod war, or the prosecution of the Quakers, to the neglect of the history of our own state? I think not. Our children are taught of the adventures of John Smith in Virginia, but are told nothing of the equally romantic life of Samuel Dale of Alabama." They read of the patriotic eloquence of Patrick Henry, but know nothing of the equally eloquent and no less patriotic appeals of William Lowndes Yancey. What citizen of Alabama does not feel a keener sense of state pride when he remembers that William Rufus King, Jabez L. M. Curry and J. Marion Sims, together with scores of others whose names would honor the pages of a nation's history, were Alabamians either by birth or adoption? Is it justice to these men whose lives have given character to our state to allow their names to be forgotten? What is more cruel than neglect? And in addition to the crime of ingratitude we are losing the greatest possible influence known in developing in our youth a feeling of state pride, that element so essentially important to a higher oder of citizenship. An individual without personal or family pride, a professional man without professional pride, or citizen without state pride is an inferior product of his kind, and can we expect to develop a feeling of state pride among our youth when they are ignorant of the history of our state?"

Source: *Memorial Record of Alabama*, 1893. Volume 1.

Note: Thomas Blake, grandfather of Wyatt Heflin Blake, was a brother-in-law of Kerney Young and, like Kerney, was prominent in the early affairs of Carroll County, although for a briefer period. Thomas Blake was residing in Carroll County in 1830. See 1830 Census. Thomas Blake appears in the Inferior Court minutes of Carroll County from 1829 until 1833. From 1830 until 1832 he was a road commissioner in the Ninth District of Carroll County. The Inferior Court minutes mention a road "from the Court House to the Alabama line at Thomas Blake's." Thomas Blake died October 30, 1880 and is buried in Blake's Graveyard, Cleburne County, Alabama.

HENRY BONE

Henry Bone, farmer, Dallas, Paulding Co., Ga., son of Bailey and Nancy (Evans) Bone, was born in Madison county, Ga., in 1834. His grandfather, George Bone, was a native of Ireland, and migrated to this country about 1770. He was a soldier in the patriot army during the revolutionary war, and after peace was proclaimed settled in South Carolina, but soon afterward migrated to Georgia and settled in what is now Madison county, where Mr. Bone's father was born in 1800. He was reared on the farm there, received a limited education at the "old field" schools common at the time, and remained in the county until 1835, when he moved to Carroll county to engage in gold-mining, in which he was quite successful. Ten years later he moved to Paulding county, where he farmed until his death, 1859. Mr. Bone's mother was a daughter of William and Celia Evans, and born in what is now Madison county in 1802. In 1822 she was married to Mr. Bone, and in 1889 died, aged eighty-seven years, the mother of eight children: William, John, Henry, Mrs. Celia Abliss, Mrs. Mary Owens, Atlanta, Mrs. Nancy Owens, Mrs. Elizabeth Collins and Mrs. Addie Drake. Mr. Bone was reared a farmer, received a very limited education and worked on his farm until Georgia seceded. Enlisting in Company K, Sixtieth Georgia regiment, he went to the front, and with it participated in the important battles of Gettysburg, second Manassas, Wilderness and minor engagements. At Staunton, Va., he was prostrated by measles, with which he suffered some time very severely. He was captured at Winchester, Va., but escaped within an hour afterward. He was never wounded, but on one occasion a ball struck his canteen and passing through one side glanced from the other. He was sent home a few days before the surrender, and never returned to the army. Returning to his farm he re-habilitated it, and has enjoyed the prosperity due to hard work and good management. He owns and operates a fine, well-stocked farm just outside the corporate limits of Dallas, and is regarded as one of the best farmers in the county. Mr. Bone was married in 1869 to Miss Ella, daughter of Adam and Maria (Martin) Summers, formerly of South Carolina, and of the children born to them six are living: Katie M., Bertie, Mattie, Warner, Clyde and Raymond. Since 1866 Mr. Bone has been a member of the masonic fraternity.

Source: *Memoirs of Georgia*, 1895. Volume 2.

GEORGE A. BONNER

George A. Bonner, farmer, Carrollton, Carroll Co., Ga., son of Zadoc and Lucy (Ridgeway) Bonner, was born in Carroll county in 1844. His great-grandfather was a soldier in the patriot army during the revolutionary war. His grandparents, Zadoc and (Johnson) Bonner, were natives of Georgia, and his grandfather was born during the revolutionary war. Mr. Bonner's father was born in Clarke county, Ga., in 1804, and was reared there on a farm and removed to Carroll county in 1829. He was a man of great energy, progressive and aggressive, and possessed unusual force of character. During the Indian war he raised a company, but the war closed before he could be mustered in. Although the county was always overwhelmingly democratic and he was a whig in politics, he was repeatedly elected a justice of the inferior court. When he moved to Carroll county he settled in the woods, lived to accumulate a very large estate and to become one of the county's most influential and honored citizens. His maternal grandparent, Drury Ridgeway, was an old settler of Georgia, who subsequently went to Alabama. Mr. Bonner was reared on the farm and received his early education in the common schools of the county. He then entered Bowdon college, where he was when the civil war began. In 1862 he enlisted in Company D, Capt. William Tumlin, First Georgia regiment, and served about eighteen months, during which time he participated in many hard-fought battles, among them Richmond, Ky., Frankfort, Shelbyville, Camp Dick Robinson, Perryville, Crab Orchard, Murfreesboro, Stone Hill, Winchester, Tullahoma, Munfordville, etc. Returning home he was engaged in gathering saltpeter and lead for the Confederate government until the surrender, and then he returned to the old farm where he now lives. His last service was the bearing of a dispatch from Jacksonville, Ala., to LaGrange, Ga. When he reached his destination he found LaGrange in the hands of the Union forces, but he was sharp enough to escape capture. He has been a jury commissioner for the last five years. Mr. Bonner was married in 1872 to Miss Mattie E., daughter of Green and Martha (Freeze) McGuire, of Irish descent, but among the early settlers: To Mr. and Mrs. Bonner eight children have been born: Zadoc M., Ola G., George L., Bessie B., Flora I., Lona Mc., Georgia and Ruth N. Mrs. Bonner, who was a devoted member of the Methodist church, died in 1893. Mr. Bonner has been a master Mason since he has become of "full age" and is one of Carroll's public spirited and progressive citizens. His family for generations have been among the most prominent and respected, but having been members of the minority party before the war seldom held office. This family is related by blood to that so prominent in New York.

Source: *Memoirs of Georgia*, 1895. Volume 1.

FRANKLIN WELSH BOWDON

The gifted Franklin Welsh Bowdon resided in Talladega, though he was born in Chester District, South Carolina, Feb. 17, 1817. His father was a thrifty planter, and a man of piety and hospitality. His mother was a daughter of Mr. Thomas Welsh, for many years a citizen of Dallas. The parents came to Alabama about 1820, and lived and died in Shelby. The son was graduated at Tuskaloosa, and read law under Hon. Daniel E. Watrous at Montevallo. Admitted to the practice, he came to Talladega in 1838, and was successively the law partner of Messrs. Thomas and Wm. P. Chilton, and Tignall W. Jones. In 1844 and '45 he represented Talladega in the legislature. In 1846 he succeeded to the seat in congress vacated by the death of Gen. McConnell, defeating Gen. T. A. Walker of Calhoun and Mr. Benj. Goodman of Chambers. He was elected to a full term the next year, defeating Hon. S. F. Rice, and again in 1849 defeating Gen. Bradford. Soon after the expiration of his term, he removed to Tyler, Texas, where he became the partner of George W. Chilton, esq. He was an elector on the Buchanan ticket, and died in that State June 15, 1857.

To attempt a description of Mr. Bowdon's mental endowments would appear like eulogy, to which this work nowhere aspires. It is but just to say that he was the most gifted orator the State has produced. An English peer who heard him in Washington said that he had listened to the great orators of Europe and America, but this member from the mountains of Alabama excelled them all. In the forum, or on the stump, he was irresistible. The symmetry of his propositions was such as to leave no flaw, and to the mind's eye the logic was as clear as a sunbeam. His words came not only without effort, but he seemed rather to repress them than promote their utterance. His influence over an audience was wondrous, and, as Macaulay has defined eloquence to be persuasion, he fully reached that standard. Nor was he less sound and learned, for Chancellor Bowie pronounced his briefs models of legal acumen. In appearance he was prepossessing. Six feet high and well proportioned, his features were handsome and well-developed. His temperament was somewhat sanguine, and he was agreeable, polished, and full of generous impulses. His only enemy was his own appetite, which impaired his usefulness, and cut him off in the zenith of life. He married the daughter of Hon. Thomas Chilton of this county, formerly a congressman from Kentucky, and his children are now in Talladega. Bowdon College, in Carroll county, Georgia, is named in honor of Mr. Bowdon.

Source: Brewer, *Alabama,* 1872.

FRANKLIN W. BOWDON

Franklin W. Bowdon, of Talladega, was educated at the University of Alabama, and selected the law as his profession. In 1844, and again in 1845, he was elected to the House, and by the force of his talents and his skill in debate, he at once became prominent. At the session of 1845, he was the champion of "Removal," and, in framing the bill for that purpose, he used such phraseology as to combine the question of "Biennial Sessions," with that of Removal," in such a compact form, the one absorbing the other, so that no vote of the House could be taken on either as a separate proposition, under the ruling of the Chair, but both had to stand or fall together. This stroke of generalship gained the day for the friends of "Removal." The efforts and success of Mr. Bowdon on this question rendered him exceedingly popular in East-Alabama, and his reward was not long deferred.

By the death of Gen. McConnell, at Washington City, in 1846, a vacancy occurred in the Seventh Congressional District, to supply which a special election was ordered, when Mr. Bowdon and Mr. Thomas A. Walker, both Democrats, took the field in opposition — the former prevailing. In 1847, Mr. Bowdon was reelected over Gen. J. T. Bradford, his Whig competitor, and in 1849, he defeated Samuel F. Rice, Esq., who had recently forsaken his Democratic friends; or rather, who canvassed the district as a Taylor Democrat.

While in Congress, Mr. Bowdon did not shrink from the discussions usual upon the floor. He was too self-reliant, and had too much force to feel or exhibit the least degree of timidity. He rushed at once into the melee, and gave blow for blow with the grace of a veteran gladiator. The bill to establish the Territorial Government of Oregon, introduced at the session of 1846-'7, contained this provision: *That in any Territory which may be secured to the United States from Mexico, slavery and involuntary servitude shall forever be prohibited.*

While this bill was under consideration, January 16, 1847, Mr. Bowdon delivered a speech most elaborately prepared, and supported by authorities, in opposition to this feature – the Wilmot proviso renewed.

Mr. Bowdon retired from Congress in 1851, with a decided reputation for abilities; but in the meantime his habits had become irregular, and disqualified him from the proper discharge of representative duties. Here is a warning to the young men of Alabama, and they should heed its teachings. Seldom has such a prodigy appeared upon the stage of action as Franklin W. Bowdon, in physical and mental endowments, coupled with the gifts of oratory. When in 1845 he was the bold and victorious leader of "Removal," he measured strength with such men as Samuel W. Inge and Joseph W. Taylor, the young giants in opposition. Before the people he was invincible, and everywhere they crowded to hear him speak. In Congress he was a star, and shone brightly for a few short years, and returned a wreck. He removed to Texas, and in 1856 was on the Electoral Ticket for Buchanan and Breckinridge, and in a short time he died.

While rising in his profession, and just as his public life commenced, Mr. Bowdon married a daughter of the Rev. Thomas Chilton, an accomplished and elegant lady who graced society at the Federal Capitol – a fine specimen of the Southern woman in person and in mind. Higher praise cannot be awarded.

Source: William Garrett, *Reminiscences,* 1872.

S. J. BROWN

S. J. Brown, ordinary of Carroll county, Carrollton, Ga., son of Samuel and Ruth T. (Brooks) Brown, was born in Newton county, Ga., in 1842. His grandfather, Burrell Brown, came to Georgia late in the last century and settled in the woods. Mr. Brown's father was born in Burke county, Ga., in 1800. After receiving his education he taught school a number of years himself, finally settling on some lands in the woods in Newton county, living alone and working hard to open a farm. In 1836 he married his wife, a daughter of Terrell Brooks, and reared a family of nine children. In 1854 he removed to Carroll county, where the future ordinary took his lessons in and enjoyed the beauties and facilities of pioneer life. Judge Brown was reared on the farm, and attended the common county schools. In 1861 he enlisted in Company B, Capt. Charles A. McDaniel, Cobb's legion, Gen. T. R. R. Cobb, and participated in many important battles; Dam No. 1 on the Peninsula, in April, 1862; the retreat toward Richmond; in the seven days' fight, Fredericksburg, Dec. 13, 1862; Chancellorsville, May 1, 1863, when he was wounded in making a charge on the enemy's breastworks, and returned home in June. Although disabled by the loss of the use of his arm, he determined to return to the army and to his company, and as he could do nothing else he carried water and waited on the sick and wounded, exhibiting a patriotic, self-sacrificing disposition very rare. After his return he participated in the battles of the Wilderness, Spottsylvania, Hanover Junction, Cold Harbor, Petersburg and several other battles, remaining in the field until July, 1864, when he was retired on account of disabilities. After the war he attended Bowdon college, remaining from 1867 until 1871, and then he taught school until 1875. In 1876 he was elected county school commissioner, and held the office eight years. From 1881 to 1884 he taught school again. In 1885 he was elected ordinary of the county, and has held the office continuously since. Judge Brown was married Jan. 10, 1871, to Miss Charlotte C., born in Lee county, Ala., a daughter of W. T. and Ann (Stringer) Colquitt, by whom he has had eight children: Ruth, Belle, Mary Lee, Helen, George C., Samuel D., Mattie and Lamar. Judge Brown is a Primitive, and his wife a Missionary Baptist. He has made an upright, faithful officer, is esteemed by everybody, and will probably hold the office as long as he wants it.

Source: *Memoirs of Georgia*, 1895. Volume 1.

W. F. BROWN

W. F. Brown, lawyer, Carrollton, Carroll Co., Ga., son of James C. and Emily M. (Knight) Brown, was born in Carroll county in 1850. His grandfather, John Brown, was born in South Carolina, whence he came to Georgia in ox-carts and settled in the woods on land now

W. F. BROWN

included in DeKalb county. They lived in tents until they cut the logs to build their cabin, and then cleared the land for cropping. In 1832, ten years after DeKalb county was laid off, he removed to Carroll county, organized a year or two before, and again settled in the woods, practically repeating his experience in making the home he had left. Mr. Brown's father was born in what is now DeKalb county in 1815, and accompanied the family to its new home. His mother's parents, John C. and Emily (Hopkins) Knight, were among Carroll's early settlers. Mr. Brown was reared in Carroll county and received a good common school education. When nineteen years of age he began teaching school and continued it seven years, and also began reading law. In 1876 he entered the literary department of the University of Georgia, and was graduated in 1878. He was admitted to the bar, and entered upon the practice of law in 1880, and has been eminently successful. He is recognized as being as well read in law as the majority of the profession practicing in his circuit, as one of its leading lawyers, and gains his share of the cases intrusted to his management. He has a good and growing clientage. No citizen stands higher or better in the estimation of the people than Mr. Brown. In 1884, he was elected to represent Carroll county in the general assembly and served the term. Mr. Brown was married in 1873 to Miss Emily, daughter of Archey and Malinda (George) Hagan. The father was one of the early settlers in Coweta county – the mother was born in Jackson county, Ga. Of the eight children born to Mr. and Mrs. Brown these seven are living: Earl I., appointed to a cadetship at the West Point Military academy, after passing a crucial competitive examination; Ralph S, Emily, Paul F., Willie G., Harry D., and Eveline. Mr. Brown is a member of the I. O. O. F., and in masonry a royal and select master. Himself and wife are working members of the Methodist church – he being superintendent of the Sunday school. He is also one of the trustees of the Hutcheson Collegiate institute. He is now judge of Carroll City court under appointment of Ex-Gov. Northen. Altogether Mr. Brown is a thoroughgoing, progressive and most worthy citizen.

Source: *Memoirs of Georgia*, 1895. Volume 1.

O. D. BUNT

O. D. Bunt, farmer and merchant, Bowdon, Carroll Co., Ga., son of John R. and Frances J. (Morris) Bunt, was born in DeKalb county, Ga., in 1857. His paternal grandfather, Thomas Bunt, was a native of South Carolina, and came to Georgia early in this century. He was a soldier during the revolutionary war. Mr. Bunt's father was born in South Carolina in 1825, and came to Georgia with his parents when a child. In 1861 he enlisted in Capt. Potts' company for two years, and in 1863 re-enlisted and served until the surrender. He had acquired a large property before the war, but lost it all; and when he returned from the army he had to make a new start. His maternal grandparents, Obadiah and Sarah (Binion) Morris, were native Georgians. Mr. Bunt was reared on a farm, and as the war was raging, and school facilities were limited, during his boyhood he was favored with but limited schooling. But he had capacity, and with it ambition and pluck, and so he pressed forward in the race of life. Without money, but with the qualities mentioned, he is fairly on the road to wealth and position. He now owns a 350-acre farm of fine land, and has supplemented his farm with a general merchandise store, building up a good tarde and largely increasing his income. Mr. Bunt was married in 1884 to Miss Nora P., daughter of L. J. and Ada J. (Hood) Aderhold, all born in Carroll county. Her father was a son of G. W. Aderhold, who was born in 1843, and served gallantly in the Confederate army under Gen. Bragg, and was a physician of some note. Three children have blessed this union: Ethel, Leola and Hettie. Mr. and Mrs. Bunt are members of the Methodist church, with cheering prospects of a prosperous and happy future.

Source: *Memoirs of Georgia*, 1895. Volume 1.

THORNTON BURK

Thornton Burk, son of Robert and Sarah Burk, was born in Elbert county, Georgia, December 1st, 1794. In his twenty-ninth year, he removed to Monroe county, and was married shortly after, to Miss Malinda Bankston, daughter of Abner and Elizabeth Bankston. He united with Rocky Creek church in 1828, and was baptized by Rev. John M. Gray. After serving that church as deacon for three years, and exercising his gifts under a license for two years, he was ordained in 1833, at Shoal Creek church, Pike county, by Revs. William Moseley

THORNTON BURK

and Spencer Stamper. During the five years preceding his removal in 1838 to Cobb county, then a new and sparsely settled section of country, he rendered pastoral service to churches in Pike, Fayette, Henry and Monroe counties; and during the ten years subsequent to that event, the counties of Cobb, Campbell, and Paulding supplied his sphere of pastoral labor. In 1848 he removed to Van Wert, Polk county, prosecuting his ministerial work in the region round about for two years, when he settled near Villa Rica, Carroll county, where he made his home for twenty years. Early in this period he was mainly instrumental, with the assistance of Rev, James Reeves, in the constitution, near his residence, of Pleasant Grove church, now a large and flourishing body. The whole of this period was devoted to the assiduous discharge of his duties as a minister, either as pastor, or as evangelist and colporteur, within the bounds of the Tallapoosa Association. In 1871 he became a second time a citizen of Cobb county, settling near Powder Springs, at his present home, and keeping up his activities in the proclamation of the Gospel, though, for some five years or more, age and bodily infirmities have restricted his sphere of labor. The ministry thus briefly sketched covers a space of forty-four years and over, in the course of which he baptized between two and three thousand persons. Much of his toil has been given to destitute places, among the poor, with little compensation, not by appointment simply, but often voluntarily, and has led to the organization and establishment of more churches, probably, in Cobb, Campbell, Paulding and Carroll counties, than that of any other minister in his section. Through all this long and arduous career he has maintained an unsullied character as a Christian and a minister. All who are acquainted with him have the utmost confidence in the genuineness of his piety. He is universally revered as a man of God.

He was elected Moderator of the Tallapoosa Association in 1841, and served the body in that capacity for ten successive sessions – occupying the chair when the schism on the mission question occurred, and taking a decided stand with the friends of the missionary cause, while its opponents were headed by the former Moderator, Rev. Henry Haynes. This honor was rightly paid him by his brethren in view of his fidelity to truth, his zeal and his abundance in labor. And now, amid the weakness of his eighty-sixth year, reduced to destitute circumstances by the issues of the war, he lingers, after the snows of twenty winters have rested on the grave of his wife, to illustrate the power of divine grace in supporting those who trust it under the burden of old age, and to rejoice in hope of re-union with the loved ones who are "not lost, but gone before."

Source: *History of the Baptist Denomination in Georgia,* 1881.

JAMES W. BURNS

James W. Burns, farmer, Bowdon, Carroll Co., Ga., son of Samuel and Jane (Morris) Burns, was born in Florida, Dec. 19, 1838. His grandfather on his father's side, James Burns, came from Ireland to the United States early in this century, settled in North Carolina, and was a soldier in the war of 1812. He was a near relative of the poet, Robert Burns. In 1835 he came to Georgia and settled and cleared a farm in Henry county. Some years subsequently he removed to Carroll county and settled. Mr. Burns' father was born in Ireland in 1804, came to this country with his father, and with the family from North Carolina to Georgia. His grandparents on his mother's side, William and Hannah Morris, were natives of Virginia, whence they came to Georgia and made their home in DeKalb county, being among the county's pioneer citizens. Mr. Burns was reared on the farm, received only the limited education obtainable between "laying-by" and "fodder-pulling" time at the old-time school house two and a half miles away. In early manhood he taught school two years. In 1861 he enlisted in Company E (Capt. James Blalock), First Georgia cavalry; for a while he was with Gen. Forrest, and afterward with Gen. Wheeler. To have been with either of those generals means that he saw as much continuous hard service and bore a part in as much hard fighting as any one during the war. He was engaged in the battles of Perryville, Murfreesboro, Chickamauga, Missionary Ridge and Franklin, and was with Johnston and Hood all the way to Atlanta; and under Wheeler made the raid all the way to Nashville, and was with the forces that harassed Sherman when "marching through Georgia;" while in the service he was sergeant of his company. After the war he returned to Georgia. Mr. Burns was married in 1865 to Miss Elizabeth F. Moore — born in Henry county — daughter of Harrison Moore, a native of Georgia, who removed from Henry to Carroll county, and who, though starting poor, lived to become rich. To the happiness of this household eleven children were added, nine of whom are living: Sarah J., Lula, James M., Beulah, Benjamin L., Samuel H., Ed, Katie and Joseph. After his marriage he began life without a dollar, but by hard work, economy and good management he has accumulated a fine property, including 1,000 acres of excellent land, with an improved farm and a delightful home in Bowdon. He is solid, substantial, popular. Mrs. Burns is a member of the Missionary Baptist church.

Source: *Memoirs of Georgia*, 1895. Volume 1.

EZEKIEL SLAUGHTER CANDLER

E. S. Candler, Sr., is a leading lawyer of Iuka, Tishomingo county, Miss., and a prominent man in that part of the state. He is a son of Hon. Samuel C. and Martha (Beall) Candler. He is of an old and prominent family of Georgia, which, for a number of generations, has been intimately connected with the various interests of the state. Samuel C. Candler was born December 6, 1809, near Milldegeville, the former capital of Georgia. He was a son of Daniel Candler, of Columbia county, Ga., who was born in 1781, and whose father was a soldier in the Revolutionary war, and also a native Georgian. His wife was Sarah Butler Slaughter, whose father was also a rebel. Daniel Candler was a planter, and died at the early age of thirty-three years. His son, Samuel C. Candler, the father of our subject, was thus left an orphan of tender age, and was reared by his mother on the plantation, but at the age of eighteen years he moved into Cherokee county, Ga., then inhabited by the Indians, and there engaged in the mercantile business. He was elected sheriff of this county when he was barely twenty-one years old, and then was elected to the legislature, and before his term of office expired. In 1830 he removed to Carroll county, Ga., and died there in 1873, at sixty-four years of age. During this time he was a member of the legislature several times. In 1860 he was a Douglas democrat, and was a member of the national democratic convention which met that year at Charleston, S. C., and in the memorable contest in which Mr. Lincoln was elected president he was an elector on the Douglas ticket. He opposed secession with all his power and influence, but after Georgia withdrew from the Union he believed it his duty to go with the state, and gave the Southern Confederacy his sincere and cordial support. He was married, December 8, 1833, to Martha Beall, daughter of Noble P. Beall, who was born December 6, 1819, and who is still living. Noble P. Beall was born in Franklin county, Ga., in 1798, and married Justiana Hooper, who was born in 1800. Both of these were of Revolutionary ancestry. The mother of E. S. Candler, Sr., was one of twelve children. The subject of this sketch is one of eleven children: Hon. Milton A. Candler (who was a member of the XLVth and also the XLVIth congress), Ezekiel S., Noble D. (who died in 1887), Julia Florence, Jessie, William B., Lizzie F., Asa G., Samuel C., Warren A. and John S. Warren A. is now president of Emory college, at Oxford, Ga., and John S. is solicitor general of one of the judicial circuits of Georgia. Samuel C. Candler and his wife were members of the Methodist Episcopal church. Their children are all church members, being distributed among the Baptist, Methodist and Presbyterian churches. The early life of E. S. Candler, Sr., was spent on the farm and at school. He received a classical education, graduating from Cherokee Baptist college in 1859, taking the highest honors of his class. He read law and was admitted to the bar, and began the practice of his profession in 1860 in Carroll county, Ga. He was born December 6, 1838, in Campbell county, Ga., about twenty miles from the city of Atlanta. He came to Iuka, Miss., in 1870, and from then till January, 1875, was principal of the Iuka male academy, and had a large and prosperous school. In 1875 he resumed the practice of law at Iuka, which he has continued successfully until the present time. In August, 1860, he married Julia Bevill, of Bellville, Hamilton county, Fla., whose parents, Granville and Sarah Bevill, were of French descent, but natives of Georgia. The wife of E. S. Candler, Sr., was born February 27, 1842, and was the youngest of seven children. He and his wife are members of the Baptist church. Mr. and Mrs. Candler have only three children, all sons: Ezekiel S., Jr., Daniel Bevill and Milton A., the first of whom is a lawyer at Corinth, Miss., and one of the brightest and most promising of the young lawyers of the state. He was one of the electors, and as such cast a vote for Mr. Cleveland for president in 1888. He married Nannie Hazlewood, of Lawrence county, Ala., who was a daughter of Thomas B. Hazlewood. The other two, Daniel B. and Milton A., are members of their father's family, the first engaged in farming and the latter still in school. Mr. Candler is a member of the Knights of Honor and Knights and Ladies of Honor, and a democrat of the strict construction school. His interest and confidence in the improvement and development of Mississippi is unbounded. He is a strong friend to, and an active promoter of, all educational enterprises, and is a member and president of the board of trustees of the Iuka normal institute, one of the most flourishing and noted institutions of the state. He is the owner of the largest acreage of lands in his county, most of which is covered with the finest of timber, and is also fine farming land; and it being in an exceedingly healthy country abounding in fine streams of water, Mr. Candler is enthusiastic in his description of its many beauties and excellencies.

Source: *Biographical and Historical Memoirs of Mississippi*, 1891. Volume 1.

JOHN SLAUGHTER CANDLER

Col. John Slaughter Candler, of Atlanta, Ga., ranking colonel of the Georgia state troops, and the solicitor-general of the Stone mountain circuit, was born in Carroll county, Ga., Oct. 22, 1861, being the youngest child of Samuel Charles and Martha B. (Beall) Candler. Hon. Samuel Charles Candler was born in Columbia county, Ga., on Dec. 6, 1809. His father was Daniel Candler, who married Sarah Slaughter, by whom he was the father of seven children, viz.: William Love, Elizabeth Anthony, John Kingston, Frances Mary, Samuel Charles, Daniel Gill, and Ezekiel Slaughter. Daniel Candler, paternal grandfather of John Slaughter Candler, was the youngest of William Candler's children. He was only ten years old when his father, William Candler, died. Of the early history of William Candler, family tradition gives but little information. There are, however, scraps of recorded history, scattered here and there, which taken together and interpreted, the one in the light of the others, enable us to arrive with reasonable accuracy at a correct conclusion as to his origin and ancestry. There is now in the possession of the Candler family a manuscript, written sixty years ago in his family Bible by Rev. Ignatius A. Few, D. D., LL. D. (the first president of Emory college, at Oxford, Ga.), which manuscript may be relied on for correctness as far as it goes, for its author, Dr. Few, was born a hundred years ago; lived, in point of time, near to his grandfather; was a man of profound learning and piety; and came fully up to Cicero's definition of a good historian, "a man too brave to tell a lie and brave enough to tell the truth." The manuscript says: "William Candler was probably born in Ireland; his parents certainly were. He held the rank of colonel in the American army during the war of the revolution, and died and was buried in Columbia county, Ga., in 1789, four miles east of Mount Carmel." Lyman C. Draper, LL. D., secretary of the State Historical society of Wisconsin, says: "Maj. William Candler, who, with Capts. Carr and Johnson, commanded the small party of Georgians at the battle of Kings mountain, was born of English parents in Dublin, Ireland, in 1738, and was brought to North Carolina when a mere child. He married, in 1761, Elizabeth Anthony, and the next year migrated to Georgia. In 1771 he was a deputy surveyor. During the war he served under Col. Clarke, was in the attack on Augusta, at Kings mountain and Blackstocks, and rose to the rank of colonel. He was a member of the legislature in 1784-5; was appointed a judge, and died at his seat in Columbia county, in 1789, at the age of fifty-one years, leaving several children, his oldest son, Henry, having served in the army with him." These two accounts from sources so far apart in point of time and distance agree substantially as to the main facts. Col. William Candler was, as Draper says, in the siege of Augusta, and in all the other affairs in upper Georgia, and those in which Sumter was engaged in his campaign in South Carolina, in 1780. With the return of peace and the establishment of the independence of the colonies, the Candlers returned to their devastated homes in Columbia county, on Little river. William Candler and William and Benjamin Few were named in the act of the royal legislature of Georgia, in 1780, proscribing certain prominent rebels in that colony who were especially obnoxious to the crown, and disqualifying them from holding office, from sitting on juries, and even from testifying as witnesses in the courts; but this ostracism continued for only a short time. The patriots soon recovered possession of the state, and these ostracized rebels, in their turn, passed laws confiscating the property of those who had mustered under the flag of the enemies of their country, and making the name of tory so odious that to-day, after the lapse of more than a hundred years, is a stench in the nostrils of the great-grandchildren of the heroes of Savannah, Augusta, Kings mountain, Cowpens, and the numerous other less noted fields on which they shed their blood in defense of their homes and firesides. William Candler was a member of the first general assembly of Georgia that met in that state under the constitution after the close of the war of the revolution. Subsequently he became a judge of the highest court then known to the judiciary of that state, and died at his seat in Columbia county, Ga., in 1789. He married, in 1760, Elizabeth Anthony, whose grandfather was a Genoese Italian and her mother a Clark. She was the eldest of a numerous family, and one of her nephews was governor of Kentucky. William Candler and his wife, Elizabeth Anthony, had children: Mary, Henry, Falby, William, Charles, Elizabeth, John Kingston, Amelia, Joseph, Mark Anthony and Daniel. We will now proceed to speak more at length of Daniel, the youngest of the children of William Candler, as he was the progenitor of most of the Candlers who still live in Georgia, Louisiana, Texas and Arkansas. He was born in Columbia county, Ga., in 1779. Samuel Slaughter came with his brother, Reuben, from Virginia to Georgia, prior to the war of the revolution, and Daniel Candler was married to his daughter, Sarah Slaughter. Samuel Slaughter was a very successful planter of Baldwin county, Ga., and both he and his brother were ardent patriots and both served in the armies of the colonies during the war of the revolution. Both reared large families, and their descendants are to be found scattered all over the south, especially in Georgia. Daniel Candler died in Columbia county, Ga., in September, 1816. Cut off at that period of life before which few men ever accomplish much, his life was devoid of special incident. He and his wife, Sarah Slaughter, had seven children, viz.: William Love Candler, born in Milledgeville, Ga., Sept. 1, 1801. He married Martha Moore in Upson county, Ga., about 1824. He died and was buried in Bienville parish, Louisiana, in 1868. He had eight children. Elizabeth Anthony Candler, born on March 30, 1803. She was twice married, first to Owen H. Myrick, by whom she bore a son, and after his death to Corley, by whom she had five children. She died in Bienville parish, Louisiana, Dec. 20, 1872. All of her children in life reside in Louisiana except the Rev. Daniel G. Myrick, who has been for many years a leading Methodist minister. John Kingston Candler was born in Columbia county, Ga., in 1804. He married Caroline Smith in Baldwin county, Ga., in his twenty-second year. He reared a numerous family, and all, if alive, are thought to be in Louisiana. He is a substantial farmer, unostentatious and unambitious. He still lives in Bienville parish, La., and is ninety-one years old. Frances Emily Candler was born in Columbia county, Ga., in 1806. She was married in her eighteenth year to Wilson Simpson, a native of Tennessee, by whom she was the mother of ten children, some of whom reside in western Texas and others in Louisiana. She died near the Brazos river, in western Texas, about 1856. Hon. Samuel Charles Candler, father of the distinguished gentleman whose name heads this sketch, was born in Columbia county, Ga., on Dec. 6, 1809. At the age of twenty-four he married Martha B. Beall, a daughter of Noble B. Beall, of Cherokee county, Ga., a niece of Gen. William Beall, for a long time prominent in the history of Western Georgia. Samuel Charles Candler represented at different times two different counties in the Georgia legislature; first, Cherokee, in 1835, and afterward, for several terms, Carroll, in which he spent most of his life. He was also, for two terms, a member of the state senate. In his earlier life he was a merchant, and, later, devoted much of his time to politics. He was a member of the convention which met at Charleston, S.C., was an ardent supporter of Douglas, and, together with Absalom H. Chappell, of Muscogee, Hiram Warner, of Meriwether, and James L. Seward, of Thomas, was burned in effigy at Macon, Ga., by the supporters of Breckinridge and the other presidential candidates for having refused to withdraw from that convention. He was also very prominent in Masonic circles, and was a member of the Methodist Episcopal church south. He served as a soldier in the war with the Seminole Indians in Florida in 1836. He died on Nov. 13, 1873, but his widow is still living and resides in Atlanta. He left eleven children, of whom we shall speak more particularly hereafter. Daniel Gill Candler was born in Columbia county, Ga., Feb. 22, 1812, and married Oct. 8, 1833, to Nancy Caroline Matthews, of western Georgia. He was a lawyer and at one time a judge, served in two Indian wars, in the army of the United States, and was the captain commanding the famous Banks county guards, one of the companies of the Second regiment that left Georgia in the army of the Confederate states. He was thrice elected mayor of Gainesville, Ga., and died in that city Oct. 17, 1887. He left twelve children, the eldest being Hon. Allen Daniel Candler, who was a colonel in the army of the Confederate state, for five years a representative in the Georgia legislature, for two years a senator in the same state, for eight years a member of the United States congress, and is now serving his second term as secretary of state for the state of Georgia. Ezekiel

JOHN SLAUGHTER CANDLER

Slaughter Candler, youngest of the children of Col. William Candler and his wife, Sarah Slaughter, was born in Columbia county, Ga., Aug. 5, 1815, married Miss Jane Williams, a native of Tennessee, in Coweta county, Ga., Aug. 19, 1839, and died in Atlanta, Ga., January 12, 1869. He was sheriff of Carroll county, Ga., when a very young man, subsequently represented that county in the Georgia legislature, and in 1851, was elected comptroller-general of Georgia, holding that important office twelve years. He left seven children, who, if in life, reside in Georgia. The foregoing are the lineal descendants of Daniel, the youngest son of Col. William Candler, of the American revolution of 1776. The descendants of his brothers are not so numerous. They live in the counties of Columbia, Talbot and Muscogee, in Georgia, and in the state of Alabama; some of them probably live in other states. Having thus traced the history of William Candler, of Richmond county, Ga., and his descendants from his first appearance, in 1771, as a land surveyor under the royal government, we will now proceed to speak more particularly of the descendants of Samuel Charles and Martha B. (Beall) Candler, of whom there were eleven, viz.: The Hon. Milton A. Candler, born Jan. 11, 1837. He is a lawyer and lives in Decatur, De Kalb Co., Ga.; has represented his county several times in the state house of representatives, his district in two constitutional conventions and once in the state senate, and his district in the forty-fifth and forty-sixth congresses of the United States. He married Eliza, daughter of the Hon. Charles Murphy, at one time a member of congress from Georgia. They have several children, most of whom are living, and the eldest of whom, the Hon. Charles Murphy Candler, was a member of the legislature of Georgia during the session of 1889-90; Ezekiel S. Candler, a lawyer and Baptist minister, of Mississippi; he married Miss Julia Bevel, of Hamilton county, Fla. They have several children, of whom the eldest, E. S. Candler, Jr., is a prominent lawyer of Iuka, Miss.; Julia Florence, wife of J. Watt Harris, of Cartersville, Bartow Co., Ga.; Noble Daniel, who was much afflicted from youth and died since the death of his father; Sarah Justana, married J. J. Willard, deceased, of De Kalb Co., Ga.; she has several children, the eldest of whom, Samuel, is in business in Atlanta, Ga.; William Beall Candler, of Carrollton, Carroll Co., Ga.; he is a merchant, and married a daughter of Dr. Slaughter, of that county, by whom he has several children; Elizabeth Frances, who married H. H. Dobbs;

JOHN SLAUGHTER CANDLER

she has several children; Asa Griggs Candler, a very prominent druggist of Atlanta, Ga.; he married Miss Howard, daughter of his former partner in business, by whom he has several children; he is now president of the Georgia Sunday-school association, and is exceedingly prominent in the lay service of the Methodist Episcopal church, south; Samuel Charles Candler, a merchant of Carrollton, Carroll Co., Ga.; he married a Miss Bevel of the state of Florida; the Rev. Warren Akin Candler, D. D., of Oxford, Ga., of whom a sketch appears elsewhere in these Memoirs; he is president of Emory college, of which his second cousin, Rev. Ignatius A. Few, LL. D., was the first president more than half a century ago; he was a doctor of divinity at less than thirty years of age, and is probably the youngest man in the service of the Methodist Episcopal church, south, who has ever been prominently mentioned in connection with the highest office in the gift of that denomination, that of a bishop; Col. John Slaughter Candler, whose name heads this article, is the ranking colonel of the Georgia state troops; he resided in Carroll county until thirteen years of age, receiving his earlier education in the rural schools of that county and at Cartersville, Ga., under the tutorage of his sister, Mrs. Florence Harris. November, 1876, he entered the boys' high school, at Atlanta, Ga., and was graduated therefrom in June of the following year; attended Emory college, at Oxford, Ga., for three years and was graduated from that institution, with the degree of bachelor of arts, in 1880. For two years next after his graduation, he taught school in the county of De Kalb, studied law while not engaged in his school duties and was admitted to the practice at Decatur, Ga., but removed soon thereafter to Atlanta, Ga., and has since pursued his profession at that city. In 1883 he was admitted to practice in the state supreme court, and in 1892 he was admitted to the United States supreme court. On Nov. 26, 1887, Mr. Candler was appointed by Gov. John B. Gordon solicitor-general of the Stone Mountain circuit, to fill an unexpired term, and in November, 1888, he was elected by the state legislature to the same position for the full term of four years, and in November, 1892, re-elected, without opposition, by the same body. His recognition by the state's executive dates back , however, to 1882, when he was appointed lieutenant-colonel and aide-de-camp on the staff of Gov. Alexander H. Stephens, holding that rank under Govs. Boynton and McDaniel until the office of judge-advocate general was created by act of the legislature. He was then appointed to that important post by Gov. Henry D. McDaniel, re-appointed to that place by Gov. John B. Gordon, and again held it four years under the administration of Gov. William J. Northen, resigning in 1893 to accept the command of the Fifth regiment of infantry, Georgia Volunteers, of which regiment he is colonel at the present time. In December, 1894, Col. Candler was appointed on the commission organized for the purpose of codifying the military laws of Georgia, and is chairman of that commission. Probably no officer of the state's militia has devoted as much valuable time to the thorough organization and equipment of the militia as has Col Candler. He has ever been a champion of the establishment of an annual encampment of the state forces, for the two-fold purpose of perfecting those forces in the battalion and regimental drills and for the mutual companionship in arms arising from such annual association. He has frequently appeared before the finance committee of the state legislature in advocacy of an appropriation to defray the expenses of such encampments, and it is to his efforts, probably, that several measures looking to these annual appropriations have been carried through the legislature. Col Candler is prominent in politics, being elected a member of the state democratic executive committee from the fifth congressional district in 1884, and upon the assembling of that body, was made secretary of the committee; and is now a member of that committee from the fifth congressional district. He has acted at various times as chairman of the congressional executive committee, as chairman of the thirty-fourth district senatorial committee, and of the democratic executive committee for De Kalb county. He has also been prominently mentioned in connection with the congressional seat of the fifth district, and his friends say that his services to the democratic party have been of such character as to deserve reward at the hands of his fellow-citizens. Col. Candler is an able lawyer, quick of perception, profound in his knowledge of the law, a thorough master of the science of pleading and practice and precedent, and always courteous to opposing counsel. He was married Jan. 16, 1884, to Miss Lula Garnier, a daughter of the late Col. Isadore V. Garnier, a native of Charleston, S. C., and a grandson of Gen. Joseph Garnier, who was one of Napoleon's generals. This union has been blessed by the birth of two interesting children, viz.: Asa WarrenCandler and Allie Garnier Candler. Col. Candler is a stewardof the Edgewood Methodist Episcopal church, south, of Atlanta, and was a member and chairman of the lay delegation to the general conference which met in St. Louis, Mo., in May, 1890.

Source: *Memoirs of Georgia*, 1895. Volume 1.

MILTON A. CANDLER

Milton A. Candler. One of the leading members of the Georgia bar, and a man who has frequently been honored by the people of the state is Hon. Milton A. Candler. Mr. Candler is a native of Campbell county, where he was born Jan. 11, 1837, but his boyhood days were spent in the neighboring county of Carroll. Here the subject of this sketch received his primary education, and remained until reaching the years of mature manhood. In 1852 he became a student at Franklin college, now the state university, graduating with the degree of A. B., in 1854. Being an excellent debater and fond of intellectual employment, having received a great stimulus from his literary course at the university, and especially his debating society, the young student resolved to enter the legal profession. Accordingly, soon after graduation, he began the study of law in the office of Warren Aikin, at Cassville, Ga. He was subsequently admitted to the bar in Pickens county in 1856, launching out into the practice of law at Cassville. In 1857 he located at Decatur, Ga., a small town about six miles from Atlanta, on the Georgia railroad. Here he remained in the peaceable enjoyment of a large and lucrative practice until the spring of 1863, when the martial spirit prevailed over the demands of his profession and he entered the Confederate army as captain of Company A, Tenth Georgia state guard. He remained in the service until the spring of 1864. Mr. Candler, by reason of his strong inherent love of politics, has frequently been forced into the political forum, and numerous honors, in the gift of the democratic party, have rewarded his aspirations. During the years of 1861-62-63 he occupied a seat in the state legislature at Milledgeville. He was also a member of the convention that met at the state capital in the fall of 1865. From 1868 to 1872 he occupied a seat in the state senate. Two years later he was elected to the forty-fourth congress as a representative from the fifth congressional district. He served on several important committees, notably the committee on private land claims and elections. Mr. Candler

MILTON A. CANDLER

was recognized as one of the ablest speakers on the floor of congress. In 1876 he was re-elected to the forty-fifth congress, and his record in that body was equally as brilliant and patriotic. Returning home from Washington at the close of his second term, Mr. Candler devoted himself exclusively to the practice of his profession. He had located his office in Atlanta in 1867, though he still continued to reside in Decatur. Many important cases were voluntarily brought to Mr. Candler on his resumption of the active practice, and his reputation as an advocate daily increased with the repeated announcements of his victories in the courts. Mr. Candler has few equals at the Georgia bar to-day, and his eloquence is still as fervid and impassioned as when his boyish face first appeared on the stump in Georgia. In 1893, though not a candidate, Mr. Candler was chosen to represent his home county (De Kalb) in the state legislature. Mr. Candler has never connected himself with any secret organization, but is an influential member, and for several years has been a leading elder in the Decatur Presbyterian church. In 1857 Mr. Candler was married to Miss Eliza C. Murphy, the daughter of the late Hon. Charles Murphy, of Decatur, an ante-bellum congressman, and a delegate to the secession convention, who died on the day that body convened. Mr. Candler has five living children: Charles M., who has been a member of the state legislature, and is now connected with the George W. Scott Manufacturing company in Georgia; Samuel C., who now resides in California as special agent of the United States land service; Florence, wife of C. A. Cowles, of Decatur; Claude and Ruth, unmarried. The father of Mr. Candler, who was a native Georgian, served for several terms in the state legislature before and after the war. His name was Samuel C. Candler, and during the greater part of his life he devoted himself to mercantile pursuits and farming. He was a man of superior intelligence, who carefully observed the times, and believed in giving his children a good education as far as his means could afford. He was a man of commanding influence in his community and his death — which occurred in 1873 at the age of sixty-four years — was deeply deplored.

Source: *Memoirs of Georgia*, 1895. Volume 1.

WARREN AKIN CANDLER

W. A. Candler, D. D., eleventh president of Emory college, is the seventh son of Samuel C. and Martha Beall Candler, and was born in Carroll county, Ga., Aug. 23, 1857. His grandfather was Daniel Candler, who was the youngest son of Col. William Candler, of revolutionary fame. This Col. William Candler was at the siege of Augusta and with Gen. Sumter in his Carolina campaign of 1780. The eldest child of Col. Candler was Mary Candler, who became the wife of Capt. Ignatius Few, and the mother of Dr. Ignatius Few, the first president of Emory college. Warren Akin Candler, the subject of this sketch, was graduated at Emory college with the highest honors of his class in July, 1875, one month before he was eighteen years of age. In December, 1875, he was admitted, on trial, to the North Georgia conference of the Methodist Episcopal church south, at its session held in Griffin, Ga. From his graduation until he applied for membership in the conference (July to December, 1875), he supplied the pulpit of the Methodist church in Sparta, Ga. In 1876 he was appointed as junior preacher on the Newton circuit, with Rev. A. W. Rowland as his senior. In 1877 he served the Watkinsville circuit with Rev. W. W. Oslin as his senior. In the years 1878, 1879 and 1880, he was pastor of the Merritts Avenue church, Atlanta. In 1881 he was presiding elder for the Dahlonega district, having been appointed to the office of a presiding elder at an earlier age than any other man in the history of his church. In 1882 he was again stationed at Sparta. In 1883-84-85 and a part of 1886 he was the pastor of St. John's church, Augusta, Ga. In July, 1886, the college of bishops appointed him associate editor of the "Christian Advocate," at Nashville, Tenn., the official organ of the Methodist Episcopal church south. There he remained until June, 1888, when he was elected president of Emory college, where he has served since. He received the degree of doctor of divinity from his alma mater at the age of thirty-one.

Source: *Memoirs of Georgia*, 1895. Volume 2.

WILLIAM B. CANDLER

William B. Candler, merchant, Villa Rica, Carroll Co., Ga., son of Samuel C. and Martha (Beall) Candler, was born in Carroll county in 1847. An ancestor of the family, which is one among the most distinguished in Georgia at this time, was an officer in Cromwell's

WILLIAM B. CANDLER

army. Mr. Candler's great-grandfather, William C. Candler, came from Ireland to America before the revolutionary war and was an officer in the patriot army. His paternal grandparents, Daniel and Sarah (Slaughter) Candler, were native Georgians. Mr. Candler's father was born in Upson county, Ga., in 1809, and removed to Carroll county in 1832, where he began life by working in the gold mines at $6 a month. His life success affords another and striking illustration of of the opportunities this country affords for acquiring fortunes and achieving distinction. He served as a justice of the inferior court of the county a number of years; he represented the county in the general assembly – once as senator and twice as representative – and was in Charleston in 1860 at the democratic presidential convention. He was one of eleven children, all of whom are living but one; he was a "live" member of the masonic fraternity, and at the age of sixty joined the Methodist church. From a poorly-paid workingman he rose to wealth and honor and lived to a ripe old age. Mr. Candler's maternal grandparents, Noble and Justain (Hooper) Beall, were of Scotch descent and early settlers in Georgia. Mr. Candler was reared on the farm within a mile of where he now lives, and attended school at the "regulation" log school house. But, as during his youthhood war raged the fiercest, and there was the direst necessity for field labor, his educational advantages were seriously curtailed. After the war ended he taught school six months and after that (1868) embarked in the mercantile business, in which he has been exceptionally successful. In 1871 Mr. Candler was married to Miss Lizzie Slaughter – born in Carroll county – daughter of Dr. J. T. and Melvina (Freeman) Slaughter. Dr. Slaughter was a leading and one of the most prominent physicians in the state. Four children blessed this happy union: Eugene, Florence, Lizzie and William B. Mr. Candler and two of the children are members of the Presbyterian church, and Mrs. Candler and the other two children are members of the Methodist church. Mr. Candler rates high in the commercial world as a man of practical business and financial ability, while in social life himself and family are outranked by none.

Source: *Memoirs of Georgia*, 1895. Volume 1.

EPHRAIM CARPENTER

Ephraim Carpenter was born in Lincoln county, North Carolina, August 15, 1812. His father, Samuel Carpenter, was born in the same county and was reared and lived there all his life, was a farmer and a member of the Lutheran church. His wife, Elizabeth Rudasell, was born in North Carolina, and became the mother of twelve children, of whom Ephraim is the fifth.

Ephraim Carpenter was reared in North Carolina, but in 1836 moved to Alabama, married there and remained until 1850, when he moved to Louisiana and made that State his abiding place until 1869, when he removed to Grayson county, Texas, where he has since resided and followed farming, and now owns six hundred acres of fine land. He started in life a poor boy, and in North Carolina and Alabama was engaged in the tanning business. Up to the time of the opening of the war he had accumulated a large property and was an extensive slave-holder. His wife bore the maiden name of Dicy Clements, a daughter of William and Winfred (Whorton) Clements, both natives of Georgia. She bore her husband five children – Permalla C., Charles A., Butler T., William S. E. and Jesse C. Mr. Carpenter is a Free Mason and a member of the Lutheran church.

Source: *Biographical Souvenir of the State of Texas.* Chicago: F. A. Battey & Co., 1889.

Note: William Clements and family were residing in Carroll County, Georgia in 1830. See 1830 Census. One source gives his wife's name as Horton, not Whorton. See sketch of M. K. Clements in this volume.

BENJAMIN FRANKLIN CLAYTON

Benjamin Franklin Clayton, is actively occupied as school-master and farmer of Huston Township. A native of Arkansas, he was born in Conway County, June 20, 1858, to the union of William and Eliza (McBurnett) Clayton. The father gave his attention to tilling the soil, with good success. He was of English descent, was born in Kentucky, and died in Conway County, Ark., during the war. Benjamin's mother came originally from Alabama, being the daughter of Thomas McBurnett; she died in 1872. In the family there were four children, two now living: Benjamin and Richard T. The subject of this sketch, the third child, was reared principally in Conway County, receiving his

BENJAMIN FRANKLIN CLAYTON

early education in Arkansas, which he supplemented by a course, in 1874, in Carroll County, Ga. In 1879 he began teaching in his native county, and has followed this occupation five terms. He has 120 acres of land, about sixty-five under cultivation. In 1886 his fitness for the position led to his election as justice of the peace, and he was re-elected in 1888, proving an able and efficient officer. He was school director of his district two years. In politics he is a Democrat, having cast his first presidential vote for Hancock. In 1881 Mr. Clayton married Miss Betty Bird, who died in 1882, and in 1883 Lizzie Johnson, a native of Tennessee, became his wife. She died in 1886, and in August, 1888, Mr. Clayton married Katie Latham, whose birth occurred in Missouri in 1871. They have one child, Lillie. Mr. Clayton's farm is well improved, and on it is a living spring of water. He and his wife are members of the Methodist Episcopal Church, South.

Source: *Biographical and Historical Memoirs of Pulaski, Jefferson, Lonoke, Faulkner, Grant, Saline, Perry, Garland and Hot Spring Counties, Arkansas,* 1889.

M. K. CLEMENTS

M. K. Clements was born on the 18th of March, 1856, in Talladega County, Ala. His ancestors came from Europe and settled in Virginia about the close of the seventeenth century. His great-grandfather, James Clements, moved from Virginia to Georgia just before the Revolutionary War. There a son, William, was born, and about the close of the last century the family moved to Alabama and settled in Randolph County. Here William married Miss Winnie Horton, and on the 10th day of April 1820, Benjamin N. was born; he married Miss Tempa Forrel. To this couple, the subject of this sketch was born. Benjamin N. Clements is a farmer, and M. K. Clements was reared on the farm amid the romantic scenery of the Hillobee part of Talladega County. He taught school in 1872-73, and in the fall of the latter year entered the A. and M. College at Auburn, where he was graduated with distinction in 1876. Soon after leaving college he married Miss Sophia Thomas. He taught school in Clay County in 1877, in Tallapoosa County in 1878, and in the fall of that year joined the North Alabama Conference and was appointed to the Valley Head Circuit in Wills Valley, DeKalb County, Ala., which he traveled until the session of the Conference in 1879, when he was appointed principal of the Guntersville District High School, located at Collinsville. He continued in charge of this school for seven years, and succeeded in building up one of the best institutions of learning in that part of the State.

In the fall of 1886 he moved to Atalla, and established the Atalla High School, which is one of the best of the kind in North Alabama. He has three children: Edna Earl, Victor Hugo, and Merit DeWitt.

Source: *Northern Alabama Historical and Biographical,* 1888.

Note: M. K. Clements' grandfather, William Clements, was residing in Carroll County, Georgia in 1830. See 1830 Census.

FELIX N. COBB

Felix N. Cobb, attorney at law, Carrollton, Ga., was born in Carroll County, Ga., December 29, 1861. His father, James H. Cobb, a planter residing near Temple, Carroll County, was born in that county in June, 1837. He, in turn is a son of Isaac E., a native of South Carolina, of English extraction, who moved to Carroll County, Ga., in 1825, and represented that county in the legislature three terms, and was sheriff of Carroll County several terms. The mother of the subject was Sarah E. (Walker) Cobb, a native of Fulton County and a daughter of John M. Walker, a planter of Georgia. She bore her husband five children, viz: Lula, wife of James M. Wynn; Felix N., John T., William I. and Walker M.

Felix N. received his literary education in Carroll Masonic Institute. He taught school in Paulding County, Ga., for two years, and was subsequently assistant postmaster at Carrollton, Ga., for the same length of time. He then took up the study of law under Oscar Reese, and was admitted to the bar in July, 1883, since when he has been actively pursuing his profession. For two years he practiced with J. L. Cobb, but in January, 1888, he formed a partnership with his former preceptor, Oscar Reese, and this firm has since that time had a full share of the law practice of the county, having been connected with all important railroad cases. The firm of Reese & Cobb are now local counsel for the Chattanooga, Rome & Columbus R. R.

In 1882 he married Miss Mattie A. Smith, daughter of George

M. Smith, of Georgia. Their home has been brightened by one child, Hiram F.

Mr. Cobb is dictator of the K. of H. fraternity, a member of the I. O. O. F. fraternity and of the Baptist Church. Stands high in the county as a lawyer of ability, being a natural born orator, which is characteristic of the Cobb family. The subject of this sketch has a bright future and promises to be one of the leading lawyers of the State. He is Democratic in his views, but has never taken an active part in State politics; is prominent, however, in all local matters.

Source: *Biographical Souvenir of the States of Georgia and Florida*, 1889.

J. F. COLE

J. F. Cole, M. D., one of the most successful physicians and surgeons of Carrollton, Ga., was born in Carroll County, Ga., February 29, 1852. His father, S. V. Cole, is a native of South Carolina, a son of Jeremiah Cole; he is still living and engaged in planting. The mother of the subject was Nancy J. (Beall) Cole, born in Athens, Ga., and a daughter of James Beall.

J. F. Cole is the only child born to his parents. He read medicine with J. G. Arall, M. D., and graduated from the Atlanta Medical College in 1875. In 1877 he went to Craigshead, Ark., thence to Carrollton, Ga., where he practiced thirteen months; since then he has practiced his profession continuously in Carroll County, giving attention to all branches, but especially to skin diseases. He has also assisted the noted Dr. Robert Battey, of Rome, Ga., in many of his surgical operations.

In 1887 he established a drug store in Carrollton, which he carries on in conjunction with his large practice.

In 1872 he married Miss Sarah Crutchfield, daughter of Jesse Crutchfield, of Georgia. To this union are born four children: Seaborn J., John F., Ella M. and Joseph Battey.

The doctor is a Royal Arch and Council Mason, and, with wife, a member of the Baptist Church.

Source: *Biographical Souvenir of the States of Georgia and Florida*, 1889.

WILLIAM A. COLEMAN

W. A. Coleman, farmer and banker, Carrollton, Carroll Co., Ga., son of Henry A. and Sarah Ann (Barnes) Coleman, was born in 1838. His paternal grandparent, George Coleman, was a native of South Carolina, and came from that state to Georgia early in this century. His father was born in Putnam county, Ga., in 1814, was reared a farmer, and was a soldier in the Indian war of 1836. For many years he was bailiff, and also a major of militia in Cobb county, Ga., when to be a major was something of a distinction locally. He was a prominent member of the Missionary Baptist church. His maternal grandparents, James and Sarah (McKenzie) Barnes, were among the early settlers of Lincoln county, Ga. Mr. Coleman was reared on a farm in DeKalb county, and what little education he received was the old-time log school so many times described elsewhere in this volume, and in obtaining it had to go three or four miles barefooted. In October, 1861, he enlisted in Company E, (Capt. Sharpe), First Georgia cavalry, and continued in the service until April 26, 1865. He was in many hard-fought battles, notably Chickamauga, Resaca, Kennesaw and Marietta – all the way to Atlanta and Savannah. He was on the skirmish line when Stoneman surrendered, and although he was neither wounded nor captured during the war, he narrowly escaped both. A spirit of enterprise and adventure took him to Honduras, Central America, in 1868, when he carried with him the necessary machinery and implements to engage extensively in saw-milling, fruit growing and cane-culture. He sawed the first lumber ever sawed and baled the first cotton ever baled for shipment in that country. His extensive manufacturing, agriculture and property interests in Honduras are now in charge of his son, William F., who resides there. From that source he derives a very large income, in addition to that from a large, well-improved farm in Carroll county, for, in addition to successfully managing enterprises so large and so remote, he prides himself on being one of the best farmers in his county. His success in everything he has undertaken has been phenomenal. He changed his residence from his farm to Carrollton, where he has an elegant home, so as to educate his children. He is one of the directors of the Carrollton bank. Mr. Coleman was married in 1858 to Miss Cynthia Riggs – born in Butts county, Ga. – daughter of John and Jane (Florence) Riggs, early settlers. Mr. Riggs was born in South Carolina, ran away from home and came to Georgia when sixteen years of age, and afterward became a Baptist minister of note. This wife died in 1877, leaving one child, William F., now in Honduras. In January, 1879, Mr. Coleman married Miss Clara, daughter of Valentine and Eliza (Gant) Kolb, a family of wealth, and among the first settlers of Meriwether county, Ga. By this marriage two children have been born to him – Laura and James. Mrs. Coleman is a member of the Missionary Baptist church and Mr. Coleman is a master Mason.

Source: *Memoirs of Georgia*, 1895. Volume 1.

GEORGE WASHINGTON COLQUITT

George Washington Colquitt, only son of Wm. T. and Ann Colquitt, was born in Russell county, Alabama, on the 16th of August, 1841. The early part of his life was spent on the farm and in school, his parents being careful to give their children the benefit of the best facilities offered at that time within their means.

Surrounded by a large family of children, whose education depended on their limited resources, his parents found it necessary to seek some locality affording better advantages for this purpose, and they accordingly removed to Carroll county, Georgia, in the fall of 1858, when the subject of this sketch entered "Bowdon College," in his seventeenth year. With his love of books and thirst for knowledge, he readily availed himself of the opportunities given at this institution. Flattering prospects were before him, and plans were already maturing to bring to perfection the hopes of his young heart, when it pleased God to awaken him to a consciousness of his wretched condition as a sinner. Although he was a constant reader of the Bible and had good instructions from a pious mother from youth he was not convinced that an honest purpose to live uprightly availeth nothing, till a sister (the only one of the nine that rests from her labors) joined the church. Upon hearing that she was to be baptized, he laid aside his books and sought peace with God through Jesus Christ our Lord, which he hopes to have realized on the 25th of August, 1859. On the same day he was received into fellowship with Eden church, and the day following was baptized by Rev. George W. Burson.

Full of joy and peace, he longed to tell others of the goodness of God, scarcely realizing that this was an *impression* of the great work of the ministry. Several years passed, during which there was a struggle amounting almost to agony; a conviction of duty and a disposition of the flesh never to yield. Finally, in 1863, the regiment (7th Georgia Infantry) of which he was a member, petitioned the church to grant him license to preach, with a view to his appointment as chaplain. The license was granted, but the War Department did not see proper to make the appointment. On his return home at the close of the war, he was ordained to the full work of the ministry in Eden church, June 15th, 1867. The presbytery consisted of Revs. George W. Burson, George W. Tumlin, James Barrow, W. S. Tweedell, and M. D. Robison.

He took charge of the church at Indian Creek, immediately after ordination and remained as pastor till the close of the following year. With no resources except his own labor, he taught school in connection with pastoral service two or three years, but failing health and a conviction that a minister should give himself "wholly to the work," induced him to abandon the school-room. After four years' connection with the churches at Bowdon and Carrollton, commencing in 1869, he removed to Heard county, Georgia, and was pastor of bethel and Western churches, in Heard, and of Antioch, in Troup county; six years at Bethel and five years at each of the others.

In 1877, he received a call from the church at Ramah, Campbell county, and in the hope that the change in location would be an advantage to his health, he came to Palmetto in December, 1877, and is at present, preaching to three churches in Campbell county, and one in Coweta county.

He was married on the 8th of March, 1864, to Miss Mary F. Word, who has shared with him the trials and comforts of a minister's life.

Brother Colquitt's ministry was, at the beginning, unpromising, and therefore somewhat discouraging; and although it has not been marked by a large increase of members, yet it is not without evidence of success. He has the confidence and esteem of his brethren; his piety and exemplary life exert an influence which greater talent sometimes fails to command. He is firm in his convictions, simple and earnest in his manner.

It has been his aim to commend the truth to every man's conscience, and to show the beauty and efficacy of divine grace in an humble life, consecrated to the glory of God in the salvation of souls.

Source: *History of the Baptist Denomination in Georgia*, 1881.

HENRY F. CRAWFORD

Henry F. Crawford, farmer, Temple, Carroll Co., Ga., son of Gallant and Katie Crawford, was born in what is now Spalding county, in 1846. His paternal grandfather, William Crawford, was a native Virginian, came to Georgia in ox-carts in 1810, and settled in the woods. He was a soldier in the war of 1812. Mr. Crawford's father was born in what is now Henry county, in 1816, and was reared a farmer, and followed farming all his life. He was a soldier in the Indian war of 1836. His maternal grandparents were among the first settlers and wealthy citizens of that part of the state. Mr. Crawford was reared on the farm and had to work hard, and so had to be content with a very limited education. In 1864 he enlisted in Company F (Capt. Thomas), Phillips' legion, and, although his service was not lengthy, it was rough and arduous. He participated in the Bellfield creek raid – three days' fighting – the battle of Petersburg, and the stirring events of the closing scenes of the war. He was in the engagement at Orangeburg, S. C., and Salisbury, N. C., and was at Charlotte, N. C., at the time of the surrender. After the war he came home and engaged in farming. In 1870, Mr. Crawford was married to Miss Nancy, daughter of John and Eliza (Weidner) Lee. Mr. Lee, her father, was born in Kentucky in 1818, and when seventeen years of age ran away from home and came to Georgia with some hog drivers, and never returned. Having fine business capacity, and being a shrewd trader he became very rich, but the war about ruined him. When Mr. Crawford married he was very poor, but not discouraged, and his wife proved a helpmeet, indeed; she worked with him in the field during the day, and at night spun and wove the cloth and made the clothing for the family. Thus they worked together and struggled on as plain farmers, until now he has a good 200-acre farm and comfortable home where he lives, and, nearby a 250-acre tract of choice land. To them six children have been born: Alice, wife of Cas. Cantrell; Robert, Frank, William H., Rilla, and O. V. Mr. and Mrs. Crawford are members of the Missionary Baptist church, content with their success in life, and happy in the consciousness of having the confidence and esteem of their neighbors.

Source: *Memoirs of Georgia*, 1895. Volume 1.

ELISHA CREEL

Elisha Creel, farmer, Mandeville, Carroll Co., Ga., son of George and Harriet (Belcher) Creel, was born in Fayette county, Ga., in 1847. His maternal grandfather, William Belcher, was a Clayton county, Ga., pioneer and was a soldier in the war of 1812. Mr. Creel's father was born in what is now Monroe county, in 1816; but while yet a young man he removed to Fayette county, among its earliest settlers, settled in the woods and cleared a farm. From this small beginning he has become by hard work and economy, and careful management, one of the wealthiest men in the county. Mr. Creel was reared on the farm and received but a limited education. In 1866, he married Mary Ann Miller – born in Campbell county — daughter of Jefferson and Eliza (Eidson) Miller, early settlers of Campbell county. Of thirteen children born to them these nine are living: George J., Joe, Wiley, Robert, Alice, Alvin, Hattie, Mary and Anna. Mr. Creel began life without a dollar and for some years had a very hard time. He moved to Carroll county in 1869 and in a few years began to prosper. He has now an excellent 750-acre farm, well improved, is recognized as one of the best farmers in the county, and is getting rich. He is another and a convincing example of what can be done in farming in Georgia when the farmer works intelligently, and works hard and early and late, saves a surplus and judiciously invests it. He commands the confidence and respect of all who know him. Mrs. Creel is a member of the Baptist church.

Source: *Memoirs of Georgia*, 1895. Volume 1.

JOHN F. CULPEPPER

John F. Culpepper, Sr., Whitesburg, Carroll Co., Ga., son of Joel and Elizabeth (Whitaker) Culpepper, was born in Coweta county, Ga., May 17, 1835. His paternal grandfather, Malachi Culpepper, was one of the early settlers of Morgan county, and was a soldier in the revolutionary war. His maternal grandparents, John and Polly Whitaker (nee Holliway), were among the early settlers of Coweta county. His father was born in Morgan county, April 1, 1802, where he was reared, and lived until 1827, when he removed to Coweta county and settled in the woods. Mr. Culpepper was reared in Coweta county, and received a good common school education, earning the money himself that paid his school expenses one year. In 1855, he engaged as a clerk in a store in Carrollton, and after one year's experience "opened up" for

JOHN F. CULPEPPER

himself, and continued in business until 1862, when he enlisted in Company B, Seventh regiment, Confederate cavalry (Capt. L. J. Smith). At the end of a year he hired a substitute, and entered into a contract with the secretary of war to gather material for the manufacture of ammunition for the armies, which contract continued until the surrender. After the war he entered mercantile life again in Newnan, Ga., and in 1877 lost everything, and went on the farm where he now lives. He made two starts in life, and failed to attain his end; but in his last undertaking, that of farming, he has succeeded beyond his most sanguine expectations, and rightly feels proud and exultant over his success. Mr. Culpepper was married in 1857 to Miss Epsie Boon – born in Carroll county – daughter of Jesse and Nancy (Lester) Boon, old settlers of the county. To them five children have been born – three living: Lucinda, wife of W, C. Branan; Anna, wife of T. E. Walten; and Vela. Mrs. Culpepper is a member of the Methodist church, and he is a royal arch Mason. Mr. Culpepper is a wide-awake, progressive farmer, and very much respected by all who know him.

Source: *Memoirs of Georgia*, 1895. Volume 1.

WILLIAM HARRIS DABNEY

William Harris Dabney, lawyer, Rome, Floyd Co., was born near Shady Dale, Jasper Co., Ga., in 1817. His father, Anderson Dabney, was born in Virginia about 1774, came to Georgia when a young man, and after living awhile in Greensboro, went to Jasper county, where he died about 1821. In 1829 his mother died also, and then he went to live with his uncle, Garland Dabney, in De Kalb county, Ga. He received his primary education at the "old-field" school, and in 1833 went to Decatur and entered the academy, where he remained three years preparing for college. Four years later he entered Franklin college (now the university of Georgia), at Athens, from which he graduated in 1839. During this period (in 1836) he served in the Creek Indian war three months. Returning to Decatur after his graduation he studied law under the direction of his brother-in-law, Hon. James M. Calhoun – afterward the war mayor of Atlanta – and in the spring of 1840 was admitted to the bar at Greene county superior court. Entering into partnership with Col. Calhoun, he practiced in De Kalb county until 1850, when he moved to Calhoun, Gordon Co., Ga. He remained and practiced law there with the exception of the last two or three years of the civil war until 1873, when he moved to Rome, where he has since made his home and practiced his profession. He was prevented by ill health from entering the Confederate service. In 1854 he was elected senator from Gordon county to the general assembly, and in 1860 was elected to represent the county in the convention which passed the ordinance of secession the January following – for which he voted. Mr. Dabney was admitted to practice in the federal courts both before and after the war. He confined himself to the practice of law and never cared for or sought office, though no citizen, by intellectual endowments, legal training and public spirit, was better qualified for it. At the bar he has been the peer of any, and in private life the embodiment of the true old-time southern gentleman. Mr. Dabney was married in Decatur, Ga., in December, 1842, to Miss Martha B., daughter of Ami Williams, one of the oldest settlers of De Kalb county. Of the children born to them four survive: William A., a Presbyterian minister; Tyree J., at Decatur, Ga.; Frank B., civil engineer, and a member of the international commissioners appointed by the United States and Mexico to settle boundary lines, and Mary V., unmarried. His wife died in 1885. Mr. Dabney is a master Mason, and although not a member, affiliates with the Presbyterian church.

Source: *Memoirs of Georgia*, 1895. Volume 1.

Note: Martha B. Williams' father, Ammi Williams was residing in Carroll County in 1830. His stay was apparently a brief one. Ammi Williams became one of the foremost citizens of DeKalb County. He and Reuben Cone at one time owned the lot of land on the other side of the railroad in Atlanta, later known as the North Atlanta District. Mr. Williams was a great believer in the growth of Atlanta. Ammi Williams and his wife, also William Harris Dabney and his wife, are buried in Oakland Cemetery. Another daughter of Ammi Williams, Laura Loomis Williams, married Lemuel P. Grant, for whom Grant Park is named.

ALFORD H. DARNALL

Alford H. Darnall is a native of Gibson county, Tennessee, and was born January 22, 1839. In 1855 he was brought by his father, Robert C. Darnall, to Texas, and here he has resided ever since. He was married in June, 1860, to Miss Barbara McRae, a daughter of

ALFORD H. DARNALL

Malcolm A. McRae, a native of Georgia, but an early pioneer of Texas. To this union were born six children, named as follows – Robert A., Mary E., Celia J., William H., Melissa A. and John F.

Robert C. Darnall was born in Murray county, Tennessee, and was a farmer all his life. After coming to Texas he served three years in the home guards during the Civil War, and failed to save his live stock. At the close of the conflict he had little or nothing left, and, although he had recuperated his fortune to a great extent by 1872, a disastrous cyclone in May of that year struck his house, destroying it, and inflicting injuries on all the family, Mr. Darnall being the most seriously hurt, and dying in April, 1878. The wife of Robert C. Darnall, Rachael E. Simpson, was a daughter of Charles Simpson, a native of Georgia and a physician, who was assassinated while sitting at his fireside, by a brother-in-law, who shot through the window. The assassin was captured, tried and convicted, but managed to escape.

The marriage of Robert C. Darnall to Rachael C. Simpson took place in Tennessee in 1837, and to their union were born ten children, named as follows – Alford H., Mary A. C., Robert, Martha E., Sarah E., Enoch G., Narcissa E., Dasigna I., Susan and Melissa J.

In June, 1860, Alford H. Darnall, as stated above, was married. He was well settled upon a farm when the war opened in 1861. It was not, however, until 1862, that he enlisted and served in Company A, Ninth Texas regiment a year or more. His army services were rendered in Texas, Arkansas and Louisiana, and one year east of the Mississippi river, taking part in the battles of Indianola, Port Hudson and Magnolia. At the last named place he was taken prisoner, but, being sick, was paroled. He returned to his regiment, and was near Mansfield, Texas, when the war was concluded. On his return home he resumed farming and added stock breeding, and is now one of the most successful hog raisers in Texas. His standing as a member of the Methodist Episcopal church South is exceptionally good.

Source: *Biographical Souvenir of the State of Texas*, 1889.

Note: Malcolm A. McRae was a resident of Carroll County.

BARNEY DAVIS

Barney Davis is a planter, residing in Bear Creek Township, Sevier County, Ark., but was born in Carroll County, Ga., February

27, 1844, a son of Jonathan W. and Rachel K. (Bridges) Davis, both of whom were born in North Carolina, the former in 1799, and the latter in 1802. They were married in their native State, and their union resulted in the birth of twelve children – six sons and six daughters – six of the family being now alive: William L., Mary (widow of C. C. Williams), Martha (widow of B. F. Booth), Julie (wife of James H. Hedley, a farmer, residing in this county), Amanda (wife of W. R. Woodruff, a resident of Howard County, Ark.) and Barney (who is the youngest of the family). Mr. Davis first removed with his family to Georgia, but in 1858 came to Arkansas, and settled on a farm in Bear Creek Township, Sevier County, where he was called from the scene of his earthly labors in 1881, his wife dying in 1879, both being earnest members of the Baptist Church. Barney Davis, the subject of this sketch, came to Arkansas with his parents at the age of fourteen, and was united here December 20, 1866, to Miss Nancy J. Hadley, and his second union took place December 1, 1886, Miss Lucinda Meriditt, who was born in Arkansas, in 1860, becoming his wife. They have one daughter, Amanda A. Mr. Davis is the possessor of a fine farm, comprising 160 acres, and his property is well improved with buildings, orchards, etc. He is a Democrat in his political views, and his wife is a member of the Christian Church.

Source: *Biographical and Historical Memoirs of Southern Arkansas,* 1890.

JACOB DOROUGH

Jacob Dorough, planter, Paris, Ark. Mr. Dorough's first impression was that of assisting on his father's farm, and it is but natural, perhaps, that when it became necessary for him to choose some occupation in life, he should select the one to which he had been reared. He was born in Georgia, October 22, 1849, and his parents, Milton B. and Emily M. (Casper) Dorough, were natives of Georgia and South Carolina, respectively, the father born in 1820 and the mother in 1819. They were married in Carroll County, Ga., and to them were born ten children, five besides our subject now living: William T., Margy M., John R., Simeon H., and Nancy R. Those deceased were Louisa S., James P., Milton W. and George H. The parents died in Georgia, the father in 1890 and the mother in 1884. Both were church members. The father was in the Indian wars. Jacob

JACOB DOROUGH

Dorough attained his growth on his father's farm, and was married in Heard County, Ga., in 1865, to Miss Susan L. Mosely, a native of Georgia, born April 14, 1850. Twelve children have blessed this union, nine now living: James W., Milton M., Charles F., George S., Henry E., Robert S., Elbert R., Sarah C. (died November 8, 1890), Rhoda J., Adolphus W. (deceased), Jacob H., and Emily R. (died November 15, 1890). Mr. Dorough enlisted in Company H, infantry, in 1864, and served until 1865. He was paroled at Athens, Ga., and then returned home, where he engaged in tilling the soil. He is now the owner of 270 acres of land, and has 100 acres under cultivation. He was elected justice of the peace of Mountain Township, in 1878, and has discharged the duties of that office ever since. He is a blacksmith, and works for the neighborhood. He is a member of the Farmers' Alliance, and a member of the Presbyterian Church. Mrs. Dorough is a member of the Methodist Episcopal Church.

Source: *Biographical and Historical Memoirs of Western Arkansas,* 1891.

W.S. DOWNS

W. S. Downs, blacksmith, and one of the skillful workmen of the county, is a native of Georgia, born in 1848, and the son of Shelly Downs, who was born in Virginia. The latter was married in his native State, and afterward moved to Georgia, where the mother died shortly afterward, and where the father died in 1861, leaving a family of three children. W. S. Downs was but thirteen years of age when his father died, and for three years after this, and during the war, he drove a team from Atlanta to Bowden, Ga., and was with his teams near Franklin, Ga. (which is 100 miles from Atlanta), when that city fell into the hands of the Federal troops. At the age of sixteen Mr. Downs went to work to learn the carriage and wagon-maker's trade with the firm of J. W. Downs, and afterward with Downs & Langford, at Conyers, Ga., remaining in their employ for three years. He then came to Clay County, Ark., where he has resided ever since, with the exception of about three years, two of which he spent in New Madrid, Mo., and one year at his old home, where he worked for Mr. Langford, who was carrying on the same business. During his stay here six years were spent in the mill business, the second steam-mill in the county, and he afterward followed farming until about 1888, when he opened up his old business in Boydsville. He has built a shop for general repair work, and is having a fair trade. He was married in 1869 to Miss Martha A. Arnold, daughter of Andrew Arnold, of Clay County (but which at that time was Greene County), and nine children have been the result of this union, eight now living. They are named as follows: Lenora J., wife of J. A. Burton, of Tennessee, and the mother of one child; J. H., at home attending the farm; L. R., at home; William E., J. B., Florence A., Matthew A. and Alvin Shelly, who is named after his grandfather. Mr. and Mrs. Downs are members of the Methodist Episcopal Church, South, and he is a Democrat in politics.

Source: *Biographical and Historical Memoirs of Northeast Arkansas,* 1889.

MELVIN NATHANIEL DYER

Hon. Melvin Nathaniel Dyer. Prominent in the ranks of the foremost of the brilliant circle of lawyers of Baxter County, Ark., stands the name of Melvin Nathaniel Dyer, who has a most thorough and practical knowledge of the complications of law. He was born near Lawrenceville, Gwinnett County, Ga., in 1833, and reared in Walker County, Ga., a son of Edwin Dyer, who was a native of Virginia, and was reared on Blue Grass soil. His father, Wiley Dyer, made fifty-three moves during his lifetime and died in Texas. He was a farmer by occupation, was quite a Nimrod in his day, and while in Kentucky, developed some salt wells, from which he netted a good income while boating up and down the Big Sandy and Ohio Rivers. In 1849 he went to Texas, where he was called from life in 1850, at about the age of seventy years. Edwin Dyer was a minister of the Missionary Baptist Church, became well known as an eminent divine, and when the subject of this sketch was a boy preached at Lafayette, Ga., Rome, Ga., and Chattanooga, Tenn. He afterward came to Arkansas and for some time preached at Mountain Home, after which he removed to Texas and died at Breckenridge in 1876, at the age of seventy years. His wife, Nancy Austin, the mother of the subject of this sketch, is still living and has attained to the advanced age of eighty-eight years. She resides in Rome, Ga. There were born to her marriage with Mr. Dyer five sons and three daughters, and four of these sons took part in the great Civil War as members of the Confederate Army. Edwin belonged to the First Arkansas Rifles, Churchill's old regiment, and was at the

MELVIN NATHANIEL DYER

battles of Oakhill, but later died from exposure. He was a graduate of the Macon Medical College. Wiley, another son, was inspector general with the rank of captain of Reynold's brigade, was for some time a prisoner of war at Johnson's Island; he is still living. Simpson was a member of the Dalton Guards, served in the Army of Virginia and died during the war. In 1862 Melvin N., the subject of this sketch, joined Company E, Fortieth Georgia Infantry, but after serving with that regiment one year went into the Third Georgia Cavalry, which was a part of Wheeler's command, and saw some hard service. At the close of the war he surrendered at Kingston, Ga. In 1856 he graduated from Mercer University, at Penfield, Ga., and after some preparation he was, in 1858, admitted to the bar, and from that time until the opening of the Civil War he was engaged in teaching school and practicing his profession. When hostilities ceased he located in Gordon County, Ga., where he taught school and operated a sawmill until 1870, when he moved to near Salem, Fulton County, Ark. Since 1874 he has been a resident of Mountain Home and has since been a successful legal practitioner and farmer. In 1882 he was elected prosecuting attorney for the Third Judicial District, when this district was among the largest in the State, and this position he filled with marked ability until 1886. In 1861 he was married to Miss Annie Field of Georgia, by whom he has four children: Wiley M., who is an attorney and is associated with his father in the practice of law. [Other three children omitted in original] Mr. Dyer is a Royal Arch Mason, has represented his lodge in the Grand Lodge of the State, and also belongs to the I. O. O. F., in which he is a member of the Encampment and has served as noble grand. He and his wife are members of the Missionary Baptist Church and he was very active in the organization of the Baptist College of Mountain Home. He is an excellent citizen, a shrewd lawyer and a man of much intelligence and force of character.

Source: *A Reminiscent History of the Ozark Region*, 1894.

Note: Wiley Dyer and family were residents of Carroll County in 1830 See 1830 Census.

C. C. EAVES

C. C. Eaves, farmer, Buchanan, Haralson Co., Ga., son of L. B. and Lavinia (Camp) Eaves, was born in Paulding county, Ga., in 1834.

His father came from Rutherford county, N. C., where he married his wife, a daughter of Cleburne Camp, who came to Georgia in 1832. When his parents settled in Haralson county they were in moderately good circumstances. His father died at the age of sixty-five, and the mother at the age of seventy-two years. Mr. Eaves was reared on the farm, but like thousands of others, children of frontiersmen and pioneers, received very meager schooling, owing to inconveniences and disadvantages, both of accommodations and teachers. He, however, by studying at home at night by fire-light, improved himself very much in that respect. In 1862 he enlisted in Montgomery's artillery, with which he remained about six months, when, being taken sick, he returned home and sent a substitute to the army. His attention has been given principally to his farm, although at one time he engaged in merchandising, and now, in addition to his farm, runs a grist mill. A plain, common-sense, unostentatious farmer, he is entirely content with his vocation, with its sufficient income, and with being regarded by his neighbors as an honorable man and good citizen. Mr. Eaves married in 1865, for his first wife, Miss Amanda, daughter of John and Betsy Kuhrt [Kirk, sic.], of Pike county, Ga., by whom he had nine children: Johnnie Cleburne, William Taylor, Benjamin Franklin, Davy Alonzo, Davis, Lovie, Bailey, Sedford and Jackson. He married for his second wife Miss Jennie, daughter of Absolom Wilson. Himself and wife are consistent and zealous members of the Primitive Baptist church. About the close of the war he was elected a justice of the peace.

Source: *Memoirs of Georgia*, 1895. Volume 1.

Note: Lavinia Eaves was listed as head of the household on the 1830 Census of Carroll County, Georgia, although it appears her husband was living with her. The 1840 and 1850 Censuses of Paulding County list L. B. Eaves as head of household.

WILLIAM R. EDGE

William R. Edge, a prosperous citizen of this county [Meriwether], has passed through many vicissitudes in the years of his life. He is the son of Joseph and Margaret (Flint) Edge, the former born in Wilkes county in 1803, and died in Meriwether county in 1886; his father, Nehemiah Edge, a South Carolinian, was one of the earliest

WILLIAM R. EDGE

settlers of Wilkes county. Here in 1826 William R. was born and here he passed his boyhood, obtaining such education as he was able to do in his country home. Later he began working for himself at the rate of seven dollars per month, at which rate he worked for three years; then he was overseer for a time, after which he went into the milling business. He fell a victim to the "gold fever," and spent some time in California in search of that much-sought mineral. He served also through the war, enlisting in 1862 in Company B, First Georgia cavalry, under Capt. J. W. Trammell; he was in the battle at Philadelphia and was in all the engagements during the memorable "march to the sea," being in those forces before Sherman all the way. Since the war he has been engaged in several different kinds of business, but has been especially successful in farming, as his large and beautiful and well-kept plantation on the Flint river bears witness. Mr. Edge married in 1855 his wife, Miss Catherine Boyd, being the daughter of Milton and Jane (Douglass) Boyd, of South Carolina, who came to Georgia in 1830. One daughter, Emma C., was born to Mr. and Mrs. Edge; she is now the wife of W. P. Lovelace. Mrs. Edge died in 1875 and in 1877 Mr. Edge married Mrs. Amanda (Miller) Knowles, a daughter of Jacob and Mary (Lovelace) Miller, of Wilkes county. Mrs. Edge is a member of the Methodist Episcopal church; her husband is a member of the masonic fraternity.

Source: *Memoirs of Georgia*, 1895. Volume 2.

Note: William R. Edge's father, Joseph Edge, was residing in Carroll County, Georgia in 1860, 1870, and 1880. See Censuses for those years. It is probable that his mother, Margaret Flint, is buried in Carroll County. However, Joseph Edge died in Meriwether County, Georgia and is buried at Mt. Carmel Methodist Church there.

CALVIN S. ELLIS

Calvin S. Ellis, farmer-mechanic, Oval, Paulding Co., Ga., son of Isaac C. and Elizabeth (Smith) Ellis, was born in Cass (now Bartow) county, in 1841. His grandfather, Calvin Ellis, was a North Carolinian, a soldier in the early Indian wars, and the son of a soldier in the revolutionary army. Mr. Ellis' father was born in North Carolina in 1812, raised on a farm and educated in the common schools of North Carolina and Georgia. His parents migrated from North Carolina to

CALVIN S. ELLIS

Georgia when he was a lad, and settled in Cass (now Bartow) county, and soon afterward apprenticed him to a blacksmith to learn the trade. Some time after this he went to Carroll county, but in 1845, moved to Marion county, Ala., where he lived until he died, Feb. 5, 1892. His mother, daughter of Simeon and Eleanor Smith, was born in North Carolina in 1814, and came to Georgia when a child, with her parents, who settled in Gwinnett county, and afterward moved to Cass county, where, in 1832, she married Mr. Ellis. She died in 1855. Mr. Ellis was raised on the farm, and educated in the "old-field" school, common to that locality and period. In 1861 he enlisted for twelve months in Company C, Seventh Georgia regiment, and the next year re-enlisted in Company I, Nineteenth Georgia regiment, with which he was in the seven-days' fight around Richmond, and the battles at Gaines' mills, Cold Harbor and Chancellorsville. May 3, 1863, Mr. Ellis was shot entirely through the body and sent to the hospital at Richmond, from there to Atlanta, and afterward to his home. He so far recovered by February, 1864, as to be able to rejoin his command at Charleston, S. C., which he did, and was with it in the famous charge on Fort Fisher. Soon after this his wound broke out afresh, and he was again sent to the hospital. After remaining there four months, he rejoined his regiment, then in North Carolina, having had the ball extracted from his back only six days before the surrender of Gen. Johnston. The wound troubles him now at times; and he still has in his possession the ball which came so near ending his life. Returning from the war, his first work was splitting 1,000 rails for a pair of trousers. He next went into a shop and made spinning wheels and chairs, which he sold to pay for making his first crop. The next year he worked on the telegraph line and worked his farm. In 1868 he resumed blacksmithing, in connection with his farming, and has conducted both successfully since. A good farmer and mechanic, industrious and thoroughly practical, his precept and example make him a useful citizen, and one highly esteemed. Mr. Ellis was married April 11, 1869, to Mrs. Lydia (Clinton) Roberts, daughter of John and Elizabeth Clinton – a union unblessed by children; two children of Mrs. Ellis, however, by her first marriage, are members of the household.

Source: *Memoirs of Georgia*, 1895. Volume 2.

GILES WINFIELD FEATHERSTON

Giles Winfield Featherston, merchant, Cedartown, Polk Co., Ga., son of L. H. and Mary Ann Featherston, was born in Heard county, Ga., June 10, 1842. His father was a lawyer, and early in life came from Maury county, Tenn., to Georgia, and settled in Heard county. In 1867 he removed to Newnan, Coweta Co., Ga., where he continued the practice of his profession. In 1866 he was appointed judge of the Blue Ridge circuit, and held the office four years. He was a prominent member of the constitutional convention of 1877. Mr. Featherston enjoyed excellent educational advantages – having attended good schools when a boy and youth, and subsequently graduating himself. In 1861 he enlisted in Company G, Capt. Joseph Brown, Heard county, Seventh Georgia regiment. This company was mostly composed of school boys connected with Franklin institute, Heard county. He was a participant in the first battle of Manassas, where he was shot through the left shoulder, which disabled him for service, and he was discharged. Before the war closed, however, he served with the state troops, and participated in the battles around Atlanta, and was finally assigned to duty in the ordnance department. In 1867 he left Heard county and came to Cedartown and engaged in merchandising, in which he was very successful, and which he continued until 1884, when he embarked in the wholesale lumber and manufacturing business and a ginnery. Beginning life with nothing after the war he has by cautious enterprise and judicious investments accumulated quite a large and valuable property. He is governed by an intelligently progressive spirit on all lines, a promoter of all movements promising development, and is a useful and much esteemed citizen. Mr. Featherston was married Jan. 16, 1868 to Miss Rosaline, daughter of E. H. and Mary C. (Jones) Richardson of Putnam county, Ga., who has borne him three children: Annie Estelle, Lucius Ernest, and Rosa May. Mr. Featherston is a master Mason, and a prominent member of the Presbyterian church.

Source: *Memoirs of Georgia*, 1895. Volume 2.

Note: Giles Featherston's brother, John, was a teacher residing in Villa Rica District, Carroll County, Georgia in 1870. Giles' uncle, Winfield Scott Featherston, was a general in the Confederate army.

F. M. FIELDER

F. M. Fielder, retired farmer, Villa Rica, Carroll Co., Ga., son of Terrell and Rebecca (Nolan) Fielder, was born in Morgan county, Ga., in 1823. His great-grandparents, Jasper and Mary (Stewart) Fielder, came from England to America before the revolutionary war, and settled in Virginia. Among the passengers aboard the same vessel was a Welsh family named Stewart – husband and wife and little daughter. The parents died during the voyage, and the little girl was reared by a family named Fielder. She afterwards became the wife of James Fielder and lived to be nearly 100 years old. Mr. Fielder's grandparents, James and Sally (Benga) Fielder, migrated from Virginia to Georgia and settled in the woods in Greene county, whence in a few years they removed to what is now Morgan county and cleared another farm, where they made a permanent home and remained until they died – he in 1813 and she in 1830, aged seventy years. Mr. Fielder's father was born in what is now Morgan county in 1797, and was a soldier in the war of 1812. On reaching manhood he was ordained a minister of the Missionary Baptist church, and preached in Morgan and adjoining counties. Having drawn some land in Meriwether county for his services in the war of 1812, himself and his brother-in-law, Sam Harris, removed to Meriwether county, in 1833. They settled in the dense unbroken forest, in which Indians and wild animals roamed and prowled at will. His father organized a Baptist church – the first in that part of the state – in an old dilapidated log house, which had been built and used for a sheep pen. He afterward, in 1851, moved to Tallapoosa county, Ala., where he died in 1873, aged seventy-six years, peacefully closing a life faithfully spent in doing good and preaching the gospel. His maternal grandparents, George and Rebecca Nolan, were natives of South Carolina, who, coming to Georgia, settled near Madison, Morgan county. Mr. Fielder was mostly reared in Meriwether county, and had the benefit of but a few months' schooling, and that was obtained at the old sheep pen where his father organized the church, after a four-mile walk, barefooted. He began life with nothing, and the first land he had he bought on credit, and before the war owned a 600-acre farm and ten slaves. Farming has been the pursuit of his life; and, although not wealthy, he has a fine farm, and a beautiful, comfortable home in Villa Rica. He served as notary public, ex-officio justice of the peace, two years. He was too old for regular service in the army, but served about six months in the Home guard. Mr. Fielder was

F. M. FIELDER

married in 1848 to Miss Martha Dobbs — born in South Carolina — daughter of Silas and Nancy (Myers) Dobbs, natives of South Carolina, who settled in Carroll county, in 1852. To them four children have been born, two of whom are living: Rebecca, wife of Dr. G. W. Strickland; and Silas O., who married Florence, daughter of William Candler. Mr. Fielder joined the church when seventeen years of age and has lived a consistent Christian life; and himself and his devoted companion are both members of the Missionary Baptist church.

Source: *Memoirs of Georgia*, 1895. Volume 1.

W. W. FITTS

W. W. Fitts, physician and surgeon, Carrollton, Carroll Co., Ga., son of Walker and Ann P. (Christian) Fitts, was born in Elbert county, Ga., in 1830. His grandfather, Tandy Fitts, was born in Virginia, and was a soldier during the revolutionary war. His father was also born in Virginia, and came to Elbert county and settled in the woods in 1820. In 1829 he went to Monroe county, Ga., and again cleared a farm in the woods. His grandfather on his mother's side, William Christian, was born in Virginia, moved to Georgia, and was among Elbert's early settlers. Dr. Fitts was reared in Monroe county, and was educated in an old-time log schoolhouse with dirt floor, lighted through apertures cut in the logs, the seats being of slabs from the near-by sawmill, with holes bored in them in which to insert the legs. There he was instructed in the old blue-back Webster's speller, reading, writing, and in Smiley's arithmetic, by Prof. Newnan. In after years he attended a good school, taught school himself and studied medicine. In 1856 he went to Atlanta, placed himself under the preceptorship of Drs. J. G. and W. F. Westmoreland, and entered Atlanta Medical college, where he graduated in 1860, and located in Calhoun county, Ala. In 1861 he enlisted in Company K (Capt. Ridley), Forty-fourth Alabama regiment (Col. Dent). Before the command went to the army he was made surgeon. He remained in the service until 1863, when he resigned on account of sickness and returned home. Dr. Fitts was married in 1855 to Miss A. W. Brown — born in Newton county — daughter of Samuel and Ruth (Brooks) Brown, who has borne him six children: Emma, wife of C. B. Simonton; William L., M. D., a graduate of the Atlanta medical college, and eleven years in practice; Robert H., druggist; Anna, wife of R. N. Moses, postmaster, Carrollton, Ga.; Eugenia, wife of Frank Weens, of Rome, Ga., and James W., merchant. Dr. Fitts moved to Carrollton in 1863, took the lead there at once in his profession, has established a large and remunerative practice, and enjoys the esteem and confidence of his fellow citizens. He has been a Mason since 1855, and is a member of the Council of Royal and Select Masters. He has filled all the offices below that of W. M. in the blue lodge, and was a representative of the lodge many years. Himself and wife and family are members of the Baptist church.

Source: *Memoirs of Georgia,* 1895. Volume 1.

JAMES B. FOOTE

James B. Foote, hotel-man and merchant-farmer, Dallas, Paulding Co., Ga., son of George W. and Amanda (Greenwood) Foote, was born at Powder Springs, Cobb Co., Ga., Jan. 5, 1843. His father, James Foote, of English descent, was born in Union district, S. C., in 1814, came to Georgia with the family when a boy, in an ox-cart, and settled near Powder Springs. His father was educated in the common schools at that place, and while yet a young man began his career as a merchant there, and was very successful. In 1853 he moved to Dallas, where he continued his merchandising with even greater success, and built the Foote hotel. Mr. Foote's exceeding geniality, good humor, and large-hearted hospitality made his hostelry one of the best-known and best-patronized of any in this part of the state. He died March 22, 1892, sincerely mourned by a wide circle of appreciative friends who had been cared for and entertained by him. Mr. Foote's mother was born in 1816, in Lawrenceville, Gwinnett Co., Ga., where she was raised and educated. She was married to Mr. Foote in 1834, and died in her seventy-seventh year. Mr. Foote was raised and educated at Powder Springs and Dallas, and received an excellent business training in his father's store. In his eighteenth year he enlisted in Company C, Seventh Georgia regiment, served faithfully and suffered bravely to the end. He was in the battles of Yorktown, Fort McClellan, and Knoxville, Tenn. At this last-named battle, Nov. 23, 1863, he was shot through the thigh, and was soon afterward captured and sent to Fort Delaware, was kept a prisoner sixteen months, suffering untold hardships. He was exchanged in 1865; but such a short time before the surrender that he could not re-enter the army. He walked much of the way home from Richmond, and when he reached home he found himself impoverished by the combined ravages of the Confederate and Union armies. With the $4 of available capital he had, he engaged in the liquor business, which he followed one year, and then began farming. In 1870 he embarked in a general merchandise business, and prospered, as he had done in his other undertakings. In 1877 he assumed the management of the Foote hotel, and has fully sustained the wide-spread reputation and popularity gained for it by his lamented father. Mr. Foote's uniform success in all his enterprises marks him as a man of more than usual business sagacity and financial ability; while his high standing socially, commercially, and as a citizen, indicates that he possesses to the fullest extent the confidence of his fellow-citizens. Mr. Foote was married in 1866 to Miss Rebecca J., daughter of Simeon J. and Matilda (Mayo) Tidwell, of Coweta county, Ga., formerly of South Carolina, who bore him five children: Lelia, Homer, James, Hattie, and Harry. Their mother died Nov. 20, 1890. Mr. Foote was made a master Mason in 1865. He has been a leading citizen of Dallas for years, and is favorably known throughout Paulding and adjoining counties.

Source: *Memoirs of Georgia*, 1895. Volume 2.

Note: Simeon J. Tidwell was residing in Carroll County in 1870 and is buried at Wesley Chapel Cemetery, Carroll County, Georgia.

THOMAS S. FREEMAN

T. S. Freeman, M. D., one of the early settlers of Grayson county, and in point of practice its oldest physician, is a native of Newton county, Georgia, where he was born July 18, 1827. He comes of Southern parents and English ancestry. Both his father and mother were natives of South Carolina, and lived to maturity in that State, moving to Georgia at an early date, where they spent the greater part of their lives. Dr. Freeman's father, Rev. Bailey M. Freeman, was a minister of the Methodist Episcopal church, South, and led a life of great piety and usefulness, dying in 1851, and leaving to his children the rich heritage of an honored name and a Christian character eminently worthy of their emulation. The lady who shared his pleasures and sorrows for many years as companion and helpmeet bore the maiden name of Elizabeth A. Smith, a daughter of a respectable and well-to-do South Carolina planter, Andrew Smith, and herself distinguished as a woman possessing many domestic virtues and a noble Christian character, which left its impress on her surviving children.

Dr. Freeman was the fourth child in a family of six children. His youth was spent on his father's farm, and he received only such an education as could in those days be had in the "old field schools" of middle Georgia. He supplemented this, however, with some study in private, and in this way, by the time he was ready to begin life on his own account, he was the possessor of what was equivalent to at least a fair academic education. He selected medicine as his profession, and began the practice in the town of Ellijay, in Gilmer county, Georgia, in 1850. In about a year following, or, more exactly, on July 31, 1851, he married Miss Lois E. Perry, daughter of R. B. Perry, of Gilmer county, who bore to him eight children, and who abided with him many years as a faithful friend and companion. She died April 14, 1876.

At the breaking out of the Civil War Dr. Freeman moved to Springville, St. Clair county, Alabama, and there continued in the practice of medicine till the surrender. In the fall of 1865 he started by wagon to Texas. Stopping a short time in Fannin county, he settled in October, 1866, in Sherman, then a frontier town of about one thousand population, and there again resumed the practice of physic. At that time there were five physicians practicing in Sherman and the surrounding country. Dr. Freeman is the only one of the number that now remains in the practice. He has seen the home of his adoption arise from an obscure village to a thriving city, and he knows the agencies and the various steps by which this change has been wrought. To this growth he has contributed his part in his own way. He has not been a "boomer" nor a blusterer in this nor in any other matter. He has devoted his life to his profession, and through it to his neighbors, friends and fellow-men. He was among the first to organize a medical society in Grayson county, and with this society, as well as with the North Texas Medical Association, he has been identified for many years and has been one of the leading spirits of these organizations.

In December, 1879, Dr. Freeman married Mrs. Augusta C. Sadler, a Georgia born lady – then, however, of Sherman, Texas. Dr.

THOMAS S. FREEMAN

Freeman has had born to him nine children – William M., now deceased; Thomas H.; Elijah S.; James L.; Elisha P.; Edwin V.; Thenie O. and Lois E. by the first marriage, and Glennie by the second.

Dr. Freeman clings to the traditions of his family in matters of religion, having been for many years a faithful and efficient member of the Methodist church.

Source: *Biographical Souvenir of the State of Texas*, 1889.

Note: Bailey M. Freeman and family were residents of Carroll County, Georgia in 1850. See 1850 Census. His occupation is listed as miner.

JUDSON T. FULLER

Judson T. Fuller, farmer, Villa Rica, Carroll Co., Ga., son of Alfred and Amanda (Evans) Fuller, was born in Meriwether county, Ga., in 1851. His paternal grandparent, William Fuller, was a native of South Carolina, and came to Georgia in 1828 and settled in the woods in Meriwether county. He was one of the pioneers, started on labor and pluck, and became one of the county's leading and wealthy citizens. Mr. Fuller's father was born in South Carolina, came to Georgia with his father, and helped to clear and then work the farm. His maternal grandparents, Elijah and Mary (Reed) Evans, were also natives of South Carolina, who came to Georgia about the time Meriwether county was laid out, and were among the early settlers in its woods. He was a tanner by trade and became rich. Mr. Fuller was reared on the farm, and as he passed through youth during the war enjoyed quite limited educational advantages. In 1866 he came to Carroll county and began life by hiring out. By persistent, well-directed effort, economy and good management he has acquired a fine property – 1,400 acres of good land, including a large, well-improved farm within five miles of Villa Rica, and an elegant home in the little city, where he is living a contented life, happier than if he were a millionaire. Such men are the nation's reliance in extreme emergencies. Mr. Fuller was married in 1872 to Miss Mary E. Johsnon – born in Walton county, Ga. – daughter of William and Elizabeth (Malcom) Johnson. This marriage has been blessed with seven children: Beulah, Lela, Maggie, Hardy, Thomas, Maude and De Witt. Mrs. Fuller is a consistent and devoted member of the Baptist church. It is almost needless to add that Mr. Fuller is one of the little city's most substantial and reliable citizens, and he and his interesting family rank with the best.

Source: *Memoirs of Georgia,* 1895. Volume 1.

NATHAN A. GANN

Nathan A. Gann, a prominent citizen of Eagle Township, Polk County, Ark., was born in Paulding County, Ga., on August 27, 1844, and is one of five living children born to Hiram and Elizabeth (Goggins) Gann, natives also of Georgia, the father born in 1824, and the mother in 1826. The father is still living, is a resident of Eagle Township, Polk County, Ark., but the mother died in this county in 1879. They resided in Georgia, until 1857, and then moved to Marion County. Ala., in 1867. From there they moved to Hardin County, Tenn., thence in 1869 to Cook County, Tex., and thence to Polk County, Ark., in the latter part of the same year. The father has always followed farming and for fifteen years was engaged in merchandising at which he was very successful. He is a Mason, a member of the Missionary Baptist Church, being clerk in the same, and is a Democrat in politics. Of his children, William A. is a farmer in Archer County, Tex., Melissa is the wife of J. B. Green of this county, John D. is a farmer of this county and Hiram F., is also in this county. Nathan A. Gann received a good practical education in his youth, and in 1862 joined the Fourth Mississippi Cavalry. Eighteen months later he joined Pierce's battalion and was lieutenant until cessation of hostilities. He was in the battle of Thompson's Station in Middle Tennessee, and was very seriously wounded by a bullet which entered just under the left collar bone and passed clear through. His recovery was considered a miracle. He served in Mississippi, Tennessee and Alabama. After the war he commenced working for himself as a farmer and after residing in Alabama, Tennessee and Texas he came to Arkansas and located in Polk County, on Two Mile Creek, where he bought a claim. Later he sold this and settled at Eagle Hill, where he is splendidly located and where he has 600 acres with good houses and outbuildings on the same. He owns another tract of 200 acres south of his present residence. He has been in the mercantile business most of the time for the last twelve years and was postmaster at Eagle Hill for five years. On March 17, 1864, he was married to Miss Mary E. Hughes of Alabama, a native of Marion County of that State, born in 1842. By this union they have five children: John R. (farming with our subject), James H. (also at home), Celia Melissa, Nathan F., Jr., and Mary who is usually called Mollie. Two children are deceased: William H. and Laura L. Mr. and Mrs. Gann, are members of the Missionary Baptist Church, and in his political views the former is strictly Democratic.

Source: *Biographical and Historical Memoirs of Western Arkansas,* 1891.

Note: Nathan A. Gann's grandparents, Nathan and Priscilla Gann, were residents of Carroll County in 1830. In 1840 Priscilla Gann was residing in District 649 of Carroll County, her husband being absent. In 1850 Nathan and Priscilla are residing in District 858 in Paulding County, Georgia.

JOHN W. GARDNER

John W. Gardner is the editor and proprietor of the Nevada County Picayune, a representative journal of this portion of the State, and under his able management this periodical has proved a decided success. It has a circulation of over 1,100, is all printed at home on a power press, and its editorial policy is directed by a man of sound judgment, whose experience in the newspaper business dates from the time he was eighteen years of age. Mr. Gardner was the son of George A. and Mary A. Gardner, both of whom are natives of Georgia, from the oldest and best families of the State, and still alive, residing with their son, on whom they lean in their old age. They were the parents of nine children – five girls and four boys – a boy and girl dying in infancy; the others are alive and in good circumstances, some living in Georgia and some in Arkansas. John W. was born in Upson County, Ga., January 21, 1857, and the most of his time, until he arrived at the age of eighteen, was spent in the best high schools of his native State. He was quick to learn, possessed a retentive memory, and as a natural consequence made rapid progress in his studies being, at the time he entered the Times office at Carrollton, Ga., an intelligent and wide-awake young man. After serving an apprenticeship on this paper for three and a half years he came out an expert printer, with the world before him, and after working at his trade in Atlanta, Rome and other places, and merchandising a while at Cedartown, Ga., he located at West Point, Ga., in 1881, where he purchased the Enterprise, which he continued to publish until 1884, when his office was destroyed by fire, which originated in an adjoining building. Although he had been successful in business he lost quite heavily at this time, as his establishment was not fully insured. Hard times prevented him from starting up again at once, and another journal soon took the place of his. In September and October, 1884, he was associate editor and publisher of the Times at Carrollton, Ga., but in November, of that year, he threw up his position to come West, and located at his present home. October 7, 1885, he was united in marriage to Miss Lena White, of Prescott, Ark., who died on June 15, 1888, leaving, besides her husband, one child, a daughter. Mr. Gardner began the battle of life without capital, and although he has received no assistance from any one since, he has been a successful journalist and now has, besides a valuable newspaper office, a good home and a small farm, unencumbered. It has ever been his purpose as a journalist, to conduct his paper on a high moral plane and accomplish all the good possible. He has been a consistent member of the Methodist Episcopal Church, South, since sixteen years of age; also joined the K. of P. at West Point, Ga., in 1883.

Source: *Biographical and Historical Memoirs of Southern Arkansas,* 1890

FRANCIS B. GARNER

F. B. Garner has been familiar with farm life from his earliest youth, and ever since he attained his eighteenth year, he has been engaged in tilling the soil on his own responsibility. His birth occurred in Georgia, in 1835, and there all his early life was spent, and his education, a somewhat limited one, received. In 1855 he concluded to make a change of location, and came to Arkansas, from Cass County, Tex., whither he had moved a number of years earlier, and upon his arrival here, he purchased a good farm of 176 acres, which he has since devoted principally to the raising of cotton and corn, the yield of the former being about one bale to the acre, and of the latter twenty bushels. All other farm products can be raised with but little trouble, and Southern Arkansas seems to be the land of delicious fruits of all kinds. Miss Elizabeth Porterfield, a daughter of Nelson Porterfield, a pioneer planter of Georgia, who now resides in Cass County, Tex., became his wife in 1853, and their union has been blessed

FRANCIS B. GARNER

in the birth of a son – Nelson, who married Rebecca Fuller, of Hempstead County, Ark. In 1862 Mr. Garner enlisted in the Confederate army, becoming a member of Company H, Twenty-eighth Louisiana Regiment, and was in the engagements at Franklin, Mansfield, Pleasant Hill, and numerous skirmishes. He was so fortunate as to escape being wounded or captured, and finally received his discharge. He is a member of the Baptist Church, a Democrat, politically, and is a liberal contributor to schools, churches and other worthy enterprises. His father, T. W. Garner, was a farmer by occupation, took part in the Creek and Seminole Indian War, and died in 1879, an earnest Christian.

Source: *Biographical and Historical Memoirs of Southern Arkansas,* 1890.

Note: In 1850 F. B. Garner was residing with his parents, Thomas W. and Sarah Garner in Carroll County, Georgia. F. B. Garner married Elizabeth A. Porterfield in 1853 in Carroll County, Georgia. He is a brother of John M. Garner, the subject of the following sketch.

JOHN M. GARNER

J. M. Garner was born in Georgia, in 1833, but his father, Thomas Garner, was a South Carolinian, a farmer by calling, and was a participant in the Creek and Seminole Indian War. J. M. Garner received a somewhat limited education in a private school, but afterward acquired a thorough knowledge of matters and events by contact with the world and by reading. He remained with his father until he was twenty-two years of age, when he began doing for himself, and in 1855 was married to Miss Isabella Blanchard, of Georgia, a daughter of a wealthy planter and merchant of that State, T. J. Blanchard. Nine children have been born to their union: Thomas Jefferson (who was married to Miss Ida H. Haynes), Mollie (wife of James Talley, of Texas), John Lucius (who is a physician of Houston, Tex., having graduated from the Medical University of Louisville, Ky., in 1887), Margaret (wife of Henry Reece, of this county), Emma (wife of William Rogers), Sallie (wife of John Card), Lula, Florence and Flora. Mr. Garner joined the Twenty-eighth Louisiana Infantry in 1862, under Capt. Brice, and was in the battles of Franklin, Mansfield and Pleasant Hill. After his company was disbanded, Mr. Garner returned home to his family in Nevada County, Ark., and after remaining there, engaged in farming for three years, they came to Hempstead County, and in 1887 settled on their farm of 245 acres, which yields from 800 to 1,000 pounds of cotton, and from twenty to twenty-five bushels of corn to the acre. Mr. Garner and his wife are members of the Baptist Church, and in his political views he is a Democrat. He is a man who has made a success of his life, and he gives liberally of his means in the support of worthy enterprises.

Source: *Biographical and Historical Memoirs of Southern Arkansas,* 1890.

Note: In 1850 John M. Garner was residing with his parents, Thomas W. and Sarah Garner, in Carroll County, Georgia. John M. Garner married Isabella Blanchard 22 August 1857 in Carroll County, Georgia. He is a brother of F. B. Garner, the subject of the preceding sketch.

JAMES H. GARRISON

One of the positive truths taught by modern science is that mental and physical qualities are hereditary in man, and this statement of fact is as old as Moses, who declared that the generations to come should bear the results of the father's actions. No doubt the subject of this sketch inherits much of his vigor of body and his strong mentality from his parents, and his parents' parents, but this can in nowise detract from the splendid success he has achieved, for he began life with but little means, and what he ahs acquired has been almost wholly through his own unaided efforts. The same will apply to his education. His schooling was limited, but years passed in the school of experience, his keen observation of persons and events, together with desultory reading, have made him one of the well-informed men of the day.

Captain James H. Garrison is a native of Polk County, Ga., his birth occurring May 1, 1836. Judge George M. Garrison, his father, was also a native of Georgia, where he grew to manhood, married Mary Ann Cosper and where, for many years, he resided. By occupation Judge Garrison was a merchant, farmer and trader, and for years served as judge of the inferior court of his county, besides holding other positions of local honor and trust. He emigrated to Texas with his family in 1854 and located on a farm near Caledonia, in Rusk County, but later moved to his farm near Mount Enterprise, where he died in 1883 at the age of sixty-two years. His widow yet survives, hale and hearty, at the age of seventy years, and makes her home with her children.

The youth of Captain James H. Garrison was passed in his native county in the usual manner of the boys of that day. He came to Texas with his parents in 1854 and assisted in clearing and improving the home farm. In 1862 he enlisted in the Fourteenth Texas Cavalry, was made sergeant and later elected lieutenant of his company. About two months after the reorganization of his regiment at Corinth, he was promoted to captain of his company, in which capacity he served until the close of the war. Perhaps no man in all Texas saw harder service than did Captain Garrison and his devotion to the cause of the Confederacy was heroic and unswerving. Among the more important events of his military career was his participation in the battles of Farmington, Miss.; Richmond and Perryville, Ky.; Murfreesboro, Tenn.; Jackson, Miss., where they were besieged for eight days by the Federals; Chickamauga; the engagements in and immediately surrounding Dalton; Lovejoy's Station, and the siege of Atlanta, including many of the adjoining engagements. After the fall of Atlanta, Captain Garrison was detailed to recruit absentees, leaving his command at Lovejoy's Station. He succeeded in securing sixty-three of his command and was trying to transport them across the Mississippi River when he heard of General Lee's surrender at Appomattox to General Grant. With this remnant of his command he returned to Shreveport and there disbanded.

With undaunted courage Captain Garrison laid aside his sword for the ploughshare and for years followed farming in Rusk County. By good management he has become one of the largest holders of real estate in the county, now owning about 3,000 acres in Rusk County and 500 acres in Nacogdoches County, and began to improve the village named in honor of his family. He was associated with Captain Z. B. Garrison, his cousin, for a number of years in merchandising, and after the retirement of his cousin from active business pursuits he has continued mercantile pursuits, buying and selling cotton and dealing in real estate. Captain Garrison is one of the progressive and prominent men of Eastern Texas. He has acquired much wealth by good business methods and from his large means he is a liberal contributor to all laudable public enterprises.

Although radical in his political views and an outspoken advocate of the principles of the Democratic party, Captain Garrison has invariably discouraged any attempt toward office holding so far as he was concerned, preferring to confine his attention exclusively to his large business interests. While this is true as to political matters, it does not apply wholly to social matters. In religion he is a member of the Methodist Episcopal church. Socially he is a member of the Masonic fraternity, in which order he was duly entered, passed and raised, and exalted to the sublime degree of Royal Arch Mason.

October 27, 1864, occurred his marriage with Miss Mary C. Young, a native of Polk County, Ga., and a daughter of William Young, whose family was prominently connected in that state. This marriage occurred near Henderson, Rusk County, Tex., whither the father had some years previously removed. Two sons have blessed this union: William Young, a successful druggist of Garrison, and George F., who is connected with Dotson Brothers, extensive merchants of Garrison. Captain James H. Garrison is one of the well-known men of Texas and he stands deservedly high for his many sterling qualities of mind and heart.

Source: *Memorial and Genealogical Record of Texas (East),* 1895.

Note: James H. Garrison's grandfather, Caleb Garrison, was residing in Carroll County in 1830. His father's brother, James Freeborn Garrison, married Abigail Bonner, daughter of Zadock Bonner, Sr., and was a prominent citizen and longtime resident of Carroll County, dying in Carroll County on September 24, 1860.

Z. B. GARRISON

Nothing is truer than the statement that in this country alone, of all countries upon the face of the earth, a man's family connections do not assist him to positions of honor and distinction, but he must win his way by his own honest merit. In the old countries the accident of birth usually determines the preferment of an individual, and if he is not born to a title, or is not the near relative of one who is, he might as profitably seek a mode of travel to the moon as to try to gain social or political equality with the eminent men of the locality. This government of the people is no discriminator of persons, but opens

Z. B. GARRISON

wide its doors for the entrance of all such persons as possess the requisite qualifications for success in any particular calling, and birth is not one of these by any means.

In the particular instance of Captain Z. B. Garrison, whose name forms the subject for this sketch, he fortunately springs from an honored and respectable ancestry, but his success in life is almost wholly the result of his own efforts. He was born in Carroll County, Ga., April 20, 1829, his parents being the Hon. James F. and Abigail (Bonner) Garrison, both of whom were also natives of Georgia, their nuptials being celebrated in Fayette County of that state. James F. Garrison was one of the typical ante-bellum Southern gentlemen, a man whose word was the soul of truth, dignified, courteous in demeanor and a man beloved by his fellow-men. Although born and married in Fayette County, he removed to Carroll County in 1827, where he was engaged in planting and milling for many years. He was a participant in the Seminole War, and died in Carroll County in 1860. His widow moved to Texas, in order to enjoy the companionship of her children, where she passed from life in 1892 at the advanced age of eighty-four years. The statement will not be disputed that to the mothers of our race is mainly due the moral status of our wonderful civilization. To them is confided the training for good or evil of our youth, upon whom the morality of future generations will have to depend, and as the moral condition of humanity shapes its destiny the state itself is guided by the influence of the mothers. The life-work of Mrs. Garrison was well done in this respect, and she lived to see her children honest, honored and God-fearing people before being called to her just reward above.

Capt. Z. B. Garrison was the second in the family of six sons and four daughters, one son, John H., having been killed at the battle of Atlanta in 1864, while serving the cause of the Confederate States. Until the age of nineteen years Capt. Garrison resided in his native county, his education being largely acquired under that hard task-master, "Experience." Believing that the great west afforded better opportunities for a young man, he emigrated to Texas in 1850, arriving in Rusk County on the 27th of January, and for a time was employed as a clerk at Caledonia. Later, in partnership with a brother and cousin, he embarked in mercantile pursuits, which he continued for several years; then purchasing a tract of unimproved land he turned his attention to its tillage and improvement. His efforts have been crowned by success, as is proven by his fine tract of about 1,400 acres on which he has a steam gin, although at one time he was the owner of about 5,000 acres.

Loyal to the Confederate States, he recruited Company C of the Fourth Texas Cavalry in 1861, and equipped it with seventy head of horses and mules. As first lieutenant of this company he went to the front, but after being dismounted the company returned home; later was ordered to organize into companies and regiments. Then Mr. Z. B. was elected captain and joined the army at Knoxville, Tenn., and soon after disbanded and Captain Garrison was then commissioned quartermaster of the Fourteenth Texas Regiment, in which capacity he served until the close of the war.

The devastating effects of war did not diminish the ardor with which Captain Garrison had previously conducted his business affairs. He accepted the results of internecine strife with becoming fortitude and resumed farming, milling and ginning with his accustomed energy in Rusk County until 1886. In that year he moved to Garrison (the town was named after Z. B. and J. H. Garrison) and in partnership with Captain J. H. Garrison erected a large business building and embarked in mercantile pursuits. In addition to this he not only built for himself a beautiful and commodious home, but has erected and owns several other residences in the town, besides being the owner of considerable real estate in the immediate neighborhood. For the past few years Captain Garrison has been retired from active business pursuits, his time being principally occupied in simply looking after the details of his large estate and in spending his later years in comfort and peace. He began life's battle at the lowest rung of life's ladder and from this meager beginning has, unaided, carved his way to wealth and, what is still better, has gained a name that is honored and respected in Eastern Texas.

March 20, 1851, occurred his marriage with Miss Elizabeth H. Lacy, a native of Tennessee, and to their union have been born five children, the oldest being Hon. James G. Garrison, a well-known lawyer of Los Angeles, Cal. The other children are: Beth, the wife of Dr. Barham, of Nacogdoches, a sketch of whom appears elsewhere in this work; John L., a leading merchant of Garrison; Henry D., a commercial traveler for a wholesale house at Houston, and Nora B., who resides at home with her parents.

A stanch Democrat in politics, Captain Garrison has never been an aspirant for public office, although he at one time by appointment held one term in the Legislature in order to attend to special business for his county. Captain Garrison and wife are members of the M. E. church. For a period of nearly half a century (forty-five years) he has been a resident of Eastern Texas, identified with its commercial prosperity and advancement, instrumental in promoting industries and contributing liberally from his means for the welfare of its people. The name of Captain Z. B. Garrison will be remembered for the many good deeds he has accomplished years after the present generation has passed away.

Source: *Memorial and Genealogical Record of Texas (East),* 1895.

WILLIAM GAULDING

William Gaulding, physician, Waco, Haralson Co., Ga., son of John and Jane Gaulding, was born in Oglethorpe county, Ga., April 15, 1833. His parents subsequently removed to Troup county, where he was reared and received the very indifferent education he started in life with. Having more fully educated himself and studied medicine, he attended Georgia Medical college, Augusta, from which he graduated in 1856, and immediately afterward located at Haralsonville, Troup county. After remaining there twenty years, and establishing a very large and remunerative practice, he removed, in 1876, to Carroll county, where he remained until December, 1893, adding to his reputation as one of the most skillful and successful physicians in that part of the state. At the last-named date he moved to Waco, where he is still actively practicing his profession, enjoying the unreserved confidence of a large and still increasing constituency. He was postmaster a number of years at Haralsonville, conducted a drug store at Carrollton and Waco, and engaged extensively in farming during his professional life, and has accumulated a quite large estate. Dr. Gaulding was married May 6, 1856, to Miss Amanda R., daughter of R. W. and Elizabeth Brown, a union which has been blessed with eleven children: Aldora, Lizzie Love, Henry Valentine, Benjamin Holmes, deceased, Lizzie Thomas, J. W., Odessa, Seaborn May, Exar, deceased, Clyde Speer, and Luella, deceased. Dr. Gaulding was originally an "old-line" whig, and voted against secession, but is now affiliated with the populists. He is a master Mason, and himself and wife are prominent and influential members of the Methodist church.

Source: *Memoirs of Georgia*, 1895. Volume 1.

ALLEN M. GAY

Allen M. Gay, farmer, Bowdon, Carroll Co., Ga., son of Gilbert and Sarah (Stamps) Gay, was born in Coweta county in 1831. His paternal grandparents, Allen and Abigail (Castleberry) Gay, were Virginians by birth, and he was a soldier in the patriot army during the revolutionary war. Some years after that they migrated to Georgia and settled in Hancock county – bona fide pioneers. Here Mr. Gay's father was born in 1811. When he was thirteen years of age he went to Wilkinson county, Ga., whence a few years afterward he moved to Coweta county. In 1848 he removed to Heard county and settled on Jumping Creek, where he ended his days. Mr. Gay's mother was a daughter of Moses and Ann (Eason) Stamps, who came to Georgia and settled in the woods in Jackson county in 1795. He cleared a farm and also did work as a gun and blacksmith. Leaving Jackson, he went to Gwinnett, and after two years went to Clarke county, where he staid two years, and then went back to Jackson county. From Jackson he went to Fayette, and lastly to Coweta county, where he died. June 29, 1894, Eason Stamps, Mr. Gay's uncle, his mother's brother, was one hundred years old, and he was given a birthday dinner – spread picnic style on the grass under the trees – at Mr. Gay's house. There were about 500 people there, of whom he fed 300. The Grandfather Stamps was a soldier during the war of 1812, in the wars with the Indians, and was captain of a company in the Indian war of 1836. Mr. Gay was reared a farmer, and was given such education as the schools afforded during his boyhood – taught as they were in log houses, with dirt floor and slab or split log seats. In 1851 he was married to Miss Martha Stamps – born in Jackson county in 1822 – daughter of Eason and Polly (Watts) Stamps, who has borne him five children, of whom only one, Sarah F., wife of Jeff Butler, is now living. When he married himself and wife had but one change of clothing, but now he has a well-improved 350-acre farm and is a well-to-do farmer. Himself and wife are members of the Missionary Baptist church and are much respected by all who know them.

Source: *Memoirs of Georgia*, 1895. Volume 1.

W. F. GOLDIN

W. F. Goldin, physician and surgeon, Draketown, Haralson Co., Ga., son of Seaborn and Sarah Goldin, was born in what is now Haralson county, near where he now lives, Feb. 6, 1851. His father was born in what is now Walton county, Ga., in 1817, and his mother was born in the same locality. His parents moved from Walton to Paulding county in 1844, and settled on a tract of land, which he subsequently converted into a fruit and nursery farm. Dr. Goldin's educational advantages during his boyhood and youth were of the most limited and indifferent sort; but after he attained manhood he attended the Tallapoosa, Ga., high school, where he acquired a very good education. He then read medicine, and under a temporary license practiced awhile. In 1875 he entered Atlanta Medical college, from which he was graduated in 1877, and located in Draketown. In 1888 Dr. Goldin went to London, England, and took a special course in surgery in the London medical colleges, and has since built up a large and very remunerative practice. He stands at the head of his profession in that part of the state, is very popular, and is steadily growing in reputation. In addition to his practice Dr. Goldin conducts a general merchandise store and is engaged in saw-milling. He not only excels in his profession, but is regarded as possessing superior business and financiering ability. In 1890 he was elected to represent the Thirty-eighth senatorial district in the general assembly, and established a reputation as a wise and able legislator. Dr. Goldin was married in 1878 to Miss Sarah Louisiana, daughter of Dr. R. B. and Sarah Hutcheson, and to them six children have been born: Grover Cleveland, Sarah Effie, Robert Battey, John Maddox and Arlina and Cora Glenn, the last two deceased. Dr. Goldin is a master Mason, and himself and family are very prominent members of the Missionary Baptist church.

Source: *Memoirs of Georgia*, 1895. Volume 1.

Note: Seaborn Goldin and family were residents of Carroll County, Georgia in 1850.

CHARLES P. GORDON

Chas. P. Gordon, attorney at law, Carrollton, Ga., was born in Coweta County, Ga., September 8, 1849, and is a son of David N. and Talitha W. (Culpepper) Gordon. The father served in both the civil and Indian wars, doing duty in the former as captain. He was justice of the peace for about fifteen years, until his death, which occurred in 1882. He was born in North Carolina and was the son of John Gordon, a distant relative of Governor Gordon.

The mother of the subject was a native Georgian and a daughter of Joel Culpepper.

Chas. P. Gordon is one of five children born to his parents, viz.: Octavia O. R., Sarah E. A., David E., Chas. P., and Susan S. He was named for the Hon. Chas. P. Gordon, of Eatonton, Ga., who is now deceased. He was taken to Carrollton by his parents when but an infant and there grew up and attended the public schools. He read law, was admitted to the bar in 1877 and located in Whitesburg, Carroll County, where he practiced until he removal to Carrollton. In 1884 he was appointed solicitor of the city court of Carrollton.

Mr. Gordon was married May 25, 1872, to Miss L. C. Gilbert, daughter of John Gilbert of Georgia. They are the parents of four children, viz: Edna E., Lillie, Oscar H. and Chas. P., Jr. Mr. Gordon is an enthusiastic Mason, having served as master of Rotherwood lodge, No. 170, for three years.

Source: *Biographical Souvenir of the States of Georgia and Florida*, 1889.

FRANK C. GREENWOOD

Frank C. Greenwood, book-keeper of Homer National Bank, like many other prominent citizens of Louisiana, owes his nativity to Alabama, having been born in Cherokee County on June 4, 1838, and is the son of William K. and Polly (Morgan) Greenwood, natives respectively of Georgia and Kentucky. The father went to the Blue Grass State when a young man, and there met and married Miss Morgan, after which they removed to Georgia, where the father was engaged in tilling the soil for a number of years. They then moved to Alabama, locating in Cherokee County, and here the father continued his former pursuit for one year. From there they removed to Talladega County, but at the end of seven years they removed to Arkansas, and located in Union County. Here the father followed agricultural pursuits

FRANK C. GREENWOOD

until his death, which occurred in December, 1880, when in his eighty-eighth year. He held several local offices in the county where he resided, and was a stanch Democrat, although he took no very active part in politics. He volunteered in one of the old Indian wars (1815), but was not called to active service. His wife died in June, 1879, in her eighty-third year. Their family consisted of eleven children, all of whom grew to years of discretion, and became heads of families, but two sons. Two brothers and two sisters are living at the present time.

F. C. Greenwood grew to manhood in Arkansas, received a limited education, and is mainly self-educated since grown up. He was early taught the duties of the farm, and in 1859 he came to Louisiana, locating in Jackson Parish. He entered the Confederate service in the first company from that parish in 1861, went to New Orleans, and was put in the Second Louisiana Infantry, with which he served until the close of the war. He participated in the battles of Malvern Hill, Cedar Mountain, Second Manassas, Gettysburg, battle of the Wilderness, Chancellorsville, and was taken prisoner at Spottsylvania Court House on May 12, 1864. Mr. Greenwood is proud of his army record, and went through the war up to the time of his capture, without even a personal reprimand. He was wounded four times, being shot in the arm and shoulder, and wounded in the breast by a bayonet. He also received a bad wound in the head at Gettysburg. He was held a prisoner at Point Lookout, Md., and Elmira, N. Y., until the close of the war, and was then paroled, and came home in April, 1865.

After returning to Jackson Parish, La., he resided there several years, and was married there on June 14, 1865, to Miss Alice A. Otts, a native of Alabama, who was reared and educated in Jackson Parish, and who is the daughter of Joel B. Otts. Mr. Greenwood then farmed in Jackson Parish for several years, after which he engaged in book-keeping there. In 1869 he moved to Union County, Ark., remaining there two years, and then removed to the Lone Star State, Sabine Pass, where he tarried for about two years, after which he returned to Arkansas, Union County. In January, 1878, he came to this parish, engaged in book-keeping here, and when the Homer National Bank opened in 1890, he took his place as book-keeper.

Mr. Greenwood is a strong Democrat, but never takes an active part in politics. He and wife are members of the Methodist Episcopal Church South, and he is recording steward of the same. Socially he is a member of the Masonic order, being a Master Mason, and serving as secretary for a number of years. He is now demitted. He is also a member of the K. of P. Mr. greenwood is a pleasant gentleman to meet, and is held in high esteem by all who are favored with his acquaintance.

Source: *Biographical and Historical Memoirs of Northwest Louisiana*, 1890.

Note: Thus far the author has only found one mention of Frank C. Greenwood's father, William K. Greenwood, in the Carroll County records, so his residence here must have been brief. On March 17, 1828 he was appointed a road commissioner in the Fourth Captain's District.

WASHINGTON L. GRICE

Col. Washington L. Grice, attorney, Hawkinsville, Ga., was born in Carroll County, Ga., February 22, 1832. He is the son of Garry Garry and Ann (Lamar) Grice, the former from North Carolina and the latter from Georgia. Garry Grice was a farmer and held various responsible county offices; was judge of the inferior court, tax-collector, census taker, and served in the legislature one term. His death occurred in 1879, at the age of seventy-four. His wife died in 1841.

These parents had three children, viz.: Q. C., married a Miss Gray and is living in Fayette County; T. C., wife of M. L. Yates, is living in Douglas County.

Washington L. began teaching at eighteen years and taught for four years with good success. He studied law, was admitted to the bar in 1854, and has practiced continuously since, with the exception of the time spent in the war. He enlisted May 24, 1861, in the Sixth Georgia regiment, but was afterwards transferred to the Forty-fifth, of which he was lieutenant-colonel. March 4, 1862, he was elected major and served until the spring of 1864, when he resigned to serve in the legislature. He afterward served in the State militia in Captain W. H. Pruden's battery. On the promotion of Col. Simmons he became lieutenant-colonel of the Forty-fifth Georgia by appointment. At the close of the war he again resumed practice of his profession, serving as judge of the Macon court for awhile, but retiring, as he did not desire official life. He was married in 1870 to Miss Mattie V. Warren, daugh ter of Gen. Eli Warren, of Perry, Ga. To this union were born two boys, Warren and Herbert. Col. Grice is a member of the Methodist Church, and his wife is a member of the Baptist Church. The Colonel is an enterprising business man, as well as a reliable and influential citizen.

Source: *Biographical Souvenir of the States of Georgia and Florida,* 1889.

JAMES P. GRIFFIN

James P. Griffin, merchant, Temple, Carroll Co., Ga., son of Charles W. and Sarah (New) Griffin, was born in De Kalb county in 1838. His paternal grandparent, James P. Griffin, was a native of South Carolina, came to Georgia in 1818, and settled in what is now De Kalb county. At that time they had to tramp their wheat out on the floor. He was a soldier in the war of 1812. Mr. Griffin's father was born in Abbeville district, S. C., in 1811, came to Georgia with his parents when he was seven years old, and was reared on the farm originally settled. He followed farming all his life, was a soldier in the Indian war in 1836, and was a member of the Methodist church. His maternal grandparent, Joel New, was a native of South Carolina and among the early settlers of De Kalb county. Mr. Griffin was reared on a farm in Carroll county, where he went with the family when he was eight years old. His father being a very poor man, and he the eldest boy of eleven children, had to work very hard, and was almost entirely deprived of the school advantages he yearned for. Oftentimes, too, he had to plow through briar patches and his feet would get so badly torn he could hardly walk. After he became of age he "boarded himself" and went to school. In 1862 he enlisted in Company E (Capt. Blalock), First Georgia cavalry, and during the war was in many hard-fought battles, among them Richmond, Ky., Wheeler's Gap, Murfreesboro, Chickamauga, Resaca, and thence to Atlanta and on to Macon. At the time of surrender he was at Greensborough, N. C. He was in numerous minor engagements, and during his service had several horses shot from under him, but was so fortunate as to escape being wounded or captured. A part of the time he acted as orderly-sergeant. After the war Mr. Griffin worked a farm at fifty cents a day and taught school. Struggling on, working hard, and saving his money, he at last came into the ownership of a 500-acre farm of good land, and well improved. In 1881 he engaged in a general merchandising business at Temple, where he has built up a good and profitable trade and has made and is making money. For six years he served as justice of the peace. Intelligent, industrious, and economical, in connection with energy and judicious enterprise, it may be expected his achieved success will be far exceeded by that of the future. Mr. Griffin was married in 1868 to Miss Sarah A. Adams – born and reared in Carroll county – daughter of Absalom and Elizabeth (Reid) Adams, by whom he has had seven children: Joseph, Ryburn, M. E., Bettie M., Lewis, Ella and Claudie. Mr. griffin is a member of the Masonic fraternity, and himself and wife and all the children except the baby are members of the Methodist church.

Source: *Memoirs of Georgia,* 1895. Volume 1.

R. L. GRIFFIN

R. L. Griffin, farmer, Carrollton, Carroll Co., Ga., son of Charles W. and Sarah (New) Griffin, was born in De Kalb county, Ga., in 1848. His father was born in what is now De Kalb county in 1812, where he was reared a farmer, and moved to Carroll county in 1850. He settled on a farm about eight miles from Carrollton. His mother was the daughter of John and Mary New. Mr. Griffin was reared mostly in Carroll county, a plain farmer, and was educated at the "old field" school, taught in a log cabin. After reaching manhood he taught school about ten years and then engaged in farming. In 1887 he was elected tax collector and served two terms (four years) and discharged the duties of that office to the entire satisfaction of the people. In 1869 Mr. Griffin was married to Miss Georgia Holmes – born in Coweta county – daughter of Thomas and Mary Holmes, by whom he has had nine children: Charles M., Mattie, Thomas, Percy, Herbert, Mary, Lee, Ellen and Barron. Starting with nothing, Mr. Griffin has now one of the best improved farms, containing 360 acres, in his locality, and is well thought of as a wide-awake, progressive farmer. Himself and wife are members of the Methodist church.

Source: *Memoirs of Georgia*, 1895. Volume 1.

ASA W. GRIGGS

Asa W. Griggs, M. D., of West Point, Ga., one of the most skillful and experienced practitioners of western Georgia, was born in Putnam County, that State, December 11, 1827. His father, Judge William Griggs, was born in Hancock, Ga. in 1794. He was a son of John, the son of William, both born in Virginia. The last-named William was a son of John, who in company with a brother William, came from Ireland and settled in North Carolina. William Griggs, the father of Asa W., was a planter by occupation, but for a number of years was judge of the inferior court of Harris County, Ga. He married Miss Louisa C. Maxwell, daughter of William Maxwell, of Savannah, Ga., and died in 1850.

Asa W. Griggs is the eldest in a family of four living children born to William and Louisa C., the others being John G., William M., and Marshall W. When a child he was taken to Harris County, Ga., by his parents, was there reared and there received his preliminary education, which was finished at the State University at Athens. He read medicine with Dr. William B. Jones and graduated with the degree of M. D. from the University at Nashville, Tenn., as valedictorian of his class, in March, 1855. For three years he practiced at Newnan, and was then appointed to the chair of surgery at the Oglethorpe Medical College at Savannah, which chair he filled for three years, and then moved to his present place of practice, West Point, his residence being just across the county line, in Alabama. He has secured a lucrative practice, not only in the city, but in the surrounding country on both sides of the border. He is not only popular professionally, but politically, and in 1878-79 represented Chambers County, Ala., in the State legislature. He is a Master Mason and a Knight of Pythias, and enjoys the esteem of a large circle of social acquaintances.

January 25, 1848, the doctor married Miss Elizabeth R. Davenport, who bore him two children, and died in 1860. The doctor's second marriage was to Lois A. McCants, daughter of Dr. R. P. McCants, and this union has been blessed by the birth of five children, viz.: Carrie L., Robert S., Asa W., Jr., Imogene and Alfred T.

Source: *Biographical Souvenir of the States of Georgia and Florida*, 1889.

Note: Asa Griggs was residing in Carroll County in 1850. The Census lists him as an instructor.

SAMUEL EMERSON GROW

Col. S. E. Grow, attorney at law, Carrollton, Ga., was born in Carroll County, Ga., August 30, 1851, and is a son of P. P. and Elmira (Wolcott) Grow, both natives of Vermont. The father, a son of Samuel Grow, was a planter and a school teacher, and died in September, 1861; the mother is a daughter of Emerson Wolcott, was born August 11, 1812, and still survives.

Samuel Emerson Grow, the youngest in a family of three living children, was educated at "Carroll Masonic Institute," Carrollton, Ga., and began his business life by clerking three years in a store at Newnan, Ga. He then read law in Carrollton with W. W. Merrell, and in Lake City, Fla., with A. B. Hagen. He was admitted to the bar in Lake City, May 10, 1875. Since that time he has resided in Carrollton with the exception of two years passed in Texas. On his return to Carrollton he was elected mayor of the city, having gained the confidence of his fellow-citizens through his uniform good conduct and the business ability he displayed in all his previous acts.

Mr. Grow, in October, 1877, married Miss Leonora McDaniel, daughter of Charles A. McDaniel, the founder of Bowdon College. Five children have blessed this union: Samuel E., Dudley M., Victor D., Thomas L. and Elmira Grow.

Mr. Grow is a Royal Arch Mason, and also worshipful master of Carroll Lodge, No. 69, F. and A. M., and high priest of Carrollton Chapter, No. 22, R. A. M. He is past grand of the I. O. O. F., Carrollton Lodge, No. 96, and regent of Carrollton Council R. A., and with his wife is a member of the Presbyterian Church. The position of Mr. Grow, socially, politically and professionally, is a most enviable one, and few deserve a higher place in the esteem of his fellow-citizens than he holds.

Source: *Biographical Souvenir of the States of Georgia and Florida*, 1889.

SAMUEL EMERSON GROW

S. E. Grow, lawyer, Carrollton, Carroll Co., Ga., son of Paschal P. and Elmyra (Wollcott) Grow, was born in Carroll county in 1851. The family is of English origin, and among the early settlers of Vermont, in the person of John Grow, the great-great-grandfather of the subject of this sketch. His great-grandparents were Joseph and Tirszah (Sangor) Grow, and his grandparents were Samuel and Jerushia

SAMUEL EMERSON GROW

(Stowell) Grow. His great-grandfather and his grandfather were soldiers in the patriot army during the revolutionary war. His parents were school teachers, and migrated from Vermont to Georgia, and settled in the woods in Carroll county in 1836 – bona fide "pioneers." In the early history of the county his father was one of its leading citizens. Three of his sons were in the Confederate army: Paschal P., who was in the battle of Manassas, died while in the service; Jacob C., now a Presbyterian minister in Llano, Tex., and Lewis K., who was killed in the charge at Petersburg. Mr. Grow's father died in 1861. Mr. Grow was reared in the county and received a good common school education. He began teaching in 1874, also read law and was admitted to the bar in Florida, May 10, 1875. Returning to Georgia, he was admitted to the bar in Carrollton, June 1, 1875, and has been in the practice in Carrollton ever since, holding his own with his professional compeers. No one of the local bar outranks him, and he is held in the highest esteem professionally, politically and socially. A safe counselor, and an able and impressive advocate, he has secured a valuable clientage which is augmented every year. In 1882 he was mayor of Carrollton. He was chairman of the democratic fourth congressional committee in 1892, and for four years was chairman of the democratic executive committee of his county and has been re-elected for another term. In 1893 he was appointed clerk to the committee on pensions in the fifty-third congress. He has been a delegate to several state conventions, but although he has always taken great interest in politics, he has never sought or been a candidate for office. Mr. Grow was married in 1877 to Miss Lenora, daughter of Col. Charles A. and Victoria A. (Hines) McDaniel. Her father was colonel of the Forty-first Georgia regiment, and was killed at the battle at Perryville, Ky. When the civil war began he was president of the college at Bowdon, Carroll Co. – a college and town which he founded – and very many of his pupils went with him into the army. To Mr. and Mrs. Grow these children have been born: Samuel E., Dudley M., Victor D., Elmyra, Stephen and Helen. Mrs. Grow was born in Bowdon. Mr. Grow is a member of the I. O. O. F., and is a member of the council and a select master, of which he has been thrice illustrious master. He has also been worshipful master of his local lodge seven years. He is now district grand deputy. Himself and wife are members of the Presbyterian church. A record such as Mr. Grow's needs no comment – it speaks for itself with emphasis.

Source: *Memoirs of Georgia*, 1895. Volume 1.

GEORGE R. HAMILTON

George R. Hamilton, merchant-farmer, Bremen, Haralson Co., Ga., son of John L. and Marguerite (Reid) Hamilton, was born in Carroll county, Ga., Sept. 6, 1830. His father was a son of Archibald Hamilton, and was born in Abbeville district, S. C., March 10, 1800, was a poor man, and came to Georgia on a wagon in 1812, and settled in what is now Gwinnett county, and in 1829 moved to Carroll county. He was a volunteer in the company of Capt. Wagnon, which accompanied the Indians as a guard on their removal from Georgia. Mr. Hamilton's maternal grandfather was George Reid. Mr. Hamilton received only the very limited and indifferent education obtainable at that time and locality, and began life for himself as a farmer on rented land. In 1856 he was elected ordinary of the county, serving efficiently and acceptably, and just before the war was appointed postmaster at Buchanan. His only experience during the war was in capturing deserters near Bowdon in Carroll county. He is still conducting his farm, and in addition is keeping a general merchandise store at Bremen. He is one of the oldest settlers in Haralson county, popular, and has been very successful. He has never married.

Source: *Memoirs of Georgia*, 1895. Volume 1.

DENNIS FLETCHER HAMMOND

Judge D. F. Hammond was born in Liberty Hill, S. C., December 15, 1819, and is one of nine children born to Ebenezer and Maria (Moon) Hammond, the former a native physician of Massachusetts, of English extraction. He was educated in Cokesbury, S. C., and commenced to read law in 1839 in Newnan, Ga.; was admitted to the bar in 1840, and practiced in Newnan for several years. In 1863 he moved to Atlanta, Ga., where he practiced his profession for twenty years, and in 1883 he settled in Orlando, Fla. He was judge of Coweta circuit in Georgia for four consecutive terms, having been twice appointed by governors of the State and twice elected by the people. In 1873 he was elected mayor of Atlanta, Ga., and served one term. He was married in 1844 to Adaline E. Robinson, daughter of John Robinson, of Tallapoosa, Ga., of which marriage there were born nine children, four of whom are now living, viz.: Hon. William R., of Atlanta, Ga.; Octavia S., wife of A. D. Adair, Atlanta, Ga.; Rev. John D., president of Central College, Mo., and Edward M., an attorney of

DENNIS FLETCHER HAMMOND

Orlando, Fla. Judge Hammond is a Master Mason, and has been a local preacher of the Methodist Church for thirty years.

Source: *Biographical Souvenir of the States of Georgia and Florida*, 1889.

Note: John Robinson, who resided at Tallapoosa, was an early settler of that part of Carroll County which later became Haralson County.

WILLIAM ROBINSON HAMMOND

Judge William R. Hammond. Few men have reached a higher distinction at the bar or enjoyed, in fuller measure, the respect and confidence of their fellow-citizens than Judge William Robinson Hammond. Though just in the prime of life, at an age when the greatest legal successes are usually attained, Judge Hammond has been recognized, for a number of years, as one of the foremost members of his profession. A native of this state, Judge Hammond was born in Franklin, Heard Co., Ga., on Oct. 25, 1848. His father, Judge Dennis F. Hammond, was a man of distinguished ability and of great usefulness. His attainments at the bar and in private life were such as to merit incidental mention in this connection. He was born at Newberry, S. C., in 1819, but came to Georgia in his youth, settling first in Lincoln county. He was subsequently united in marriage to Miss Adeline Robinson, of Carroll county, and nine children sprang from this union, four of whom survive: Octavia, wife of A. D. Adair, of Atlanta; William R., the subject of this sketch; Dr. John D., president of Central college, Missouri, and Edward M., a practicing lawyer of Orlando, Fla., and formerly a member of the state senate. Judge Hammond, the elder, was admitted to the bar in 1840. He moved to Newnan, Ga., in 1850, and five years later was elected to the superior court bench as judge of the Tallapoosa circuit. Leaving the bench in 1862, after an able and fearless administration of the law, Judge Hammond came to Atlanta and entered upon the active practice of his profession. In 1870, during a period of great disturbance and of frequent violations of the law, Judge Hammond was elected mayor of Atlanta. His administration was one of the most conservative the city has ever enjoyed and its influence was felt in the superior moral tone imparted to the city's daily life. Judge Hammond remained in the practice of law with his son until 1881. Leaving Atlanta, he then removed to Orlando. Fla., to engage in the orange industry, and devoted himself to that pursuit, though not giving up his professional practice entirely, until his death in 1891. The passing away of this great and good man was sincerely mourned. Among the tributes of sympathy received by the afflicted family were letters from Senators Alfred H. Colquitt, John B. Gordon and one from Judge B. H. Bigham. The press of the state teemed with eulogies upon his noble and useful life and the memory of his stainless record is still fresh in the minds of his fellow citizens. Returning to Judge William R. Hammond, the son of the foregoing: he lived only two years in Heard county, removing with his parents to Newnan, Ga., where he received his primary education. In 1862 the family came to Atlanta and William attended the private schools of that city for three years. He then entered the state university at Athens, Ga., in 1867, graduating from that institution in 1869, with the highest honors of his class. Dr. A. A. Lipscomb was the chancellor of the university at that time, and the class was one of the brightest and largest that ever graduated, several of its members having since attained both state and national distinction. After graduating the young student entered the law office of his father, Judge Dennis F. Hammond, and after preparing himself for the practice was admitted to the bar in 1870. Forming a partnership with his father they continued to practice, as a law firm, until 1881. In the following year William R. was elevated to the bench of the Atlanta circuit, having been elected by the general assembly to fill the unexpired term of Judge Hillyer, who resigned. He was subsequently re-elected for a term of four years but after serving for only a few months he resigned in November, 1885, to resume the active practice. As a judge his decisions were sound and logical and he enjoyed the confidence of both the bar and the public. During the period of his practice from 1870 to his election as Judge in 1882 Mr. Hammond had charge of, and successfully conducted, some of the most important and difficult litigation in the state. One of these was the case of the state against the Scofield Rolling Mill company, brought under a special act of the legislature, in which Mr. Hammond was for the defense. He obtained a new trial in the supreme court, after a heavy verdict for the state, and got a verdict for the defendant, on the second trial. Another case was the state vs. Cox, charged with the murder of Alston. He was convicted, and Mr. Hammond was selected, by five or six prominent lawyers who represented Cox, to argue his case in the supreme court. He obtained

WILLIAM ROBINSON HAMMOND

a strong dissenting opinion from Chief Justice Warner, on which Cox was pardoned. Mr. Hammond was highly complimented by the supreme court in both these cases, Judge Warner having said that his argument in the Cox case was the finest he had ever heard. These cases attracted a great deal of attention, and his management of them made him a great reputation and character as a lawyer throughout the state. After leaving the bench he formed a partnership with Judge John I. Hall, the present assistant attorney-general of the United States. Judge Hammond was elected a member of the board of education of the city of Atlanta in 1887, for a term of six years, and was subsequently re-elected in 1893, serving with pay. His work on the board has demonstrated his abiding love for the public school system of Atlanta, and his desire to elevate the masses by giving to all the wholesome advantages of a good education. Judge Hammond is a man of deep religious convictions, and has always been active in the affairs of his church. He is chairman of the board of trustees of Trinity church, and is also chairman of the board of stewards. In addition to these religious offices Judge Hammond is a life trustee of Wesleyan Female college, the oldest institution of its kind in the world. He is also president of the board of trustees of the Atlanta Dental college, and a member of the board of trustees of the colored branch of the state university, located in Savannah, Ga. Judge Hammond has always taken a profound interest in this work, and has made it a matter of careful study. He has also been engaged, as a prominent factor, in some of the leading enterprises of the city. In the early period of his professional life Judge Hammond was united in marriage to Miss Laura Rawson, the daughter of Hon. E. E. Rawson, one of the most prominent and enterprising citizens of Atlanta. In his private, as well as in his professional life the career of Judge Hammond has been above reproach, and his integrity has never been assailed. The firm of Hall & Hammond is one of the ablest in the state, and controls an extensive general practice, not only in Atlanta but throughout the state. His success as a practitioner, with his natural business capacity, has brought Judge Hammond a handsome competence, and in the financial world he enjoys a high rating. He exercises the same prudence, consideration and sagacity in his business interests that he brings to bear in his profession, and with a corresponding result. Judge Hammond is held in the highest esteem by all classes and his career of public service has not only been one of honor to himself but of usefulness to the community.

Source: *Memoirs of Georgia*, 1895. Volume 1.

Note: William Robinson Hammond's mother was a daughter of John Robinson of Tallapoosa, a prominent citizen and early settler of that part of Carroll County which later became Haralson County.

JAMES D. HAMRICK

James D. Hamrick, M. D., an eminent practitioner of Carrollton, Ga., was born in Carroll County, Ga., March 12, 1858. His father, James D. Hamrick, was born in Meriwether County in 1830, is still living and engaged in planting. The father of James D., Sr., was H. Harrison Hamrick, a native of Georgia, born in Jasper County in 1805. James D. Hamrick, Sr., married Miss Susana Scogin, daughter of Gilliam Scogin, of Troup County, Ga., and is the father of nine living children, viz.: Margaret E., Frances, James D., Gilliam A., Elizabeth, Mary, D. Harrison, William and Lula.

James D. Hamrick, the subject of this sketch, received his education primarily in the schools of Carroll County, Ga., but finished in the academy of Paulding County, that State. He read medicine with Dr. John W. Hallan, and graduated from the University of Georgia, at Augusta, in 1884. He immediately located in Carrollton, and his skill there as a physician is duly recognized. He is particularly successful in treating diseases of women and children. In 1885 he went into partnership with S. M. Crider, in the drug business, and the firm has a flourishing business.

In 1886 Dr. Hamrick married Miss Priscilla N. Gardner, daughter of Rev. G. A. Gardner, of Tennessee. Their home has been made happy in the birth of one child, James D., Jr.

Source: *Biographical Souvenir of the States of Georgia and Florida*, 1889.

ARTHUR D. HARMAN

Arthur D. Harman, a farmer, and engaged in milling and cotton ginning business, Carrollton, Carroll Co., Ga., son of William M. and Nancy (Dillard) Harman, was born in Monroe county, Ga., Nov. 14, 1832. His great-grandfather, Hezekiah Harman, emigrated from England to Virginia some years before the revolutionary war, and then

ARTHUR D. HARMAN

moved to North Carolina. His grandparents, Merriman and Nellie (May) Harman, were born in North Carolina, migrated to Georgia in 1828, settled first in Monroe county, and then went among the first settlers to Meriwether county. There they lived the first year on a dirt floor, and as there was no sawmill near, he split out puncheon with which to lay a floor. Mr. Harman's father was born in Chatham county, N. C., in 1805, where he grew to manhood; then (1826) he came to Georgia and settled in the woods. In 1830 he was married to Nancy, daughter of Arthur and Mary (Abney) Dillard, who were born in South Carolina, and moved thence to Georgia and settled in Jones county in 1826. Both families for generations were farmers. To this union five children were born: Eliza J., Emeline E., Nancy A., Martha F. and Arthur D., the subject of this sketch — all of whom are now living except the eldest daughter. Mr. Harman was reared in Meriwether county and was schooled in the log cabin of that day and locality, with dirt floor, puncheon seats, a chimney made of clay and sticks and square holes cut through the logs for windows. The only time he had for schooling was between "laying-by" and "fodder-pulling" time. Before the war he was captain of the militia, when the position had some local distinction, but in 1861 he enlisted as a private in Company A (Capt. J. D. Frederick), Tenth Georgia battalion (Maj. Rylander). He was on some of the most hotly contested fields — the Wilderness, Petersburg, Davis Farm, Blow Up, Deep Bottom, Turkey Ridge, Hatcher's Run, Suffolk, etc. After Suffolk he was transferred to Gen. Ranse Wright's brigade and remained with it until the surrender at Appomattox. For a considerable time during the war he acted as commissary, and in this position was faithful and prompt in the discharge of every duty. After the war he returned to his farm and has since engaged in farming. In 1892 he moved to Carrollton and invested in milling and cotton-ginning. Mr. Harman was married in 1857 to Miss Jane I. Fincher — born in Troup county — daughter of Isaac and Elizabeth (Brooks) Fincher, who were among the early settlers of Meriwether county. To them eight children have been born: William I., born March 26, 1859; Arthur D., born July 11, 1861; John A., born July 13, 1864; Betsy B., born February 15, 1867; James R., born March 3, 1870; Luther M., born Jan. 26, 1872; Edgar S., born March 21, 1875; and Anna I., born Nov. 12, 1878. Mr. Harman is a royal arch Mason and himself and wife are members of the Baptist church. He

is a man in whom everybody has the utmost confidence and possesses
no inconsiderable influence, and he and family are highly esteemed.

Source: *Memoirs of Georgia*, 1895. Volume 1.

SAMPSON W. HARRIS

Sampson W. Harris, of Coosa, was a native of Georgia, and a graduate of the University of that State. He was a son of the Hon. Stephen W. Harris, a Judge of the Superior Court from 1813 to 1816, whose death in 1822 was considered a great loss to the State.

In September, 1831, the first Internal Improvements Convention ever held in Georgia, assembled at Eatonton, where Mr. S. W. Harris resided, of which he was appointed one of the three Secretaries. Wylie W. Mason, Esq., afterward a Chancellor in Alabama, was a member of that Convention.

About the year 1838, Mr. Harris settled in Wetumpka, in the practice of the law, and at once took high position. A Democrat, he soon attracted popular notice, first in a State Convention held at Tuskaloosa, where he made a speech which placed him at once on the road to preferment. In 1841, as noticed in another place in this volume, he was elected Solicitor of the Eighth Circuit, the duties of which office he discharged with such ability, and faithfulness, that the partiality of friends, more than any desire on his part, presented him as a candidate for Judge of the Circuit Court, in which election he was defeated. In 1844, he succeeded Mr. Yancey in the Senate, for the District of Coosa and Autauga, and again in 1845. The session of the latter year terminated his connection with the State Legislature, and his rapidly developed powers sought a wider field, where he might win laurels more suited, it may be, to his taste and ambition.

In 1847, Mr. Harris was nominated as the Democratic candidate for Congress, in the Third District, and was elected, if I mistake not, without much show of opposition. In 1849, he defeated Judge John S. Hunter, who was an antagonist of no ordinary strength. In 1851, his opponent was Judge William S. Mudd, who with the issue pending that year, was the most popular man that could be placed in competition with him, and he was defeated by Mr. Harris. In 1853, his opponent was Judge Moore, of Lowndes, who shared the like fate. In 1855, by a new arrangement of the district, he was thrown upon several counties of territory new to him, and he had to confront a new political organization, the Know-Nothing or American party, headed by Col. William B. Martin, of Benton. That was a year of much political excitement and activity, and for sometime, during the Spring and early Summer, the future of parties and aspirants was veiled in uncertainty. Mr. Harris was timid and easily alarmed, and that was the time for the exhibition of his great powers before the people. I remember the day that he and his competitor, Col. Martin, opened the canvass, at Nixburg, in Coosa county. By consent, among several of his friends, Mr. Harris was to be alarmed to a degree that would arouse him. This was not hard to do, when he came to look over the large concourse of people in attendance, many of them from adjoining counties, and the debate opened under the firm belief of Mr. Harris that it would give direction to the canvass and the result, which I have no doubt was the case. His speech, on that occasion, astonished even his most sanguine friends, in the force and power of his arguments; and yet the softness and elegance of his manner as a public speaker, was fully preserved. The people turned out *en masse,* and would follow him from one appointment to another to hear that wonderful orator. He defeated his opponent by a majority of 800 votes. This was his last canvass, and it is quite probable that, by his extraordinary labors, his health was impaired, so that he did not long survive. He served the people ten years in Congress, and died at the city of Washington, during the Winter of 1856-'7, an humble Christian, leaning on the merits of his Redeemer.

The foregoing sketch of Mr. Harris' public life and positions vindicates, in unmistakeable terms, the character of the man, and his high grade of talents. Well educated, with the advantages of much reading and study, which accorded with his taste and habits, he was fitted for any position in the State. In person, he was tall and spare, with a fine head and face, while his manners were graceful and captivating, his voice soft and musical, and his conversational powers of a high order. All these advantages were at his command in social life, and with men of every station; and then, when he came upon the hustings, and with the conviction that what he would say was to have its influence in the success or failure of the principles he had adopted, as the best for the administration of the Government, he was instructive and eloquent.

In Congress, Mr. Harris spoke a few times, and at every effort advanced further to the front rank of speakers in that body. But with all his vast powers and attainments, he was indolent, and this indulgence, or rather injustice to himself, eclipsed greatly the rising splendor of his political star. He did not take the commanding position in the councils of the nation that was his due, nor in any public situation that he held, and therefore he was never known or appreciated as he should have been. Let him be aroused to a proper sense of the importance of an occasion, and he was a full match in all that constitutes an able, eloquent speaker, with any man of his day in the State. He died in the meridian of life.

At an early age, Mr. Harris married Miss Thomas, an accomplished lady, of Athens, Georgia. One of his sons, Sampson W. Harris, Jr., commanded the 6th Georgia Regiment in the late war, as the successor of Gen. A. H. Colquitt, promoted. He now resides at West-Point, Chambers county, engaged in the practice of the law. Another son, Dr. Hugh Nisbet Harris, married a daughter of the Hon. B. C. Yancey, and resides at Athens.

Source: Garrett, *Reminiscences of Public Men in Alabama, For Thirty Years,* 1872.

Note: Sampson W. Harris, Jr. was a resident of Carroll County.

SAMPSON W. HARRIS

Sampson W. Harris, judge of Coweta circuit, Carrollton, Carroll Co., Ga., son of Sampson W. and Paulina (Thomas) Harris, was born in Alabama, in 1838. His great-grandfather, Simpson Harris, was a native of Wales, and emigrated to Virginia before the revolutionary war. He came to Georgia in 1795 and settled in the woods. His grandparents were Stephen W. and Sarah (Watkins) Harris. His grandfather was one of the first graduates of the university of Georgia, Athens, Ga., was an eminent lawyer, and for many years a judge of the superior court. The father of the subject of this sketch was born in Elbert county, Ga., Feb. 23, 1809, graduating from the university of Georgia in 1828, and removed to Alabama in 1837, where he practiced law and rose rapidly professionally and politically. He represented the Fourth congressional district of Alabama for ten years and died in Washington, while in congress, in April, 1857. Judge Harris was reared on the plantation, and received a good common school education. He entered the university of Georgia, in 1853, and graduated in 1857; studied law and was admitted to the bar in Oglethorpe county, Ga., and entered upon the practice. In 1861 he enlisted in Company K (Capt. John T. Lofton) Sixth Georgia regiment, which was assigned to Gen. A. H. Colquitt's command. He served through the war, and was in many hard fought battles. He was seriously wounded and was captured by Sherman's army just before the surrender, but was paroled. He entered the army as first lieutenant, and was gradually promoted until he reached a colonelcy just before the close of the war. After the war he planted a few years, in Chambers county, Ala., and then resumed his law practice. He moved into Georgia in the seventies, and was a member of the constitutional convention of 1877. That same year, also, he was appointed solicitor-general of the Coweta circuit, which office he held until 1880, when he was elected judge of the circuit – a position he still holds. In May, 1894, Gov. Northen tendered him the office of secretary of state to fill a vacancy, but he declined the appointment. In 1866 Judge Harris was married in Alabama to Miss Lucy, daughter of Henry and Emily (Watkins) Todd. This union has been blessed with six children: H. F., physician, graduate of Atlanta medical college, and of Jefferson medical college, Philadelphia, been in practice three years; Sampson; Stephen, graduate of Atlanta medical college; Isabella, Paulina, and Lucy. Judge Harris is a master Mason.

Source: *Memoirs of Georgia*, 1895. Volume 1.

JAMES R. HEAD

James R. Head, farmer, Tallapoosa, Haralson Co., Ga., son of D. B. and Harriet Head, was born in Baldwin county, Ga., Sept. 12, 1823. His grandfather and grandmother on his father's side were born in Virginia, his grandfather, James Head, coming to Georgia just before the revolutionary war. Mr. Head's father was reared a farmer, but in 1837 he engaged in merchandising, which he continued until 1842, when he returned to the farm. In the meantime he studied medicine and in 1845 entered upon the practice, which he successfully followed until his death, which occurred in 1887, and was occasioned by a fall from a wagon near Gadsden, Ala. Mr. Head was reared in Fayette county, Ga., until he was thirteen years of age (1836), when his parents moved to Carroll county. His education was limited to what was obtainable at the common country schools within the brief time then allowed farmers' boys. Mr. Head enlisted in a company commanded by Capt. William Potts of Newnan, Ga., which became a part of the Second regiment, Georgia state troops. With his command he participated in the battle at New Hope church, went thence to Marietta, then to Atlanta and Jonesboro. From there the command went with Gen, Hood when he made his flank movement to Nashville, Tenn. Beginning life with nothing, he has by industry, upright dealing and good management, acquired a quite large property and is accounted one of the most substantial and responsible citizens of the county. Farming has been his life-pursuit; but he was a justice of the peace five years, and is now a member of the board of education. Mr. Head was married Feb. 24, 1842, to Miss Amanda A., daughter of Solomon and Mary Stisher of Carroll county, who has borne him three children: Mary Ann Harriet, Marguerite Roberts and Elizabeth Missouri. Mr. Head is a master Mason and an exemplary member of the Missionary Baptist church.

Source: *Memoirs of Georgia*, 1895. Volume 1.

JAMES J. HENDON

James J. Hendon, M. D., physician and surgeon of Mobile, was born in Carroll county, Ga., November 13, 1853. His father was James H. Hendon, a native of Georgia, and a farmer by occupation. His father was Elijah Hendon. The mother of J. J. Hendon was Diademah Smith, a native of Georgia, and her father was Gabriel Smith. Both parents of Dr. Hendon are now living in St. Clair county, Ala. He took a high school education and in 1876 began the business of life as a school teacher, teaching and attending school alternately for several years. In 1881 he took up the study of medicine under the instructions of Dr. D. E. Cason, of Ashville, Ala. He took a full course of medicine at the Medical college of Alabama, and graduated in 1886. He at once began the practice of medicine in Mobile, where he has since remained, and where he is in possession of a lucrative practice. He is a member of the Mobile county Medical society and the Alabama state Medical association. He is a member of the democratic party, and the Methodist Episcopal church, south. He is an Odd Fellow, and a member of the Knights and Ladies of Honor, and of the Legal Friendship. He was married October 14, 1885, to Miss Laura A. Moore, of Mobile, by whom he has two children, both daughters. Dr. Hendon is the proprietor of a drug store which he conducts in connection with his practice, which is very extensive.

Source: *Memorial Record of Alabama*, 1893. Volume 2.

J. B. HERNDON

J. B. Herndon, the popular merchant of Bradley Station, was born in this county on February 9, 1860, and here he attained his growth and was schooled, received the best education that the common schools afforded. He was married September 20, 1888, to Miss Lola Velvin, who was born in Georgia in 1867. Her father, R. C. Velvin, is now living in Texas. Their marriage has been blessed in the birth of one child, a daughter – Ella W. In 1885 Mr. Herndon began life's battles for himself by engaging in the saloon business on Red River, but in 1888 he disposed of these interests, and opened a general store in Walnut Hill, continuing there about one year, and then came to Bradley. Here he commenced a general merchandise business, which he has successfully conducted ever since, carrying a stock valued at $2,500, and he is conceded to be a very capable young business man. His wife is a member of the Baptist Church, in which she is one of the most active workers, and is an intelligent and amiable lady. J. B. Herndon is one of seven children – three boys and four girls – born to the marriage of J. D. and Eliza (Cramtree) Herndon, both of whom were natives of this county and are now deceased. The father departed this life in March. 1872, and his widow on January 1, 1880. The paternal grandfather was a native of Kentucky, and emigrated to Arkansas at an early day, being one of the early pioneers of this State, and here he passed the remainder of his life. He was a farmer by occupation, as was his son also, the father of our subject. Five of the seven children born to the parents are still living: Zurie (deceased), Mattie (deceased), Ida, J. B., R. F., Lola and J. D.

Source: *Biographical and Historical Memoirs of Southern Arkansas,* 1890.

Note: The R. C. Velvin mentioned in this sketch is Robert J. Velvin who was a resident of Carroll County, Georgia. See the 1870 and 1880 Censuses. Annual Returns of Carroll County, Book M, page 2, lists Mrs. Lola Herndon as a daughter of Robert J. Velvin.

FRANCIS MARION HICKS

This prominent old settler of Texas was born in Georgia, November 16, 1826, being the fourth of five children born to William A. and Margaret (Moon) Hicks, who were married near Raleigh, N. C., and were born in Tennessee and North Carolina respectively. The parental grandfather, John Hicks, was born in Virginia, and was a soldier of the Revolution. After that great strife was over he moved to Tennessee, of which state he was among the first settlers. He came of English ancestors, who settled in Virginia during colonial days. William A. Hicks settled in Georgia when a young man and engaged in planting and trading, but afterwards moved to Alabama and then to Mississippi, thence to Arkansas, and finally to Texas in 1849. Here he settled in Cherokee County, and became one of the settlers of Rusk. He was an old line Whig politically, and was elected to the Legislature from Cherokee County, which was strongly Democratic. He was also a county clerk in Georgia, and was quite a party leader of the Whigs there, and a strong Henry Clay man. He became a prominent planter of Cherokee County, and there made his home until death closed his career. His wife died when the subject of this sketch was a boy, in Hickstown, Ga., which place was named in his honor. It was a gold mining town, and his early days were spent as a miner. He was a Royal Arch Mason, and was an active and enterprising citizen.

Francis M. Hicks was educated in Mississippi, was married at Paulding, Jasper County, and began life as a merchant. In 1852 he came to Cherokee County, Tex., but shortly after removed to Corsicana, Navarro County, Tex., and began business as one of the early merchants of the place. Shortly after he sold out and returned to Rusk, where he was engaged in business until the outbreak of the war.

In 1861 he entered a company and went to Galveston, where he was detailed to act as commissary at Rusk, and served in that capacity about one year. He was then detailed by General Kirby Smith as the financial agent of the Government iron works at Rusk, and served in that capacity until the war closed, his assistance being most invaluable to the Government.

The war left Mr. Hicks almost destitute, but he at once embarked in business at Rusk, where he continued until 1868, when he went to Shreveport and opened a commission house, which is known as the Hicks Company, Limited. In 1872 he associated with him Mr. Robert H. Howell, under the firm name of Hicks & Howell, dealers in groceries and the cotton factorage business. They were very fortunate in their operations and prospered from the very beginning, and on the solid foundation which was the laid there had been builded the staunchest commercial organization in the state of Louisiana, outside of the city of New Orleans.

After sixteen years of lucrative business, the firm of Hicks & Howell was dissolved, and Mr. Howell took from the establishment a fortune without the least affecting its standing or credit. Mr. Hicks then took into partnership his son, S. B. Hicks, a young gentleman whose education, training and natural business ability peculiarly fitted him for the responsible position to which he was called. The firm name was then changed to F. M. & S. B. Hicks, and continued in existence for four years, during which time the failing condition of Colonel Hicks' health caused him to throw the burden of the extensive business, in all its multitudinous details, on the shoulders of his son, who proved equal to the occasion, and won his spurs in an arena where many older and more experienced had failed. In 1892 the present incorporation was formed under the name of the Hicks Company, Limited, whose business is exclusively wholesale grocers and cotton factors. Their place of business is admirably located where the house has for many years been established. Colonel Hicks' name is justly at the head of this establishment, though he is no longer able, on account of his health, to take an active part in its affairs. He was compelled to seek a change of climate, came to San Antonio, and has been greatly benefited thereby. The active management of the business now devolves upon his son, S. B. Hicks, vice president, who is ably assisted by Captain W. T. Crawford, secretary and treasurer. Mr. W. F. Chase is the cashier and bookkeeper, T. H. Scovell is head salesman, and F. H. Gosman has charge of the cotton department. All these gentlemen have been long connected with the business, and are by experience and special adaptability thoroughly equipped for their several responsible and exacting positions. To give an idea of the immense business transacted by this house, it is but necessary to state that its store-room, merchandise and cotton warehouses have a floor space, under roof, exceeding by 16,000 square feet, an acre of floor space, and the annual sales aggregate considerably over a million dollars.

Colonel Hicks' kindly face and genial manners endear him to all with whom he comes in contact, and socially or otherwise make him popular with all classes. He is a man of rare business qualifications and indomitable energy, and to him is due full credit for the decided success achieved by the firm, whose name will always adorn the best pages of Shreveport's commercial history. He was made a Mason in Mississippi, and in April, 1851, was married to Miss Ann E. McDugald, a daughter of James McDugald of Scotland, who became a prominent lawyer of Mississippi at Paulding, where he was an active citizen and served as State Senator.

To Colonel Hicks and his wife four sons and four daughters were given: Emma L., Lelia, wife of Dr. Lawrence of Longview, Tex.; Francis Marion, Jr., Clara, wife of Callie McArthur Walke, who is a business man of Shreveport; Samuel B., who was educated at Shreveport and graduated at Soule College, New Orleans, in which educational institution he won a medal. He is now general manager and vice president of the Hicks Company of Shreveport; Marshall was educated at Shreveport and graduated at the Southwestern University of Clarksville, Tenn. He studied law for two years at the State University, Austin, Tex., from which he graduated and began practicing at Minneola, Tex., with Captain Giles, a prominent lawyer. He came to San Antonio and was appointed district attorney of Laredo District by Governor Hogg, after which he was elected to that office and served four years. He is now a practitioner of San Antonio, but was married in Clarksville. Richard Yale is also a lawyer of San Antonio. Annie McD., and one that died early.

Francis Marion was educated at Rusk and Shreveport, La., studying medicine in the latter place also, after which he attended lectures at Bellevue College Hospital, New York, from which he graduated. He began practicing at Rusk, but in a short time went to Tyler, Tex., where he built up a large practice, but labored so incessantly that he injured his health, to improve which he went to California, and in 1890 returned to San Antonio, where he has built up a large practice. His attention is given to all branches of his profession, but he makes something of a specialty of surgery and surgical cases, and is also a member of the Texas State Medical Society; and is also a member and first vice president of the Southwest Texas Medical Association. He is surgeon of the International & Great Northern Railway at San Antonio, and while at Tyler he was chief, and later consulting surgeon of the Cotton Belt Railroad, but resigned from the former office on account

FRANCIS MARION HICKS

of ill health. While at Tyler he was medical examiner for nearly all the old line life insurance companies. The doctor is a student in his profession, and in 1882 spent six months studying at the Jefferson Medical College, and the medical department of the University of Pennsylvania at Philadelphia. In 1885 he went to New York and took a post graduate course at the New York Polyclinic Medical College, and made a special study of surgery and diseases of the eye, ear and nose, to aid him in his office of chief surgeon of the Cotton Belt Railroad. In 1887 he made a trip to California in search of health, but since coming to San Antonio he has enjoyed comparatively good health. He was married in 1887 to Miss Margaret R. Spence, a native of Texas, and a daughter of John Spence, one of the early settlers of the Lone Star State from Maryland. He belongs to an old Scotch family that came to this country during colonial times, that assisted in founding and became members of the first Presbyterian church in America, at Snow Hill, Md., and from that time down to the present day some member of the family has been an elder in that historic church. Mrs. Hicks is a highly educated lady, of decided literary and musical taste and talent. She graduated from the Augusta Female Institute at Staunton, Va., the finest young ladies' college in the South. There she won a medal for scholarship and music. Her union with Dr. Hicks has resulted in the birth of two children. The doctor and his wife are members of the First Presbyterian church, and he is an elder in the same. Politically he has always been in sympathy with the Democratic party, and has served as delegate to various conventions.

Source: *Memorial and Genealogical Record of Texas (East),* 1895. *Memorial and Genealogical Record of Southwest Texas,* 1894 contains an almost identical sketch.

WILLIAM HENRY HINES

William Henry Hines, merchant, Rockmart, Polk Co., Ga., a son of James and Winiford Hines, was born in Meriwether county, Ga., Sept. 8, 1829. His father was born in Greene county, Ga., where he was reared a farmer and as such lived and died. Mr. Hines was reared on the farm in Meriwether county, and was educated in the common schools of the county, taught in log cabins; but when he was eighteen years old he attended school at Longstreet, Ga., and obtained a good education. Returning home he farmed until the war occurred. After the war he went to Jamestown, Texas, where he merchandised for fifteen months, and then returned to Meriwether county. He left that county and came to Rockmart, in 1871, where he established a large and profitable general merchandise business in which he is still engaged. He had but little to begin life with, and has attempted nothing extraordinary; but he has been satisfactorily successful, has accumulated a good property, and has an enviable reputation as a business man and citizen. Mr. Hines was married Nov. 1, 1855, to Miss Sarah E. Mitchell, who bore him two children: Carrie and Etta. Their mother having died in 1857, in 1872 he married Miss Nannie L. Battle, daughter of Lazarus Battle, by whom he has had one child, William L. Mr. Hines is a master Mason, and a member of the Missionary Baptist church.

Source: *Memoirs of Georgia*, 1895. Volume 2.

Note: James and Winaford Hines are buried in the Whitesburg, Georgia, City Cemetery.

HAMILTON HOGAN

Hamilton Hogan, farmer, Whitesburg, Carroll Co., Ga., son of James and Elizabeth (Spraggins) Hogan, was born in Pendleton district, South Carolina, March 1, 1820. His paternal grandparents, William and Nancy (Dillard) Hogan, were Virginian born; and Mr. Hogan was a soldier in the revolutionary army. His maternal grandparent, Thomas Spraggins, was a native South Carolinian, and a soldier in the patriot army during the war for independence. In 1824, Mr. Hogan's father came from South Carolina to Georgia, settled in Habersham county, and rented a farm with a cabin on it preparatory to bringing his family. In 1825 he went for some needed articles, and to bring them he cut two poles to serve as shafts, and fastening the box containing his articles on one end, hitched his horse between the poles at the other end. He then put little five-year-old Hamilton, the subject of this sketch, on his horse, and returned to Georgia, he walking all the way. This shows one of the methods by which the "Empire State of the South" was peopled. In 1832 his father moved to Coweta county and cleared a farm on which he ended his days. Mr. Hogan attended school in the old-time schoolhouse, and after he "graduated" he taught school himself five years, by which he earned his first money. He next engaged in farming, which has been his life pursuit, in which he has been successful, and acquired a competency. In 1862, he enlisted in Company H, third Georgia battalion (Col. Stovall) and served one year, when his health failed and he was discharged. As soon as he recovered his health he re-enlisted, this time in Company H, of which he was made orderly sergeant, Sixty-sixth Georgia regiment (Col. Nesbit). He was captured at Decatur, Ala., and after being held some time was paroled. While at home the conflict terminated, and he is now the proud possessor of two one-hundred-dollar bills paid him for his services. Although he was not wounded during his service in the army, the numerous perforations in his clothes show how narrowly he escaped not only wounds but death. He was in the battle of Missionary Ridge, and the charge on Peachtree creek, and many other engagements. In 1876 he was elected a representative from Carroll county to the general assembly, and was re-elected in 1878, but did not serve out the term. He is now serving his second year as county commissioner, and while serving as such he was largely instrumental in having erected the really elegant new courthouse, as good as any in the state, and, all things considered, one of the cheapest. Mr. Hogan was married in 1846 to Miss Jane Watson – born in Carroll county – daughter of Tyre and Clarissa (Sockwell) Watson – Georgia born – by whom he has had nine children: Helen, wife of J. T. Jones; Elizabeth, wife of L. J. Jones; Sarah J., wife of John A. Byers; Ellen M., wife of N. C. Morris; Fannie; James T. and Gus A., who are living; and Louisa J., wife of Henry G. Jennings; and Hepsie A., wife of John W. Duncan, deceased. Mr. Hogan is one of the most substantial and influential citizens of Carroll county, and is held in the highest esteem by everybody. He is a member of the Masonic fraternity, and is a useful and exemplary member of the Methodist church.

Source: *Memoirs of Georgia*, 1895. Volume 1.

JOHN K. HOLCOMBE, Jr.

John K. Holcombe, Jr., farmer, Buchanan, Haralson Co., Ga., son of John K. and Rachel Holcombe, was born in Carroll county, Ga., July 4, 1848. His father was born in Laurens district, S. C., in 1810, and came to Georgia with the family in a one-horse wagon, and settled in what is now De Kalb county, in 1820. His education was very limited, and he followed farming all his life. Mr. Holcombe's mother was born in what is now De Kalb county in 1815, and was married to her husband in 1830. Mr. Holcombe received a very limited education, as he was merely a boy and lad while the war was being waged, and the schools suspended; but being ambitious he studied at home and acquired a fairly good education. He was reared a farmer, but ran machinery at one period of his life, and has also done a general merchandise business. The estimation in which he is held by the people of Haralson county is evidenced by the fact that for ten years he held the office of sheriff. He has been successful in all his undertakings, has accumulated a competency, and while one of the most popular, he is accounted one of the solidest men in the county. Mr. Holcombe married Miss Mary, daughter of Levi and Lucretia (Reeves) Stidman, of Bartow county. Her grandfather, Martin Stidman, was one of the first settlers of Bartow (then Cass) county. Six children have blessed this union: William F., Reuben Cornelius, Estelle, Sarah Elizabeth, Emma and John Kellette. As Mr. Holcombe is yet young, so popular and so well capacitated for public position, it is quite certain he will again be called into public service.

Source: *Memoirs of Georgia*, 1895. Volume 1.

JAMES EDWARD HOPSON

James Edward Hopson is one of the most successful and substantial men of Cleveland County, Ark., but was born in Coweta County, Ga., January 2, 1846, being a son of Briggs W. and Sarah (Franklin) Hopson, who were also Georgians, but removed to Arkansas in 1860, locating in what is now Cleveland County, then Bradley County. They were members of the Missionary Baptist Church, and he was a member of the Masonic fraternity and a Democrat in his political views, and while a resident of Georgia held a number of local offices. Mr. Hopson was a fairly successful farmer, was a man of many worthy traits of character, and passed to his long home in Cleveland County, Ark., in 1872. James Edward Hopson was the fourth of eleven children, seven now living, and spent his school days in Georgia. In 1863 he joined Col. Flippin's regiment, Arkansas Cavalry, Confederate States Army, afterward dismounted, and served the cause he espoused faithfully and well until May, 1865, when he was mustered out of service

JAMES EDWARD HOPSON

at Camden. He then found himself without any means, in broken health, caused by exposure during service, but he set energetically to work on the home farm, and remained with his father until the latter's death. Since then he has been very successful in his farming operations, and is now the owner of a valuable farm of 465 acres, with 130 acres in a high state of cultivation, all of which is the result of industry and business ability. June 10, 1869, he was united in marriage to Miss Harriet Elizabeth Owens, a daughter of William Owens. She was born in Georgia, in 1844, and her union with Mr. Hopson has resulted in the birth of eleven children, all of whom are living: Lila F., Augusta G., Thomas Evan, Joseph P., Beulah A., Jesse M., Charles A., Frank E., Willie W., Cal D. and James O. Mr. Hopson and his wife are members of the Missionary Baptist Church, and he, like his father, is a supporter of Democratic principles.

Source: *Biographical and Historical Memoirs of Southern Arkansas,* 1890.

Note: Briggs W. Hopson was residing in Carroll County, Georgia in 1850 See 1850 Census.

WILLIAM M. HOPSON

Rev. William M. Hopson is a member of the Missionary Baptist Church, and although born in Coweta County, Ga., January 1, 1840, he has been a resident of the State of Arkansas since 1859, in which year his parents, Briggs W. and Sarah Franklin (Walden) Hopson, came thither. They were born in Walton and Jasper Counties, Ga., respectively, and the father died in Cleveland County, Ark., when about fifty-nine years of age, his widow still surviving him, her age being about seventy-two years. She is a member of the Missionary Baptist Church, as was her husband, and during his lifetime they were well-to-do and successful farmers. He was a Mason, and in his political views a Democrat, and while in Georgia was tax receiver of Randolph County for some time. He was a soldier in the war with the Creek Indians. Rev. William M. Hopson was the eldest of eleven children, seven now living, and his youth was spent in his native State. In the fall of 1861 he joined the Ninth Arkansas Infantry, Confederate States Army, with which he remained until the close of the war, participating in the battles of Corinth, Baker's Creek, Jackson, Port Hudson, and was in the famous Georgia campaign, taking part in the battles of Jonesboro,

WILLIAM M. HOPSON

Lovejoy, Atlanta and Moon Station, after which he went back to Tennessee, and participated in the battles of Franklin, Columbia, Pulaski, Sugar Creek, Franklin, also two days' battle at Nashville, Tenn., and was wounded in the right arm by a minie-ball, in the engagement at Bentonville, N. C., this being the first wound he had received. He was in fifteen regular engagements, not counting the numerous skirmishes, and acted as a sharpshooter, at Jackson, Miss. After the war he returned home and commenced to farm for himself in the neighborhood of where he now lives, his capital at that time consisting of 75 cents. He manfully put his shoulder to the wheel, and by industry and good management has become the owner of 400 acres of land, as good as there is in the county, and has his property well improved. February 3, 1869, he was united in the bonds of matrimony to Miss Martha J. Wilson, a daughter of James and Mary Wilson. She was born in Marion County, Ga., September 1, 1844, and her union with Mr. Hopson has resulted in the birth of nine children: Annie L. (born November 25, 1869), James W. (born May 12, 1871), Mary F. (born August 3, 1872), Eugenia O. (born August 17, 1876), William B. (born October 9, 1877), Amanda C. (born November 23, 1878), Alva B. (born October 22, 1880), Charles F. (born February 22, 1882), and Laurence R. (born July 20, 1884). Mr. Hopson united with the Missionary Baptist Church, in 1861, and in 1874 was licensed to preach the gospel, and in the month of June, 1887, he took charge of the church at Kingsland. His wife and eldest daughter are also members of that church, and he is a member of the Agricultural Wheel, and a Democrat in his political views. It is characteristic of the man only to claim himself a corn-field preacher, contending earnestly for the faith once delivered to the saints.

Source: *Biographical and Historical Memoirs of Southern Arkansas,* 1890.

Note: Briggs W. Hopson was residing in Carroll County, Georgia in 1850 See 1850 Census.

JOHN HOUSEWORTH

John Houseworth, farmer, Whitesburg, Carroll Co., Ga., son of John J. and Catherine (Lyons) Houseworth, was born in Carroll county, in 1848. His grandparents on his father's side were Philip and Katie (Hollensworth) Houseworth. His grandfather's parents came from Germany to America before the revolutionary war, and his father dying when he was quite a child he was reared by a charitable institution in South Carolina. After reaching manhood and marrying he came to Georgia and settled first in Newton county, and afterward moved to De Kalb county. Here Mr. Houseworth's father was reared and married his wife, daughter of George and Kate Lyons, of English descent. Of ten children reared three sons enlisted in the Confederate army: Robert and Abraham, in Company K (Capt. Bark), Seventh Georgia regiment, which was in Early's command. Robert was a lieutenant, and he with his brother were in all the engagements in which his company bore a part, and was wounded at Knoxville, Tenn. Philip was in the western army under Capt. Kendrick. Mr. Houseworth was reared on the farm cleared by his father, and is living in the house in which he was born. He received a common school education, and started in life with a good constitution, good health, and a determined and willing spirit as his patrimony and capital. Mr. Houseworth was married in Carroll county in 1869 to Miss Harriet A. Holland – born in the county – daughter of Linsey and Elizabeth (Lassetter) Holland. Ten children are the offspring of this union: Delvous, Wyley, Walter, Della, Frank and Lee (twins); Katie, Tiney, Anna, Gordon. Mr. Houseworth is a well-to-do prosperous farmer with more than 600 acres of productive land, doing well, and is highly respected,

Source: *Memoirs of Georgia*, 1895. Volume 1.

THOMAS C. HOWELL, Sr.

Thomas C. Howell, Sr., farmer, Dallas, Paulding Co., Ga., son of Greene W. and Elizabeth (Clayton) Howell, was born in Cabarrus county, N. C., in 1833. His father, who was the son of Joseph Howell, a revolutionary soldier, was born in North Carolina in 1807. In 1836 he migrated from that state to Georgia, traveling all the distance by wagon, and settled in Cobb county, living in a tent until he could clear land and build a house. In 1846 he moved to Carroll county, Ga., whence after living there two years, he moved to Paulding county, where he died in 1852. Mr. Howell's mother was a daughter of Thomas and Sallie (Raysor) Clayton, and was born in North Carolina in 1799, was married about 1827, and became the mother of seven children: Joseph; Mrs. Mary Hardeman; Thomas C., the subject of this sketch;

THOMAS C. HOWELL, Sr.

Mrs. Sarah Walton; Mrs. Bede R. Hester; John A., and James J. His mother died in 1878. Mr. Howell was reared on the farm, and educated at the "old-field" school, taught in a dirt-floor log house without windows. In April, 1862, he enlisted in Company A, Fortieth Georgia regiment, saw much hard service, and was engaged in many hard-fought battles, among them: Baker's Creek, Vicksburg, Missionary Ridge, Resaca, and from there to, and including, Atlanta (where he was slightly wounded), and many less important engagements. Aug. 16, 1864, he was made a prisoner at East Point, near Atlanta, and sent to Camp Chase, Ohio, where he was confined ten months. After the surrender he was sent home to find it a mass of ruins 'mid a scene of desolation. Nothing daunted he went to work manfully to recuperate and rehabilitate himself. How well he has been successful is told by his comfortable home, his broad productive acres and present pleasant surroundings. Popular, progressive and prosperous, his declining years will pass untroubled by anxious cares. Mr. Howell was married in 1854 to Miss Sarah A., daughter of Sidney and Nancy (Hull) Robertson, and to them six children were born: John H., Joseph B., Green W., Thomas C., Benjamin F. and Mrs. Mollie J. Rogers. Within one year he had two sons killed on the East Tenn., Va. & Ga. railway. His second son, a conductor, was killed in a wreck in 1891, and his fourth son, a flagman, was also killed that same year in a wreck; and the next year his son-in-law, Patrick Rogers, a fireman, was killed in another wreck on the same road. His wife died May 12, 1892. On June 22, 1892, Mr. Howell was married to Miss Lucinda Bradbury. Mr. Howell is a prominent member of the Missionary Baptist church, of which he has been a deacon for thirty-four years, and possesses the entire confidence of all who know him.

Source: *Memoirs of Georgia*, 1895. Volume 2.

NEDOM W. HULSEY

Nedom W. Hulsey, merchant and farmer of Guin, Ala., is a native of Carroll county, Ga., and was born July 23, 1843. He is the third of a family of eleven children born to Kenion and Millie (Sanders) Hulsey, also natives of Georgia. His paternal grandparents were Charles and Nancy (Pate) Hulsey, and his maternal grandparents were Jonathan and Lucy (Adair) Sanders, all of the state of Georgia. In 1849 Kenion

NEDOM W. HULSEY

Hulsey came to Alabama, and settled in Cherokee county, where he followed farming until 1856, when he removed to Jefferson county, and there passed the remainder of his days, dying in 1872, highly respected by all who knew him. Nedom W. Hulsey was reared in Alabama, and here received his education. In 1862 he enlisted in company D, Third Confederate cavalry, Gen. Joe Wheeler's corps, and took part in the battles of Fort Donelson, Bowling Green, Murfreesboro, Nashville, Chickamauga, New Hope Church, Atlanta and Franklin. He rose to the rank of captain, and served in that capacity for two years. While at home on furlough, he was captured in Jefferson county, Ala., and was sent to Montgomery, and detained as a prisoner of war twenty-one days, when he was paroled.

On his return home, he engaged in farming, which vocation he followed until 1876, when he became a merchant at Guin, in which business he still continues, in conjunction with farming. He is still the owner of 200 acres of good land in Jefferson county; he owns, beside five building lots in Guin, and his store is well stocked; he does a thriving trade, which justifies him in placing some of his surplus capital at interest.

Mr. Hulsey has been twice married. His first wife, whom he wedded in 1868, was Miss Sarah A., daughter of Nicholas J. Sanders of Alabama, and to this union was born one child, Parlee. For his second wife Mr. Hulsey chose Miss Margaret, daughter of Moses Edes, of the same state, and this marriage has been blessed with one child, Julius. Mr. and Mrs. Hulsey are members of the Missionary Baptist church, while he is a Mason in good standing. He began his business life at the age of twenty-one, without any capital; but strict application to business, economy and fair dealing, have brought their reward. In politics he is a democrat, and though he aspires to no political office, he exercises his franchise toward the election of good and capable men to the various offices of the county and state, within the gift of the people.

Source: *Memorial Record of Alabama*, 1893. Volume 2.

ARTHUR HUTCHESON

Arthur Hutcheson, deceased, for many years the president of the Hutcheson Manufacturing company, Banning, Carroll Co., Ga., was the son of James and Sophia (Montgomery) Hutcheson, and was a full-blooded Irishman, having been born in Ireland in 1818. His father died in 1827 and his mother in 1856. In 1836, when eighteen years of age, he left Ireland for America, on whose shores he landed after a journey of six weeks, and came to Campbell county, Ga., and stopped with an uncle living there. This uncle, James Hutcheson, left Ireland for this country in 1818, and his first stop in Georgia was in Milledgeville. From there he went to McDonough, Henry Co., and thence, in 1827, he removed to Newnan, Coweta Co. From Newnan he went, in 1832, and settled in the woods and cleared a farm, and here on this farm Arthur Hutcheson, without education or money, started in life. But he had good common sense, indulged in no bad habits, was frugal, and invested his earnings with rare good judgment. What he amassed was not made by sharp, tricky trading nor semi-gambling speculation. No "blood money" stained his purse. He did not accumulate rapidly, but he did it safely and surely, nor was he a millionaire, nor could he ever be, but he left a comfortable fortune, though he provided generously for himself and those dependent upon or serving him. During the war he was in the commissary department under Maj. Shackelford, whose headquarters were in Atlanta. He had a cousin in the army who saved the Confederate general, Bates, from being captured on one occasion when posting his pickets. After the war he engaged in merchandising at County Line, Carroll county, and in 1878 he bought an interest in what was then known as Amos' [Amis'] factory, to which he subsequently devoted almost his entire attention. At that time there was one mill, and that supplied with old-style, run-down machinery. The old fogy shareholders were gradually bought out, and under Mr. Hutcheson's able management improved modern machinery displaced the old. He next proceeded to organize a joint stock company with a capital of $93,000, of which he was elected president and general manager. Additions and improvements were continued and now they have a 5,000 spindle (and preparation) cotton factory, a paper mill, two pulp mills, and a grist and sawmill, all fully equipped with the best made, modern improved machinery, and all within a mile along the creek, propelled by water retained by one dam. This company operates one of the three mills in the United States that make striped paper. The company owns 1,300 acres of good land, employs 210 hands, and when all their machinery is running full time,

240. Workers are furnished house room and a garden spot free, and the company has built a school house for the children and a church for them to worship in. Mr. Hutcheson looked after the physical comfort of his employes and gave attention to their moral training and conduct. He was kind and considerate, and treated them humanely, respecting them himself and stimulating them to cultivate self-respect for themselves. It is superfluous to add that Mr. Hutcheson was esteemed very highly by all who knew him in financial circles as well as in the humbler walks of life. His true worth as a man could not be better appreciated than by his employes and their families, in whose welfare he took so much interest, and to them his death fell with the heaviest hand. He was a master Mason and an exemplary member of the Methodist church. He died on the morning of April 5, 1895.

Source: *Memoirs of Georgia*, 1895. Volume 1.

JOSEPH HUTCHESON

Joseph Hutcheson, farmer, Roscoe, Coweta Co., Ga., son of James and Sarah P. (Henry) Hutcheson, was born in Campbell county, Ga., in 1839. His father was born in Ireland in 1793, and came to America in 1818. He went to Orange county, N. Y., first, but was there only a short time when he decided to come to Georgia. After reaching here he taught school a while, and then engaged as clerk in Augusta. From Augusta he went to McDonough, Henry county, where he went into business for himself. He then went to Newnan, Coweta Co., where he conducted a general merchandise business a few years, when, finally, he permanently settled in Campbell county, and in connection with a store he conducted a farm. When he came from Ireland he was nearly two months on the voyage, was poor and without relatives on this side; yet he was industrious and a good manager, and accumulated quite a valuable estate. He was married in Newnan to a daughter of William and Sarah (Pickens) Henry, Coweta county pioneers. Mr. Hutcheson received a good common-school education, but before he could utilize it the war began and he enlisted in 1861 in Company C (Capt. Kendrick) Third Georgia battalion. Capt. Kendrick was killed at Pine Mountain when he was retiring before Sherman between Dalton and Atlanta. Col. M. A. Stovall was his first commander, and he was in all the battles in which his company was engaged — the principal of which were Hoover's Gap, Chickamauga and Murfreesboro — and was wounded in each of the two battles last named. His command was in the front of Sherman from Dalton to Atlanta. At the last-named place he was captured Aug. 7, 1864, and was held a prisoner ten months at Johnson's Island. Mr. Hutcheson entered the service as a private, was made orderly sergeant, and was promoted to a lieutenancy, which he held when captured. His brother, William Hutcheson, who was first a lieutenant, rose to be a captain, and was killed in the battle of Jonesboro, Ga. Mr. Hutcheson came out of the war with very little property. But having good business qualities in connection with progressive ideas of farming, he has been exceptionally prosperous — having a farm of 1,000 acres not surpassed in beauty of arrangement in the state. He raises all he needs; has extensive fields of red clover, and fields of wheat and oats as well as corn and cotton, and has one of the most beautiful dwellings in this part of the country. Mr. Hutcheson was married in 1891 to Miss Mertis Harris — born and reared in Coweta county — daughter of C. J. Harris, whose family was among the first settlers, and now rank among the most prominent in the county. Two children have blessed this union, but only one, Louise, is living. Mr. Hutcheson ranks as a leading farmer in his county whether diversity of products, yield per acre, or progressive and improved methods be considered; and stands very high as a citizen. Mrs. Hutcheson is an exemplary and esteemed member of the Presbyterian church.

Source: *Memoirs of Georgia*, 1895. Volume 1.

Note: Joseph Hutcheson was residing in Carroll County in 1880. Typescript copies of several Civil War letters of Joseph Hutcheson are available in the Annie Belle Weaver Special Collections, Irvine Sullivan Ingram Library, University of West Georgia. Some of the letters mention events in Carroll County.

JOSEPH S. JAMES

Joseph S. James, United States district attorney of the northern district of Georgia, was born in Campbell (now Douglas) county, Ga., March 20, 1849. He received a common school education, attending the log-cabin school located near his home. At an early age his mind possessed of much firmness, breadth and power for solving difficult problems, he decided to become a lawyer, and studied with this end in view. In 1869 he married Margaret Elizabeth E., daughter of the late Dr. E. W. Maxwell, a native of Douglas county. At this time, being very poor and without a thorough education, he was disqualified for the battle of life, but gathering all his strength and ability, he applied himself to the study of law, reading and being admitted to the bar without instruction from a lawyer or attending any law school, at time poring over his books the entire night. When admitted to the bar he stood a most creditable examination and immediately forged his way to the front of the profession in his section and has maintained that position ever since. He was admitted in Douglasville in 1875, and to the supreme court two years later. When twenty-one years of age he was elected justice of the peace in Douglas county, but resigned after two years' service. He was chosen the first mayor of Douglasville in 1876, holding the office for one term, and by his executive ability obtained the regard and congratulations of the community. In 1880 he was elected to represent Douglas county in Georgia's general assembly and re-elected after the expiration of the first term. In 1886 he was elected to the state senate from the thirty-sixth senatorial district, and served two years. In 1892 he was chosen a presidential elector-at-large from the state of Georgia, and in ninety days made 102 speeches in the state, covering almost every nook and corner, his consecutive appointments sometimes being from 100 to 300 miles apart, and frequently meeting in joint debate the opponents of his party. He was appointed United States district attorney by President Cleveland on April 3, 1893. As the legal representative of the government, the sole responsibility devolved upon him of grappling with and suppressing the gigantic organization in North Georgia known as "White Caps." In his herculean task he was ably assisted by Messrs. Rucker, Bell and Camp of his office and by the internal revenue collector and marshals. Lawyers who rank among the best in the state were employed for the defendants and the nature of the cases being wholly new to the practice, it required the greatest skill and ingenuity to draft bills of indictment that would stand the test of the law's technicalities. To this effort Mr. James devoted himself, spending one whole night in his office to perfect the bill upon which the worst of the organization were put on trial. They were convicted and his bill was sustained by the supreme court of the United States, to which the case was carried. Col. James has three daughters: Margaret Odessa, Eunice Lettitia and Lois Cleveland.

He is a member of the Odd Fellows and affiliates with the Methodist church south. Mr. James is the son of Stephen James, who, with his three sons, fought valiantly in the late civil war. Those in the ranks were: George W., who gave up his life at Front Royal, Va.; John M., a member of the Twenty-first Georgia regiment, first lieutenant of Company A, who lost his right leg at Chancellorsville, and William A. James. Their bravery is denied by none.

Source: *Memoirs of Georgia*, 1895. Volume 1.

WILLIAM A. JAMES

W. A. James, lawyer, Douglasville, Douglas Co., Ga., son of Stephen and Martha (Shipleigh) James, was born in Campbell (now Douglas) county, May 7, 1847. His paternal grandparents, Stephen and Mary (Mills) James, were natives of North Carolina, whence they moved in 1825 to Walton county, Ga. They made the journey in ox-carts, in which they lived until cabins could be built. Clearing a piece of land, he engaged in farming. A few years later he moved to Cobb, and subsequently to Campbell county. Mr. James' father was born in Newbern, N. C., in 1821, and when a child came to Georgia with his parents. He became a large farmer and also a very prominent citizen of Campbell county. He was a justice of the peace for thirty years consecutively, and is credited with having married not less than 200 couples. He died in 1871. His mother was born about 1820 and was married in 1840. She is still living. Mr. James received his primary education in the common schools of his native county and finished it in the city schools of St. Louis. In 1864, at the age of seventeen, he enlisted in the Confederate service and served as aide de camp and courier to Gen. Wheeler. He was afterward transferred to the Third Alabama cavalry, in which he served until the surrender near Salem, N. C., by Gen. J. E. Johnston. He made his escape, however, and made his way home. Mr. James enjoys the distinction of having been one of the youngest soldiers in the regular Confederate service. He began life for himself as a clerk in a drug store in St. Louis, Mo. Afterward he studied law under the late Judge Dennis F. Hammond, of Atlanta, and was admitted to the bar in 1871. In 1873 he settled where Douglasville now stands, and the following year, in company with his brother James and others began the erection of the first house built in the town. In

WILLIAM A. JAMES

1876 he moved to his mother's plantation near Lithia Springs, where he remained until 1881, when he returned to Douglasville and resumed the practice of law, in which he has been very successful, representing a large and valuable clientage. In 1885-86 he was mayor of the city, and again during the years 1892-93-94, and is chairman of the board of trustees of Douglasville college, which demonstrates his efficiency and public spirit, and the estimation in which he is held by his fellow citizens. Mr. James was married Jan. 15, 1879, to Miss Mary M., daughter of William P. and Mary (McLarty) Strickland. To them five children have been born: Clifford M., Ruby L., Nettie P., William P. and James. He is a member of the I. O. O. F., and an active, influential member of the Methodist church.

Source: *Memoirs of Georgia*, 1895. Volume 1.

Note: Stephen James only briefly owned land in Carroll County, Georgia in the earliest days for his land was quite soon cut off into the new county of Campbell.

W. W. KELLEY

Rev. W. W. Kelley, Baptist minister, Whitesburg, Carroll Co., Ga., son of Andrew Wilson and Elizabeth J. (Pitts) Kelley, was born in Coweta county, Ga., in 1847. His paternal grandparents, John and Mary (Hews) Kelley, were natives of North Carolina, and came to Georgia about 1810. His grandfather was a soldier in the war of 1812. Mr. Kelley's father was born in North Carolina, came to Georgia with his father, and had a very fair education for his day. He was a member of the Baptist church and a man of considerable prominence in his day. His maternal grandparents, Archey and Charlotte (Burnett) Pitts, were South Carolinians, were Baptists, and early settlers of Georgia. Mr. Kelley was reared on a farm and received a good common-school education, and attended a theological school at Greenville, S. C., a part of one term in 1873. His father being a poor man, he earned the money himself to pay for his higher education. In 1863 he became his father's substitute in Company G, Second Georgia regiment, and served two months, when he was relieved. During this time he was sent to Grayville, Tenn., to engage in a battle, but it had been fought before he and his comrades reached the field. In 1864 he enlisted in Company I (Capt. J. Johnson), Bell's [Beall's] battalion, his company performing guard duty most of the time. He began life after the war very poor, but feels that he has been wonderfully sustained and blessed by Providence. He was ordained a Baptist minister in 1871, but the first pastorate to which he was called was that of Whitesburg in 1874, since which time he has been actively engaged in the Master's service. He is now pastor of the churches of Central Hatchee, Heard Co.; Corinth (at Banning), and Salem, Carroll Co., and Effices [Ephesus], in Douglas county, Ga. He aided in the organization of the three last named, and also in the organization of Friendship in Heard county, and Firendship and Ebenezer, in Douglas county. He was pastor of Friendship for fifteen months. In addition to this arduous work he taught school in 1874-75-76 and a part of 1877. During his ministry he had baptized about 1,000 persons and made scores of couples happy by uniting them in marriage. Rev. Mr. Kelley was married to Miss Elizabeth T., daughter of James D. Moore, a pioneer settler, in 1877, who has borne him five children, of whom three, James A., William B. and Charles S., are living, and two, Carrie E. (Mrs. Van D. Sewell) and Thomas Mercer are dead. Rev. Mr. Kelley is a master Mason and Mrs. Kelley is a member of the Baptist church. He has a fine farm and comfortable residence in the edge of Whitesburg, is an exemplary Christian minister, and a useful and very highly esteemed citizen. To Andrew W. and Elizabeth Kelley ten children were born, eight sons and two daughters. Of these W. W., Thomas A., and James M. were ordained Baptist ministers, and actively engaged in the ministry. Andrew W. died in infancy and Newton Calvin at the age of eighteen. J. M. and Mary K. were twins. The latter married Mr. Capes, and the other sister, Amanda J., is the wife of W. M. Hunter.

Source: *Memoirs of Georgia*, 1895. Volume 1.

SANFORD THEODORE KINGSBERRY

Sanford Theodore Kingsberry, lawyer, Valdosta, Lowndes Co., Ga., son of Sanford and Mary Ann (Grow) Kingsberry, was born in Carrollton, Carroll Co., Ga., Nov. 12, 1837. The American progenitor of this branch of the family, Henry Kingsberry, came to America in 1630 with Gov. Winthrop, settled first in Boston, Mass., where himself and wife united with the present First church, moved thence to Ipswich, Mass., where seven sons were born to them. Joseph (I^st), the youngest

SANFORD THEODORE KINGSBERRY

son, moved to Haverhill, Mass., where two sons, Nathaniel and Joseph, and several daughters were born to him. Joseph (2nd) was born June 22, 1682, was married Feb. 5, 1705, to Ruth Denison, moved to Norwich, Conn., in 1708, and died there Dec. 1, 1757. He was locally and familiarly known as "Deacon Joseph." They had twelve children, the fifth of which, Joseph (3rd), was born in 1714. When grown he went to Pomfret, then to Scotland, Conn., married, and raised six children, the youngest of whom, Sanford (Ist) was born in 1733, married Elizabeth Fitch, and moved to Windham, Conn., where six children were born to him. He afterward moved with his family to Claremont, N. H. About the time hostilities began between the colonies and Great Britain, King George III. Granted 100,000 acres of land on the island of Cape Breton – just east of Nova Scotia – to 100 citizens of Claremont and vicinity. Mr. Kingsberry being one of the number, was appointed agent to go to the island and survey and divide the land. He laid out the city of Mira, at the head of navigation on Mira river – which the grant included – and then proceeded to survey and subdivide the remainder. About the time he completed the survey, he and his companions were arrested and imprisoned, for the purpose of extorting from them the oath of allegiance to the king of England. All his men took the oath, but he refusing, was kept in prison on bread and water several weeks. Failing to accomplish their purpose, he was released, when he returned to Claremeont. The revolution being in progress, he at once volunteered in the Continental army at Norwich, Conn., under Gen. Spencer, who appointed him his aid. He was the author of the muster roll adopted by congress, was appointed muster master for the Connecticut troops, and commissioned major, retaining the rank to the end of the war. He participated in the battles of Bennington, Vt., and Ticonderoga, N. Y. After the war he resided in Claremont until his death in 1829, aged ninety-six years. His third son, Charles (Ist), born in 1773, moved to Derby, in the extreme northern part of Vermont, in 1790. His first deed bears date in 1797, and upon this tract was planted the first apple orchard in the township – and it is still yielding fruit. In 1820 he moved to Derby Center, living there till he died in 1843, aged seventy years. He was the first representative from his township to the general assembly, was re-elected three times consecutively and held the office of town treasurer from 1812 to 1833 inclusive. To do right was the governing principle of his

SANFORD THEODORE KINGSBERRY

life. To him nine children were born. Of these, his third child, Sanford (2nd), whose mother maiden name was Persis Stewart, was born June 24, 1805. He came to Georgia in 1822 and located in McDonough, Henry Co., where he remained about five years, and then went to Carrollton, Carroll Co., and engaged in merchandising. His friendliness of disposition and fair dealing secured the good will and confidence of the Cherokee Indians – who were then numerous there – and he was very successful and accumulated a large property. He was married Sept. 23, 1834, to Miss Mary Ann Grow, of Vermont, by whom he had ten children. He died Dec. 24, 1869, transmitting to his children, untarnished, that rich heritage – a good name – received from his father. Mr. Kingsberry remained with his parents until he attained his majority, with the exception of three years – 1849-50-51 – when he attended school at Derby, Vt. He completed his education at Carrollton Masonic institute, and in 1858 began reading law under Buchanan & Wright, Newnan, Ga., and was admitted to the bar at the March term of the superior court at Newnan in 1859. Locating at Quitman, Brooks Co., Ga., he remained there until April, 1861, when he enlisted and served as a private in the Piscola volunteers until after the seven days' fight around Richmond, in which he gallantly bore a part. In 1862, just after those battles, he was elected, without his knowledge, second lieutenant of a cavalry company organized at Carrollton, to which command he was transferred, and served in Eastern North Carolina and along Black Water river in southeast Virginia until the advance of Grant on Petersburg, when his command, the Seventh Confederate cavalry (before independent), was made part of a brigade under command of Brig.-Gen. James Dearing, with which he served until October, 1864, when his regiment was reorganized into the Tenth Georgia cavalry, under Gen. P. M. B. Young. In 1864 he was commissioned captain of Company K of the Seventh Georgia regiment, continuing as such until the surrender, when his command, under Gen. Wade Hampton, was disbanded at Greensboro, N. C. After the war he and his brothers – Joseph and Charles – met at the old homestead near Carrollton to find it almost totally destroyed, and their old father plowing in the field. These three brothers went to work, and living mainly on corn bread and sorghum syrup, made him a good crop; they then left, and each for himself commenced the battle of life anew. The two younger brothers chose a mercantile life

SANFORD THEODORE KINGSBERRY

and have won for themselves wealth and high commercial standing in Atlanta. Sanford returned to South Georgia, where he and his wife taught school during 1866, after which he resumed the practice of law at Quitman, to which he has since devoted his time and attention. During the reconstruction period he efficiently discharged the duties of secretary of the democratic county committee. In 1874 he became local attorney for the Atlantic & Gulf railway, retaining the position for that corporation and its successor until 1883, when he became assistant general counsel for the Savannah, Florida & Western and the Charleston & Savannah Railway companies, and moved his office to Savannah. In 1892, finding the labor of an exclusively corporation attorney excessive and uncongenial, he located in Valdosta, retaining his position as assistant general counsel for Georgia of the S. F. & W. Railway company, and resumed his general practice. Mr. Kingsberry ranks among the foremost in his profession and with his fellow-citizens, and enjoys a large and influential clientage. Mr. Kingsberry was married March 10, 1861, to Miss Jane Margaret Smith, daughter of Rev. John Brown Smith, formerly an eminent Presbyterian minister of North Carolina, and later in Talbot county, Ga., where he died in 1845. Mrs. Kingsberry is a lineal descendant of "Light Horse Harry" Lee, of revolutionary fame. Three children have blessed this union: James Sanford, now at Richmond, Ga.; Edwin Paschal, reading law under his father, and Helen Ann, at home. Mr. Kingsberry is a democrat, but no politician, a council Mason, and an exemplary and influential member of the Presbyterian church.

Source: *Memoirs of Georgia*, 1895. Volume 2.

J. R. LASSETTER

J. R. Lassetter, general superintendent of the Hutcheson Manufacturing company, Banning, Ga., son of William and Parthenia (Brown) Lassetter, was born in Carroll county. His grandfather, Benjamin Lassetter, came from Virginia to Georgia in 1828, and went to Milledgeville and bought the fractions of land in Carroll county on which he settled and began clearing for a farm that year. He was a soldier in the last war with Great Britain. His father, a farmer, was born in Carroll county, and was a member of the cavalry company commanded by Capt. Shuford three years during the late "unpleasantness." Mr. Lassetter received a good common-school education. His father died when he was young, but being of the stuff that men are made of, he has persistently struggled toward the front, where, before many years, he will be. As soon as qualified he began teaching, and after following it a few years engaged in merchandising. Having the misfortune to be burned out, he went back to the old farm, which he bought on credit, and after much privation and hard struggling he paid for and began to lay up money. In 1891 he went to work for the Hutcheson Manufacturing company, and in 1893 bought an interest in it. He has since been made general superintendent – a well-earned and deserved compliment to his pluck and energy and his superior general capabilities. He is a thorough-going young man, recognized as promising to become one of the most influential of his generation in the county. Little is known in Georgia of this Hutcheson Manufacturing company; on a small scale it is but a sample of many, in other localities in Georgia, of like topography and surroundings, and demonstrates the grand manufacturing possibilities of the state. Mr. Lassetter richly deserves the confidence he has secured, and the success he has attained. With the position he holds in the company, the natural manufacturing advantages of the mills' site, the possibilities of greater development and expansion, and the advantages of the experience and instruction of the company's president, Arthur Hutcheson, this rising young manufacturer has before him a brilliant future.

Source: *Memoirs of Georgia*, 1895. Volume 1.

J. W. G. LASSETTER

J. W. G. Lassetter, farmer, Villa Rica, Carroll Co., Ga., son of William and Mary Parthenie (Brown) Lassetter, was born in Carroll county in 1858. His grandfather, Benjamin Lassetter, settled in Georgia early in the present century. Mr. Lassetter's father was Georgia-born, was reared a farmer, and came to Carroll county and settled on Snake Creek when it was a wilderness, in 1841. He cleared a farm and made a home there and reared a family of fourteen children, all of whom made good citizens. His maternal grandparents were also among the early settlers of upper Georgia. Mr. Lassetter was bred a farmer, received but little schooling, but enough to enable him to teach a short time. In 1883 he married Miss Mary Barnett, born in Georgia, daughter

J. W. G. LASSETTER

of Waddie H. and Nancy (Butler) Barnett, who were native South Carolinians, but came to Georgia many years ago. Two children, Erie and William C., have blessed this union. The first died in his youth. Mr. Lassetter began life with a horse and $200, has steadily pursued farming as a business, and has succeeded admirably. He has a nice 250-acre farm, a comfortable dwelling and substantial outbuildings, and is a progressive and prosperous farmer. Himself and wife are members of the Missionary Baptist church, and are exemplary farmers, citizens and church members.

Source: *Memoirs of Georgia*, 1895. Volume 1.

JAMES R. LATIMER

James R. Latimer, merchant, Waco, Haralson Co., Ga., son of R. T. and Lovy J. (Tweedell) Latimer, was born Aug. 7, 1858. His father was born in South Carolina, and when a young man came to Georgia and settled on a small farm in Cobb county. His mother was a daughter of Rev. W. S. and Betsey Tweedell of the same county. Mr. Latimer was in his boyhood during the civil war, and received no schooling, but subsequently acquired a very good education. He worked on the farm until 1879, when, with $200 capital, he entered upon a mercantile life at Bowdon, Carroll Co., Ga. After doing a successful business there until 1886, he moved to Waco, where he continued business, and enjoyed a prosperity beyond his most sanguine expectations. He is popular with the people, a steady-going business man, enjoys the confidence of the public, and is considered one of the most prosperous young business men in the county. Mr. Latimer was married in Philadelphia, Penn., Jan. 7, 1884, to Miss Emmie, daughter of Dr. Joseph R. and Hattie E. Hood. Dr. Hood went to Philadelphia in 1881 for the purpose of advertising a patent cultivator, and returned to Randolph county, Ala., in 1887. This union has been blessed with two children: Ottie Bell and Robert Earl. Mr. Latimer is a master Mason, and himself and family are members of the Missionary Baptist church.

Source: *Memoirs of Georgia,* 1895. Volume 1.

Captain N. D. Lawler. The subject of this sketch is a native of Tennessee, and a son of Martin and Nancy (Davis) Lawler. His ancestry and kinship are Southern throughout. His father was born and reared in Fauquier county, Virginia. His grandfather, Nicholas Lawler, emigrated from Scotland to Virginia at an early day.

Major Martin Lawler moved to Henry county, Tennessee, in the year 1822 or 1823, and married there in 1824. Soon afterward he moved to Weakly county, where he spent the greater part of his life. He served in the War of 1812, and was always known afterward as Major Lawler, but whether his title came from his military rank or was simply complimentary, is not known. He was county surveyor of Weakly county for many years, being one of the commissioners appointed to locate and lay out Dresden, the county seat. He was a man who took much interest in public affairs, being elected county surveyor of Weakly twelve terms in succession. He was self-educated but of considerable attainments, an ardent advocate of education, entertained pronounced views on matters of common concern, and of strict morality and strong religious convictions. He led a life of much activity, and had he looked closely after his pecuniary interests, might have accumulated considerable property; but he was indulgent to a fault toward those who owed him, did a great deal of work gratuitously, and was more than once caught for security debts, which bore heavily upon his limited means. He died at Montpelier, Weakly county, Tennessee, September 29, 1851, in the sixty-seventh year of his age.

The mother of N. D. Lawler was Nancy Ann Davis before marriage, daughter of Robert and Elizabeth (Trigg) Davis, of Sumner county, Tennessee, one of the most respectable families of that county. She lived to the great age of eighty-three years, spending the greater part of her life in Weakly county, in her native State. She died in 1885 in the city of Martin, Tennessee.

N. D. Lawler is the fourth child and eldest son of Martin and Nancy Ann Lawler. There were three daughters older than himself – Elizabeth died in infancy; Martha Jane, now widow of Lynn Guy, and Mary Ann, wife of William Carter. She died in 1858, and there are three daughters and two sons younger, namely – Lucy Cathern Thompson, of Greenway, Arkansas; Dr. Thomas Benton Lawler, who fell leading his company of Tennesseeans in a charge on the Confederate side at Perryville, Kentucky, October 8, 1862; and Dr. William Trigg Lawler, now of Martin, Tennessee, who lost his right arm fighting under Cavalry General Forrest, of the Confederate army; Virginia and Sarah Lawler, now of Martin, Tennessee.

Nicholas Davis Lawler, our subject, was born near Dresden, Weakly county, Tennessee, May 2, 1830. He was reared there and had tolerable educational facilities until fifteen years of age, when his father, moving to the western part of the county, which was then sparsely settled, and school facilities poor; besides his father opening up a new farm in heavy timber, required his son's services in improving his new place, he was consequently deprived of further school facilities until after he reached his majority – his father dying, leaving it to him to aid his mother in settling his estate. His greatest desire was an education, but he had not the means to go off to school without selling the land his father had left him. He had improved his land and made a good crop, but produce was so low he became discouraged, rented out his farm, and tried trading to New Orleans on live stock and country produce, spending several years traveling up and down the Mississippi river on steamboats, running the gauntlet of cholera and yellow fever, besides the many other dangers and terrors of that treacherous stream. But in this business he had no better success, and becoming disgusted with a business of so much peril and so little profit he abandoned it, sold his little place, went to Virginia, and attended school three five-months' terms; his money giving out, he taught one term in that State, then went to Georgia, where he taught successfully for two years, when, the war between the States breaking out, he in April, 1861, entered Company I, Nineteenth Georgia regiment, Confederate service, as a private. After drilling two months at Big Shanty, near Marietta, Georgia, his command went to Virginia and was placed under General Wade Hampton, of South Carolina, and put into active service, forming part of the Army of Northern Virginia. He served successively under Hampton of South Carolina, Archer of Texas, and Colquitt of Georgia. He participated in every battle fought by the army under Lee, and was also in the detachment that assisted in the coast defense, as occasion demanded, a member of the special detachment that was sent to the relief of Charleston, South Carolina, in July, 1863, having a little battle of his own on James Island July 14, 1863. With his twenty-four veterans from Virginia he met and overcame seventy-five of the Fifty-fourth

Massachusetts (colored) regiment, killing and capturing the whole company without any casualty on his side. He did garrison duty on Battery Wagner until it was surrendered, also on the demolished Fort Sumter and James Island until February, 1864, when he was sent with his command to Florida, where he assisted in winning the battle of Olustee, that State. He served twelve months as a private, when he was promoted to third lieutenant and soon to first lieutenant, and was entitled to a captaincy by recent deaths of superior officers, to which he would have been promoted had the struggle continued, having acted in that capacity the greater part of the war. He was never out of the field on furlough but twice, and never absent from duty more than sixty days during the four years. He was three times wounded, and carried his arm in a sling for months while commanding his company, and in this condition was taken prisoner with his whole company at Fredericksburg, Virginia, December 13, 1862; was conducted to Burnside's headquarters and kept for five days, paroled and sent into the Confederate lines, and succeeded in getting a twenty-days' furlough in one day by seeing Generals Hill, Jackson and Lee in person, when it would have required ten days in the ordinary way. He had his thumb shot off at Shepardstown, Virginia, a continuation of the Sharpsburg fight; was shot in the ear at Grant's mine explosion at Petersburg, July 30, 1864, and was wounded in the breast and only saved from death by a blanket-roll at the battle of Bentonsville, North Carolina, April 10, 1865. He was frequently commended for his bravery and received his several promotions for gallantry and efficiency displayed on the field. His company was one of the few drilled in skirmish and Zouave drill, which caused them to be in frequent request and to suffer severely, only twenty-five living to return home out of an enlistment of 175, or one out of seven.

He was in those days, a man of iron build and steel nerves, capable of any endurance and absolutely fearless. He fought bravely — often desperately — astonished and won the admiration of those who witnessed his conduct and bearing. When he learned that Lee had surrendered and that Johnston, under whom he was then serving, was negotiating with General Sherman for terms of surrender, he organized a company of his own, mounted them on C. S. artillery horses with the intention of making his way to Texas and finally to Mexico; but after traveling several days he got among Stoneman's U. S. cavalry and learned that the whole Confederacy had collapsed, when he returned to his old command and accepted his parole not to take up arms against the U. S. government until duly exchanged, which pledge he has sacredly kept, and like a sensible man bowed gracefully to fate and accepted the results of the war in good faith. Returning to Georgia penniless he resumed school-teaching, made a little money, and in the fall of 1865 came to Texas. He taught four years in Upshur county, this State, and four years in Hunt county, abandoned the school-room at the end of that time and engaged in farming and has been a farmer ever since. It is useless to say that he has succeeded – a man of his make-up always wins.

He has a competency and is recognized as one of the best farmers of his locality and one of the most intelligent, level-headed business men. Captain Lawler married in September, 1868, Laurissa F., daughter of Nathan Morris, a native of Georgia, now of Wood county, Texas. Mrs. Lawler was born in Georgia but reared in Texas. This marriage has been a happy one and its fruits have been nine children, namely – Lee Jackson, died in infancy; the living are: Lucius Edger, May, Ambrose Archer, William Arthur, Lula D., Nina Florence, Nathan Morris and Virginia Iva Dell.

Captain Lawler is a liberal minded, public spirited citizen, a strong advocate of improved school facilities and a generous contributor to all charitable enterprises.

Source: *Biographical Souvenir of the State of Texas*, 1889.

Note: In 1860 Nicholas D. Lawler was residing with B. M. Mabry in the Bowdon District of Carroll County. He was listed as a common school teacher. The 1861 Tax Digest shows that he owned no property.

MILES W. LINER

Miles W. Liner, farmer, Tallapoosa, Haralson Co., Ga., son of Chrsitopher D. and Sarah Liner, was born in Carroll county, Ga., May 26, 1836. His parents went from Walton county, Ga., to Mississippi, in 1835, but returned to Georgia and settled in Carroll county early in 1836. Mr. Liner was raised in Carroll county, and was educated at the "old-field" common schools, taught in the dirt floor log cabins. He was exempt from military service during the war on account of physical disability. Mr. Liner was married Sept. 23, 1858, to Miss Marguerite

E., daughter of Robert A. and Jane Katharine Read of Carroll county, by whom he has had sixteen children: George Alexander, Henry Wise, Sarah Katharine, John Franklin, Robert Christopher, Mary Elizabeth, Susan Indiana, James Quitman, Harvey Washington, Rhoda Malighty, Madison, Van Buren, Jefferson, Malachi, Emma Rosella, and Simeon Jackson (deceased). Mr. Liner is a well-to-do farmer, respected by everybody, unambitious, and content with the generous yield of his well-cultivated lands.

Source: *Memoirs of Georgia*, 1895. Volume 1.

ALEX LITTLE

Alex Little is a practical, go-ahead farmer and stock-raiser, and fully appreciates the comforts of a competence gained by individual efforts. His birth occurred in 1831, in Carroll County, Ga., but his father, Theophilus Little, was a South Carolinian, born July 26, 1810. He was married, in his native State, to Miss Martha Lowry, and a short time after his marriage he removed to Georgia, where he made his home until 1861, at which time he took up his abode in Texas, coming after the cessation of hostilities to Sevier County, Ark. After living here three years, they removed to Crawford County, where the father closed his eyes in death, March 26, 1875. His widow returned to South Carolina and died in July, 1888, having been a member of the Missionary Baptist Church for sixty years, her husband having been connected with that denomination for forty-six or forty-seven years. He was a farmer and stock-raiser, and a son of Josiah Little, who was probably born in South Carolina, and died in Carroll County, Ga., where he had filled the office of sheriff for many years, his son, Theophilus, acting as his deputy. The maternal grandfather, Charles Lowry, was born in Virginia, and died in Cass County, Ga., about 1872, at the age of eighty-two years. He was a soldier in the Mexican War, was wounded several times, and until his death carried seven bullets in his body. He was helpless for many years. The subject of this sketch is the third of fourteen children, seven sons and four daughters now living, and his early days were spent on a farm and in attending the common schools. At the age of twenty-one years he began farming for himself, but in 1857 Margaret J. Ferguson, a daughter of Andrew and Dorothea Ferguson, became his wife, and in time the mother of his twelve children, five of whom are sons: of these three daughters and five sons are deceased. She was born in Calhoun County, Ga., in 1839 and shortly after her marriage, and about the same time as her parents, she came to Sevier County, Ark. Her father died in Howard County in 1886, his wife dying in 1877, both having been members of long standing of the Missionary Baptist Church. Upon coming to Sevier County, Ark., Mr. Little settled on a farm one and one-half miles north of Lockesburg and there now owns a fine farm of 320 acres, 175 being under cultivation. In addition to tilling the soil he raises considerable stock, and has become well known throughout this region as a successful man in both enterprises. In April, 1861, he joined the Nineteenth Arkansas Infantry, and served almost continuously until the close of the war, and while a nurse in the hospital at Little Rock he was captured, but soon after managed to effect his escape, and came to Washington, where he was made forage master in Gen. Kirby Smith's cavalry, and operated in Southwest Arkansas and Louisiana until the close of the war. He surrendered at Marshall, Tex., and returned home. He is a Democrat; has been a member of the A. F. & A. M. for the past eighteen years, and he and his wife have long been members of the Cumberland Presbyterian Church, their two eldest children being also members.

Source: *Biographical and Historical Memoirs of Southern Arkansas,* 1890.

BENJAMIN McFARLAND LONG

Benjamin M. Long, merchant of Cordova, Ala., was born in Carroll county, Ga., November 5, 1827. He is the second of six children born to John and Nancy D. (Long) Long, both natives of Virginia. His paternal grandparents were Robert and Isabelle Long, both natives of Virginia, and his maternal grandparents were James and Jane (Walker) Long, also of Virginia. Benjamin M. Long was reared in Georgia, and educated at private schools in that state. He is now one of the leading merchants and business men of Walker county, and also owns a large amount of real estate, including valuable coal lands, Walker county being one of the richest counties of the state in coal lands. Mr. Long is interested in four coal mines in Walker county, the Dore coal mines and the Price coal mines, of Horse creek, the Morris and Goss mines at Carbon Hill, and the Carbon Hill and Lost creek mines, of Carbon Hill. He owns 35,000 acres of land, and is the wealthiest man in the county. He served in the Mexican war, and now draws a pension for that service. He was in the late war for a short time, also, but was not in any of the principal battles. He was captain in the state troops of Georgia for six months. In 1854, he married Miss Amanda Wootten, of Georgia, and to this union have been born eleven children: Henry W., John B., Thomas L., Robert W., Pope, Jesse, Edgar, Carrie, Ida, Lou, Ada. Mr. Long and family are members of the Methodist Episcopal church, south, and he is a Mason of high degree. He is one of the most influential men of the republican party in western Alabama. Before the war he was an old line whig, and when the question of secession was uppermost in the public mind, he was strongly opposed to that policy. He was a member of the first reconstruction convention held in Alabama after the war. He was a member of the Georgia legislature in 1872-73, and was a member of the Alabama legislature in 1880 and 1881, and was the only avowed republican in that body in either branch. He was a presidential elector from the sixth Alabama district in 1884, and was a candidate for governor of the state on the republican ticket in 1890. His is an excellent family and is of that sturdy Scotch-Irish stock, which has furnished so many excellent men to this country.

Source: *Memorial Record of Alabama*, 1893. Volume 2.

ROBERT L. Y. LONG

R. L. Y. Long, M. D., one of the oldest and most experienced physicians of Newnan, Ga., was born in Granger County, East Tenn., August 20, 1822, and is a son of John and Charlotte (May) Long, both natives of Tennessee. John Long was a clerk of the superior court of Carroll County, Ga., for thirty-one years and also represented that county in the State legislature.

Upon his early settlement in Georgia his life was frequently imperiled by the Indians while on their wild raids through the country. On one occasion his house was visited by a party of these savages who were intoxicated; they took full possession of the house and attempted to kill the inmates. Mr. Long knocked one savage down with a chair just as he was in the act of striking Mrs. Long with a knife. Mr. Long ran for help and upon his return succeeded in driving the

ROBERT L. Y. LONG

Indians away. A few days after this adventure Mr. Long was thirty miles from home on an expedition to procure corn from an Indian who was indebted to him, and encountered one of the Indians who had so ruthlessly entered his home. He was recognized by the savage and followed with the vindictiveness of his race, but it happened that they took different trails and to that fact was due the preservation of Mr. Long's life.

R. L. Y. Long was taken to Carroll County, Ga., by his parents when but four years of age. His fine literary education was obtained principally from independent study evenings, after his day's work was done.

He read medicine with Dr. A. B. Calhoun, attended one course at Charleston Medical College, S. C., and graduated from the Transylvania University, Lexington, Ky., March 13, 1841. After practicing one year in Greenville, Ga., he located in Newnan in January, 1842, where he has since given his best energies to his profession.

Dr. Long has quite an extensive war experience, having served in the Indian war in 1836 for three months, and the following year as captain of a company in the Florida war for eight months. In 1861 he enlisted in the Confederate army, company D, Phillips' legion of cavalry and served in the army of Virginia until February, 1862, when he was ordered down to the coast of South Carolina; subsequently he returned to Virginia, where he served until a few months before the close. At that time he was severely attacked with rheumatism so that he was unable to walk and was compelled to return home.

October 23, 1849, he married Miss Martha Ann Powell, daughter of James Powell, of Coweta County, Ga. Their union has been blessed by the birth of five children, viz.: Edgar H., James J., Chas. D., Helen May, and R. L. Y., Jr.

The doctor has been successful in his profession and has a large circle of admirers and friends. He is a Royal Arch and Council Mason, and with his wife and all of the children, with one exception, is a member of the Baptist Church.

Source: *Biographical Souvenir of the States of Georgia and Florida*, 1889.

ROBERT L. Y.LONG

R. L. Y. Long, M. D., one of the old and leading citizens of Newnan, Ga., and a son of John and Charlotte (May) Long, both natives of Tennessee, was born in east Tennessee Aug. 20, 1822. His father, son of Robert Long, a native of Virginia, was a soldier in the revolutionary war with Gen. Sevier and Gen. Shelby, and in the Creek Indian war. John Long was the second clerk of Carroll county superior court, and served thirty-two years. The mother of Dr. Long was the daughter of John May, who was a native of Virginia, but a pioneer settler of east Tennessee. Dr. Long was reared at Carrollton, Ga., where he received his education by the fireside after his day's work. On Jan. 13, 1839; he began the study of medicine with Dr. A. B. Calhoun, and read with him one year. In 1839 he, in company with three other students, started to Charleston, S. C., to attend college, graduated from the Transylvania university in 1841, and located the same year at Greenville, Ga., where he remained one year. Then he came to Newnan, where he remained until 1844, when he went into the country and formed a partnership with Dr. Ira E. Smith; after four years he went to Louisiana and practiced until 1848, when he returned to Newnan, where he has since remained and has had a large and lucrative practice. June 1, 1836, he enlisted in Capt. W. S. Parr's company in the Creek Indian war, and on Nov. 2, 1837, he went into the Seminole war in Florida as captain of the Carroll Rangers cavalry, and with one exception was the youngest of the company and was mustered out May 13, 1838, by Maj. Churchill of the United States army. In 1861 he enlisted in Company D, Phillips' legion cavalry, as first lieutenant, but was chosen captain a short time after. Capt. Long was engaged in many very hard conflicts, some of which were: Spottsylvania court house, Gettysburg, Williamsburg, battle of the Wilderness and many others. At Williamsburg he, with 250 men, captured 1,100 men under Col. Campbell, the captain riding the same horse 125 miles in twenty-five hours. He served throughout the entire war without receiving a wound or being captured. His company was noted for bravery and was called upon for all particular and dangerous work. After the war he returned to Newnan, began the practice of medicine, and Oct. 23, 1849, Dr. Long was united in marriage with Martha Ann Powell, a daughter of James and Sarah A. (Summerlin) Powell. To this union five children have been born: Edgar H., James J., Charles D., Helen A. and R. Y. Mrs. Long was born and reared in this county, but her parents both died while she was yet a child and she had no way of gathering their history. Dr. Long has always been a stanch democrat, but would never consent to have his name used for public office. He is a member of the masonic fraternity, having become a member at Newnan in 1845, and is one of the leading citizens of the county.

Source: *Memoirs of Georgia*, 1895. Volume 1.

JESSE LOONEY

Jesse Looney, a farmer residing in Grayson county, about two miles from Denison, Texas, is the son of John Looney, who was living at the time of subject's birth in east Tennessee. Five years afterward he moved to Alabama; from there he migrated to north Missouri, and last of all located in Grayson county, Texas, in 1862. His wife's maiden name was Miss Betsy Short, and they were the happy parents of nine children, of whom Jesse is the fourth.

Jesse Looney received his early training in Missouri, where he remained till 1858, when he came to Grayson county. Being a poor boy his start in life was up-hill work, and it was a long time before he succeeded in getting much of this world's goods together to have ready for a "rainy day." In 1844, on the 14th day of February, he was married to his second cousin, Miss Mary Ann Looney, daughter of Alvin and Betsy Looney. Nine bright, healthy children have since been the result of this union, the names of which are – Barton A., William, Isaac, Benjamin, Elizabeth, Richard, Joseph, John and Jesse.

In 1877 death visited the family and chose Mrs. Looney as the one God required to go to the other world. In 1880 once more Mr. Looney joined hands in the bonds of holy wedlock, this time with Mrs. Edna McHenry, daughter of John and Mary Hale, and widow of Sam H. McHenry. One child, Edgar, has been born to them.

Mr. Looney now owns two hundred acres of land and is a member of the Farmers' Alliance.

Source: *Biographical Souvenir of the State of Texas*, 1889.

Note: John Luna was selected as a petit juror for the December 1827 term of court. This is the only time the author has found his name in the Carroll County records. Because some members of the Luna family went by the name Looney, this sketch is included here. However, its inclusion is questionable.

N. C. LOONEY

N. C. Looney, a prosperous farmer of Talladega county, was born in St. Clair county in 1835. He is a son of John and Cinderella (Cooper) Looney. John Looney is a native of Tennessee and his wife was a native of South Carolina. He came to Alabama about 1822 with his parents. He was a son of John and Elizabeth Looney, both of whom were of German descent. Mr. N. C. Looney was reared mostly in Coosa county, coming here in 1836 with his parents, and settling within one mile of where he now lives. The country was then new, and the work upon the farm so necessary that he had but little time to devote to securing an education. He had to help his father make a living for the family. In 1859, he married Mary E. Blakely, by whom he had eight children, seven of whom are now living, viz.: Nettie, Viola, Eliza, Ruby, Iscie, Claudius and Emma. The mother of these children was born in Alabama, and reared in that state. Both Mr. and Mrs. Looney are members of the Methodist Episcopal church, south. In 1862 Mr. Looney enlisted in company B, Thirty-fourth Alabama infantry, under Capt. John H. Slaughter, and served throughout the war. He participated in some very hard fought battles, among which may be named Chickamauga, Missionary Ridge, Dalton, Atlanta, Jonesboro, Franklin and Nashville. At the last battle he was captured and taken to one of the northern prisons, where he was held until June 22, 1865, when he was released. He then came home to begin life anew. At first he embarked in the tanning business, which he continued three years. He then engaged in farming, milling, running a saw mill, grist mill and a cotton gin. He has thus been engaged ever since, and has made his business a success. He is a member of the Masonic fraternity, is a representative farmer of the county, a prominent democrat and a leading and most worthy citizen.

Source: *Memorial Record of Alabama*. 1893. Volume 2.

Note: John Luna was selected as a petit juror for the December 1827 term of court. This is the only time the author has found his name in the Carroll County records. Because some members of the Luna family went by the name Looney, this sketch is included here. However, its inclusion is questionable.

L. T. C. LOVELACE

L. T. C. Lovelace, farmer, West Point, Troup Co., Ga., son of Lucius C. and Obedience (Robinson) Lovelace, was born in Troup

L. T. C. LOVELACE

county, on the farm where he now lives, in 1839. His paternal great-grandfather was a native of North Carolina, moved to and lived in South Carolina a short time, and then came to Georgia and settled in Columbia county, among its earliest settlers. His grandparents, James and Mary (Stapler) Lovelace, were natives of South Carolina, came to Georgia in ox-carts and settled in the woods. He was one of the pioneer school teachers in Columbia county, was excellently well educated, served as a soldier in the war of 1812 and died in 1860. Mr. Lovelace's father was born in Columbia county Feb. 6, 1806, where he was reared on the farm, and received his education. He came to Troup county in 1831 and settled in the woods when they were full of Indians and wild animals and began life in a little log hut. His mother was a daughter of Leggett and Elizabeth (Bennett) Robinson, who were natives of South Carolina, came to Georgia and settled in what is now Henry county in 1820. He served as a volunteer in the Creek Indian war of 1836. Mr. Lovelace was reared on the farm where he now lives, and was educated in the "old-field" schools and at Bowdon college. In 1861 he enlisted in Company D, Capt. Matthews, Fourth Georgia regiment, Col. George Doles, Gen. Blanchard, and participated in many hard-fought battles, among them: King's Schoolhouse, Malvern Hill, Fredricksburg, Chancellorsville, Gettysburg and Wilderness. At the last-named battle he was wounded in the shoulder, which disabled him for service and crippled him for life. He was sent to the hospital, where he remained until the surrender. He then came home and conducted the farm about five years, when he went to West Point, Ga., and embarked in manufacturing. At the end of five years he sold out and returned to the old homestead, where he has since remained, content with the enjoyments of an intelligent and delightful home circle. He has been a jury commissioner sixteen years and a county commissioner two years. No citizen of Troup county is held in higher esteem, none of more unbending integrity, or who more fully commands the public confidence. Mr. Lovelace was married in 1866 to Miss Amanda Davidson, born in Troup county, daughter of Elias and Lucretia (Leverett) Davidson, native Georgians. Four children have blessed this union: Samuel, Amanda O., Lula, and Lucius B. He is a master Mason and himself and wife and all the children are members of the Methodist church.

Source: *Memoirs of Georgia*, 1895. Volume 2.

T. J. LOVELESS

T. J. Loveless, merchant-farmer, Buchanan, Haralson Co., Ga., son of Thos. and Rebecca Loveless, was born in Newton county, Ga., in 1832. His parents were born in Greenville district in South Carolina in 1800, where they were married and lived until 1830. That year they came to Georgia in a wagon, settled in the woods in Newton county, where they cleared a farm, meantime living in a dirt-floor log cabin. Here they followed farming and raised their children. Mr. Loveless was raised on the farm, and attended school at the dirt-floor log house, lighted through the spaces between the logs, with slabs for seats and writing desks, and chimney made of mud and sticks. After his graduation Mr. Loveless himself taught school in these historical structures, and afterward farmed. In 1861 he enlisted in Company A, Capt. W. Bass, Fourth Georgia regiment, and after serving six months went into the regular army, Company C, Capt, John A. Grice, Fifty-sixth Georgia regiment, Col. E. P. Watkins. With his command he was in very active service, and participated in many important battles: Baker's Creek, where he was slightly wounded; siege of Vicksburg, where he was captured; Mission Ridge, and from there with Gens. Johnston and Hood in front of Gen. Sherman; shared in the defense of Atlanta, and was in the battle of Jonesboro. He was first lieutenant of his company, and as the captain was nearly always absent he was in command. He remained in the service until the surrender, and after that resumed the cultivation of his farm, which he did with success until 1882, when he opened a general merchandise store in Buchanan, and is profitably conducting both. He is now the leading merchant of Buchanan, and, in connection with his store, is keeping a hotel. He has been very successful as a farmer, merchant, and hotelkeeper, has made money, and is a much-liked and highly esteemed citizen. Mr. Loveless was married in 1857 to Miss Louisa J., daughter of Thomas and Letitia (Lindley) Camp, who were native South Carolinians, but who, early in life came to Georgia, where they raised their family. One child only, Robert E., has blessed this union. Mr. Loveless is a master Mason, and himself and wife are exemplary members of the Baptist church.

Source: *Memoirs of Georgia*, 1895. Volume 1.

Note: In 1860 T. J. Loveless, his wife, and young son were residing with his parents in the Ninth District of Carroll County.

W. D. LOVVORN

W. D. Lovvorn, farmer and miller, Bowdon, Carroll Co., Ga., son of James and Bashaba (Traylor) Lovvorn, was born in Henry county, Ga., in 1831. His great-grandfather, Elijah Lovvorn, came from Ireland to this country before the revolutionary war, and was a soldier in the patriot army, during which time he suffered many privations and great hardships. His grandparents, James and Hannah (Smith) Lovvorn, were born in Virginia, whence they moved to North Carolina, and afterward to Georgia, about 1800, and settled in what is now Morgan county. Subsequently they moved to St. Clair county, Ala. He was a soldier in the war of 1812. Mr. Lovvorn's father was born in Morgan county in 1807 and went with his father to Alabama, where he died. His mother was a daughter of Mijman and Lidy (Lang) Traylor. Mr. Traylor was a soldier in the war of 1812 and was captured and confined in Fort Pickens. He was fond of fun and jokes, and on one occasion when sweeping the floor an officer passed him, and on the impulse of the moment he gave him a playful swipe with the broom. The officer resented the apparent indignity, and the incident came near involving him in serious trouble. He also served through the Indian war of 1836. Mr. Lovvorn was reared on the farm, in Alabama, and was educated in the common country schools (walking three miles, sometimes barefooted in the winter), taught in a dirt floor log house with split log seats. After "graduating" he taught school himself a few years. He was a justice of the peace many years, and in 1872 was elected to represent Randolph county in the legislature of Alabama – the last republican elected from the county. In 1878 he removed from Alabama to Carroll county, Ga., and bought and settled the large farming property on which he now lives, and on which he has built and runs a large custom mill. Mr. Lovvorn was married in Alabama in 1851 to Miss Sarah D. Burden – born in Elbert county, Ga. – daughter of Henry and Sarah (White) Burden. Her parents were born in Virginia, migrated to Georgia, and settled in what is now Hart county, and afterward moved to Alabama, where he died. Ten children blessed this union: Thomas J., Mary, Gaines W., William J., Sarah R., Robert M., Martha E., Cindonia and Henry O. Mr. Lovvorn and his wife are members of the Missionary Baptist church. He was one of the first county commissioners of the county, a man of large property and a most substantial and highly-respected citizen.

Source: *Memoirs of Georgia*, 1895. Volume 1.

ALEX LUTHER

Alex. Luther, farmer and present clerk of Sevier County, was originally from Georgia, his birth occurring November 29, 1839, and is the son of Frederick and Jane (Bell) Luther, both natives of North Carolina. Frederick was the son of Solomon, and the father of the latter was a Revolutionary soldier. The Luther family is of German descent, and there is a strong probability that the family are descendants of the famous Martin Luther. Frederick Luther was among the early settlers of Carroll County, Ga., but moved to Arkansas in 1856, and there he and wife are now residing. They reared a family of eight children, seven of whom are living and reside in Arkansas. Alex. Luther resided in Georgia until nearly seventeen years of age, and then came with his father's family to Arkansas. While in Georgia he attended the subscription schools, received a good knowledge of the common branches, and remained with his father until in July, 1861, when he enlisted in Company G, Twelfth Arkansas Infantry, Confederate Volunteers. Early in the war he was at Columbus, Ky., during the battle of Belmont, and after that came to New Madrid. He was captured at Island No. 10, and for five months enjoyed a resting spell at the expense of Uncle Sam in Camp Douglas, Ill. About 10,000 others enjoyed this privilege with him. He was exchanged at Vicksburg, Miss., in July, 1862, reorganized at Jackson, Miss., where he was elected orderly sergeant, and was in the siege of Port Hudson, La. He was captured and paroled at Port Hudson, returned home, but soon after was put into active service and served for about five months in the mounted infantry. He was then in the Mark's Mill engagement, and as he was at home, sick, at the close of the war he consequently never surrendered. After the war Mr. Luther taught school several terms and also served as dry goods clerk in Lockesburg for some time. For the last ten or twelve years he has been engaged in agricultural pursuits. In 1886 he was elected clerk of the county and re-elected in 1888, and at this writing he is before the people for re-election as clerk. He has been twice married; first, to Miss Melissa J. Carlock in 1866, and one son was born to this union. About six years after marriage the mother and son both died. In 1876 he was married to Miss Mary E. Harrison, whose ancestors were originally from Mississippi, and three children were born to this union, only one now living: Lydia Belle, who is four years of age. Politically Mr. Luther is a Democrat, but is conservative, and socially he is a member of the Masonic fraternity.

Source: *Biographical and Historical Memoirs of Southern Arkansas,* 1890.

HINCHE P. MABRY

General H. P. Mabry, Fort Worth, was born in Carroll county, Georgia, October 27, 1829. His father, bearing the same name, was born in Virginia, removed to Georgia in 1806, was a soldier in the War of 1812-15, and soon after its close married Linnie Williams [Lydia Stallings], of an excellent North Carolina family. In 1827 he removed from Greene to Carroll county, Georgia. His children were – Charles W., Woodford J., Martha E., married Redmond B. Young, and died in Ellis county, Texas; Lydia, widow of Dr. W. S. Tanner; Hinche P., the subject of this sketch; Phoebe, married Abner Gunter, and died during the Civil War, leaving a daughter.

Hinche P. Mabry, after the death of his father, educated himself, chiefly at the University of Tennessee, at Knoxville, wherein he was a student under the venerable Major Albert M. Lea, of Corsicana, Texas. He located in Jefferson, Texas, in 1851, and studied law with T. J. and J. H. Rogers, till 1856, when he was admitted to the bar. In 1854, he married Abbie, a daughter of William H. Haywood, of the well known family of that name in North Carolina and Tennessee. They have three children, all born in Jefferson – Haywood Mabry, born in 1855, now a merchant in Fort Worth; Bob, born in 1857, and Hinche P., born in 1877.

General Mabry served in the legislatures of 1856, and 1859-60. He opposed secession, but followed the fortunes of his State. In May, 1861, he served in the expedition that captured Forts Washita and Arbuckle, in the Indian Territory. In June (the next month) as captain of Company G, he joined the Third Texas cavalry, commanded by Colonel E. Greer, and was in the battle of Oak Hills, on the 10th of August. In the succeeding autumn, while on a scout under orders of General Ben McCulloch, he and Captain Alfred Johnson reached the vicinity of Springfield, Missouri, after nightfall. Leaving their comrades, they entered the town on foot while General Fremont held it with over fifty thousand men. They entered the house of a widow lady with two daughters, known to them, in search of information. While there their presence was made known to a Federal officer, who sent about twenty men to capture them. Going a step or two to the front yard to see that all was well, Captain Mabry was confronted by seven of them, who took hold of him, and ordered him to surrender and yield up his arms, which consisted of a bowie knife and two revolvers. He knew that as a prisoner his fate would be that of a spy, and therefore took the hazard of resistance. With his bowie knife he cut down two and wounded a third. Captain Johnson, revolver in hand, sprang out of the back door and rapidly fired among the other thirteen in the back yard. The result, all the work of a second, was seven Federals killed and several others wounded. Johnson was severely wounded, and Mabry had his hand and entire arm shattered terribly. They escaped in the dark, rejoined their friends, mounted and eluded pursuit. Captain Mabry's wound was a dangerous one and caused great anguish, but he recovered in time to lead his company in the battle of Elkhorn, after which the whole command was transferred to Corinth, Mississippi. In April, 1862, he became lieutenant-colonel of the regiment, and a month later its colonel. He commanded it as a part of Hebert's brigade till the battle of Iuka, where he was severely wounded in three places and captured. Too badly injured to be removed, he was paroled. He was exchanged at Vicksburg late in 1862, and later re-assumed command of his regiment, then in Whitfield's brigade.

In the summer of 1863 General Whitfield came west of the Mississippi, and Colonel Mabry took command of the brigade, then composed of Whitfield's legion, Third and Ninth Texas cavalry and Croft's Georgia battery. He remained in command till March, 1864, when General S. P. Ross, of Texas, recently promoted, assumed command, uniting his own regiment (Sixth Texas) to the brigade. At the same time Colonel Mabry was raised to the rank of brigadier-general, and assigned to the command of a brigade consisting of the Fourth, Sixth and Thirty-eighth Mississippi regiments, the Fourteenth Confederate Louisiana and Mississippi regiment, the Fourteenth and Sixteenth consolidated Arkansas regiment, and an Arkansas battery. He was placed in command of Yazoo City and surrounding country, and, with cavalry, captured the gunboat Petrel, believed to be the first incident of the kind on record. He next served with Forrest in all his subsequent campaigns, but was left behind in his campaign into Tennessee. During Hood's march north General Mabry was left in command of north Mississippi and west Tennessee. He victoriously fought a severe battle to preserve Hood's connections. In the meantime he was offered a command under General Stephen D. Lee, but preferred to remain with his own men. In March, 1865, General Taylor sent him to Louisiana to conduct troops to the east side of the river, but before anything could be accomplished the surrender occurred.

General Mabry resumed his home and professional labors in

HINCHE P. MABRY

Jefferson. In 1866 he served in the constitutional convention, and under it was elected judge of the Jefferson district, but was removed a year later by military authorities. Thence, till 1879, he enjoyed a large and successful practice, enjoying the confidence of the people to a degree of which any honorable man would be proud. In the latter year he transferred his home and business to Fort Worth, where his high and chivalrous character was well known. – *Encyclopedia of the New West.*

Source: *Biographical Souvenir of the State of Texas,* 1889.

W. J. MABRY

Capt. W. J. Mabry, Jr., planter, Richland, Stewart Co., Ga., was born in 1820, in Warren county, N. C. The founder of the family in America was Charles Mabry, an Englishman who in 1717 came to North Carolina from Quebec, Canada. He had been married to a Miss Gibbs, of Irish descent, and connected with an old Quebec family. He was a planter and fought for independence in the patriot army. One of his sons, W. J., born about 1764, was married to Mary Ann Short, daughter of an old settler in North Carolina. He served with distinction in the war of 1812, and lived in the old Tar Heel state, dying in 1824. His wife survived him and was married the second time to a Mr. Baker. They moved to Quebec, where she died in 1876, at the very old age of ninety-six years. She bore to Mr. Mabry the following children: Mrs. Harriet McCartha, deceased; L. F., Atlanta; Mrs. Ann Jones, of Carroll county; Mrs. Susan Kidd, of Alabama; Seaborn, deceased, and Capt. W. J., the subject of this sketch. The Mabrys have long been democrats and members of the Methodist church. Capt. W. J. Mabry came to Georgia with his uncle when he was six years old and settled in Lincoln county. There he was educated and when the early inhabitants were harassed by the murderous Creek Indians he shouldered a musket and aided in the subjugation of that warring tribe. In 1839 he moved to Stewart county and commenced a farming life that has been continued for over half a century. He entered the Mexican war as a private and was promoted to the rank of captain. He participated in the battles of Matamoras and Monterey, was in a trip to the Rocky mountains to move an Indian tribe and back again, was in the front in the engagements at Tampico, Vera Cruz, Alvorado,

Sierra Gordo, Pero, Black Pass, and for six months was in the siege of Mexico. In 1851 he was married to Mary C. Bowers, daughter of Philemon and Mary Ann Bowers, of Stewart county. In the civil war he headed a company, but in Virginia he was put in the quartermaster's department, and was later transferred to the western army with the rank of captain. He was in the first battles in Virginia, at Bethel, first Manassas, Perryville, Ky., Murfreesboro, Tenn., Chickamauga and numerous others of smaller importance. After the war he again put his hand to the plow and once more took up the affairs of his farm. Capt. Mabry has five children: W. W., of Richland; E. N., of Terrell county; T. J. and Philip P. (twins), at home; Mrs. Mattie, wife of Isom T. Webb, of Stewart county. Mr. W. W. Mabry is a distinguished Baptist divine. Capt. Mabry, though in the last part of the three-quarter-century walk of life, is robust in appearance and enjoying splendid health, with his mental faculties strong and unimpaired. He was a boy when there was no railroad in the state, and was a visitor in the neighborhood of Atlanta when the site of that thriving city could not boast of a single house. He remembers the event of the laying of the first rail on the first railroad in the United States; of the second one, from Charleston to Aiken, S. C., and of the driving of the first spike in the first road in Georgia — from Macon to Forsyth. He was the personal friend of the first engineer to cross the Chattahoochee river — Mr. Watson.

Source: *Memoirs of Georgia*, 1895. Volume 2.

GEORGE W. MALLET

George W. Mallet, prominently numbered among the pioneer settlers of Conway County, was born in Carroll County, Georgia, in 1839, and is a son of Jesse and Tabitha (Sterling) Mallet, the former born in Hancock County, Georgia, in 1803, and the latter in Mecklenburg County, North Carolina, in 1810. They were married in Monroe County, Georgia, but afterward lived a short time in Alabama and Mississippi, and about the year 1841 immigrated to Conway County, then almost a wild waste, and thinly settled, and where game was abundant. He located in what is now Faulkner County, where he took an active part in the improvement of the county, and spent his future life as a farmer, serving as Justice of the Peace a short time. His death occurred in 1860, but his estimable wife survived him fifteen

GEORGE W. MALLET

years. They led an industrious and moral life, although not identified with any religious denomination. The grandfather of our subject (Jesse Mallet) was a Virginian by birth, but died in Monroe County, Georgia. He was a blacksmith and millstone cutter by occupation, and was of French descent. William Sterling, the maternal grandfather, died in Georgia, but formerly lived in North Carolina. G. W. Mallet was reared to farm life, being educated in the subscription schools, and aided in clearing up the old homestead farm. He enlisted in June, 1862, in Capt. J. D. Morgan's company of Arkansas Infantry, of the Confederate army, and fought at Prairie Grove and at Helena, and when the army went south he remained in Arkansas, and in December, 1863, joined Company G, Third Arkansas Cavalry, and operated in Arkansas till June, 1865, when he was honorably discharged, and returned to farm life, and the same year he was married to Henrietta Cashirighi and native of Italy, and a daughter of Gilbert and Mary M. Cashirighi, who were natives of Italy, where they were reared and married, but in an early day came to Arkansas, and lived some years in Prairie County, but prior to the war came to this county, where Mr. Cashirighi was engaged in farming. He died about 1886, and his wife followed him two years later. Both were members of the Methodist Episcopal Church, South. To Mr. and Mrs. Mallet were born ten children, three sons and five daughters, living. After his marriage Mr. Mallet continued to reside in what is now Faulkner County for a few years. He then removed to this side of the Cadron, and settled in the woods, but has since opened up about 100 acres of land, being the owner of over 600 acres in all, which is the fruit of his own industry. His aid and influence have ever been devoted to the growth and welfare of this locality. He is independent in politics, and he and Mrs. Mallet are faithful members of the Methodist Episcopal Church, South.

Source: *Biographical and Historical Memoirs of Western Arkansas,* 1891.

JAMES L. MALONE

James L. Malone. He whose name heads this sketch is one of the early settlers of Texas, was born in Georgia in 1825, and was the youngest of seven children born to Robert and Agnes (Nichols) Malone, the former of whom was born in Virginia and the latter in Georgia. The paternal ancestors came from Ireland to this country and settled in Virginia, and from this State Robert Malone removed to Georgia in his early youth, in which State he eventually married. In 1846 he became a resident of Texas, and in Hays County of this State he was called from life in 1864, having been a stanch Democrat in his political views throughout life. His wife died in Georgia, of which state her people were residents. James L. Malone was reared on a farm in Georgia, and after coming to Texas, in 1846, made his home in Austin for several years, in the vicinity of which place he was engaged in farming. In 1852 he moved to Hays County and purchased a farm of 1,000 acres, near San Marcos, on which he erected a substantial residence and made his home for over forty years. During that time he made many very valuable improvements on the place, and had about 500 acres under cultivation. In 1892 he disposed of the farm and moved to San Marcos, in which place he erected him a handsome home. When he first came to the State the Indians were very troublesome, and the family was compelled to undergo many hardships during these early times. In 1850 he led to the altar Miss Eliza P. Pitts, a native of Georgia and a daughter of Gen. John D. Pitts, who was born on the ocean while his parents were en route from London, England, to this country in 1798. His parents located in South Carolina, and later in Washington County, Georgia, where his father, who was a sea captain prior to coming to this country, died. John Pitts was his eldest son, and he was reared in Georgia, and upon reaching manhood represented Stewart County in the State Legislature for one term. He married Eliza Daves, a native of South Carolina, and in 1841 came to Texas and settled in Austin County, where he was engaged in farming the following year. He afterwards resided for four years in Grimes County, and in 1847 came to Hays County and erected about the first residence in San Marcos. The next year he was appointed Adjutant General by Governor Woods, and during the two years that he filled that office his family lived in Austin. He then returned to Hays County and made the first settlement at Stringtown, near San Marcos. He became an extensive farmer and stock raiser, and for years was very active in the political affairs of his section and a delegate to numerous conventions. He was a member of the secession convention at Austin in 1861, but was taken sick there and died on his way home, his wife having previously died in 1851. They were members of the Methodist Episcopal Church, which was the first church organized in San Marcos, and was organized in the home of Gen. Pitts, with seven members enrolled, four of whom were members of his family. Mrs. Malone is the only one of the original seven who is now living. To Mr. and Mrs. Malone the following children have been born: Mrs. E. P. Duggan, Mrs. Laura McKie, Robert Malone, Mrs. Glenn Rylander, Mrs. Pitts Hunter, William Malone, John Malone, dead; Samuel Malone, dead; Davis Malone, Ward Malone, Nina Malone, dead; B. Malone, Wilsie Malone, dead; Alma Malone, Zoe Malone.

Source: *Memorial and Genealogical Record of Southwest Texas*, 1894.

Note: Robert Malone of Snake Creek appears on a Carroll County grand jury list June 1, 1835. Robert Malone was residing with his family in District 682 in Carroll County in 1840.

WILLIAM H. MALONE

William H. Malone, merchant, Villa Rica, Carroll Co., Ga., son of J. D. and Mary (Hale) Malone, was born in Atlanta, Ga., in 1858. His paternal grandparents were Jones and Lucy (Dumas) Malone, his grandmother Dumas being a Huguenot refugee. Mr. Malone's father was born in Union district, S. C., in 1811. He was educated at the Presbyterian college at Marysville, Tenn., and came to Georgia and settled in Atlanta in 1852. He engaged in merchandising and continued in business until Gen. Sherman entered the city in 1864. He was then sent a prisoner to Cambridge City, Ind., where he remained until after the surrender, when he came back to a farm he had in Cobb county, Ga. Soon after that he re-entered business in Atlanta, but in 1869 he had the misfortune to be burned out, and returned to his farm. Subsequently he went to Villa Rica, where he died in 1887. He was a local preacher in the Methodist church, an active worker and a liberal contributor to all movements having in view the advancement of the church and the progress and upbuilding of the city. It was a genuine pleasure to him to be helpful to others, especially the poor, and many are the deeds, agreements and wills on record in Fulton county written by him. A true man and a sincere Christian, he lived beloved and died regretted.

On his mother's side Mr. W. H. Malone traces his ancestry far back and through prominent family lines. The great-great-grandfather, George Hale, came from England to America with Lord Baltimore.

WILLIAM H. MALONE

George, a descendant of his, was a soldier during the revolutionary war, and married a Miss Nancy Grant, who was a Scotch refugee. Alexander Hale, their son and Mrs. Malone's grandfather, was born in Baltimore, Md., in 1768, and some time not long afterward his parents migrated direct to territory since erected into the state of Tennessee, and settled in what is now Blount county. John B. Hale, Mrs. Malone's father, son of Alexander and Sarah (Billingslea) Hale, was born in Washington county, Tenn., and married Miss Jane McClung, daughter of William and Euphemia (Cunningham) McClung. The families of her parents were early settlers, and prominent in Savannah, Ga., in social and commercial circles. Early in the history of Tennessee her parents moved to that state, and the house they lived in is still standing. Hon. J. C. Hale, Mrs. Malone's brother, is an ex-state senator of Tennessee, and now holds a very important position under the government at Washington. Mr. Malone was reared in Atlanta, where he received a good education, and afterward took an eclectic course at the university of Georgia. At the age of eighteen he began teaching, and taught as many as six different schools in different places. A part of the time he taught in Forsyth county, where he read law and was admitted to the bar and practiced four years. He taught school in Villa Rica three years. When his father died, 1887, he abandoned all other pursuits and assumed control of his estate, in the management of which he has been pre-eminently successful, and has become the leading merchant and citizen of that part of the county. He took great interest in the establishment of a high grade school in Villa Rica and was instrumental in the accomplishment of the object. He was elected president of the board of directors, and occupies that position to-day. Every movement inaugurated for advancing the interests of Villa Rica has had his support and substantial aid, and he contributes liberally to all church and moral enterprises. In 1894 he reluctantly consented to become a candidate for the general assembly, and received 975 out of about 1,200 votes, although for competitors he had two of the best citizens of the county. As he lives in an extreme corner of the county the result is a very significant compliment. Mr. Malone was married in 1884 to Miss Mary A. Knox, born and reared in Forsyth county, Ga., daughter of Dr. J. R. and Martha (McAfee) Knox. Her parents on both sides are among the best known and most influential families in Cherokee county, Ga. To this happy union three children have been

WILLIAM H. MALONE

born: Robert K., William H., and Ralph G. Mr. and Mrs. Malone are active and prominent members of the Methodist church, and Mr. Malone is a member of the Masonic fraternity. In view of his age and what he has already attained to in general popularity, in his standing in the commercial world and in the political field, it is safe to predict for him wealth, influence and political honors – prosperity and usefulness.

Source: *Memoirs of Georgia*, 1895. Volume 1.

APPLETON MANDEVILLE

Appleton Mandeville, one of the first residents of Carrollton, Ga., was born in Delaware County, N. Y., February 26, 1802, and is a son of Benoni and Dolly (Waite) Mandeville, the former a native of Massachusets and a son of John Mandeville. The subject is the elder of two living children, the other being a sister, Mathena. At the age of six years he was taken to Massachusetts by his parents, and there he grew up and received a common school education. When twenty-one years of age he moved to Walton County, Ga., where he clerked in a store for one year. He then became a partner in a store in Salem, Clarke County, and merchandised three years, thence going to McDonough, Henry County, and thence to Zebulon, Pike County, and finally, in the fall of 1832, locating in Carrollton, where he has since resided. For twenty-five years he was a prosperous merchant of that city but retired in 1857. His has been eminently a business life, having acted one term as judge of the inferior court of Carroll County, and also served several years as county treasurer.

In 1835 he married Miss Mary Ann Stewart, of Orleans County, Vt., and daughter of John and Mary (Wilson) Stewart, of Vermont and Massachusetts, respectively. To their union were born ten children, as follows: Selina F., Patrick J., Mary S., Nellie J., Stella M., Leon P., L. Clifton, Eugenia, Willie C. and Lula.

Mr. Mandeville is a Master Mason and a member of the Royal Arch. He and wife are worthy members of the Presbyterian Church.

Source: *Biographical Souvenir of the States of Georgia and Florida*, 1889.

D. R. MARTIN

D. R. Martin, farmer, Carrollton, Carroll Co., Ga., son of John C. and Emily (Bates) Martin, was born in Coweta county, Ga., in 1846.

His paternal grandparents migrated from South Carolina to Coweta county in 1830. They came in the old-time block-wheel ox carts, and it took them three weeks to make the journey. His grandfather was born in South Carolina and was a farmer – he, however, supplemented farming with blacksmithing and wood-working. Like other early settlers, he had to clear the land on which he made his home. His father was born in South Carolina in 1821, and his mother, daughter of David and Rhoda (Evans) Bates – old settlers – was born in Wilkes county, Ga., in 1824. Mr. Martin was reared in Coweta county, and, as were other boys at that time, was educated in an old-time dirt floor log cabin and subjected to all the inconveniences incident to them. In May, 1863, he enlisted in Company K (Capt. George Short), First Georgia regiment (Col. Lester), for six months; when the time expired he enlisted in the First Georgia cavalry (Capt. H. A. North, under Col. Cruse) and was in many battles. He was in front of Gen. Sherman's army from Marietta to Atlanta, and during the "March through Georgia." He was in North Carolina at the time of the surrender. Immediately after the event he returned to Carroll county penniless, but with a firm will and a stout heart went to work. In 1869 he bought a tract of land with not a stick amiss on it, and proceeded to make a farm and lay the foundation for a fortune. He made a specialty of raising Irish potatoes and fruit, and his great success has demonstrated his sagacity and wisdom. In 1893 he bought the land on which he now lives, also virgin forest, which he has transferred into one of the best improved farms in this community, and has built on it one of the finest modern residences in the county. He is recognized as one of the leading and most successful farmers in Carroll county; rich and getting richer. In 1869 Mr. Martin was married to Miss Mary Ann, daughter of E. B. and Ruth Ann (Curtis) Martin, both born in Gwinnett county, Ga., who were among the early settlers of Carroll county, by whom he had the following children: Henry C., Lou, Ida, Mary and Claude. The mother of these children died in 1887, and in 1888 Mr. Martin married Nannie, widow of Thomas Dixon, and daughter of Otha and Eliza (Curtis) Bell [Beall], born in Randolph county, Ga. To them two children – Laura and Susie – have been born. Mr. Martin is a Knight of Honor, and himself and wife are members of the Methodist church. In farm management Mr. Martin is acknowledged to have few equals – no superiors. Content with the superior management of his 240-acre farm, its profitable returns and the esteem of his neighbors, he is unambitious of public honors. Whatever he has is the result of honest toil.

Source: *Memoirs of Georgia*, 1895. Volume 1.

JAMES J. MASSEY

James J. Massey, a respected and enterprising planter of Nichols Township, was born in Cumberland County, North Carolina, July 19, 1819. His parents, Warren and Nancy (McDougal) Massey, were natives of Virginia, to which State his ancestors were among the earliest pioneers. To that union were born seven children, three of whom only are now living. He served as a soldier in the war of 1812-15; followed farming for a livelihood, and died in 1826. His wife survived him over forty years, and died in 1870. They both embraced the faith of the Methodists, but were not connected with any church. The subject of this sketch was educated in the common private schools of his county, in North Carolina, and at his majority began for himself by engaging in mining for gold. He followed that pursuit as an occupation for some time, and in 1849 crossed the plains, to try his fortune in the gold fields of California, but returned to North Carolina in 1851. In 1841 Mr. Massey had married Barbary Mangrum; she died in March, 1857, and left one child, James, which also died a few years after. In 1858 Mr. Massey married the second time to Miss A. Perkins. To this union have been born four children, all sons, and all married. They are named in order of birth: Leonis, Joseph M., John E., and Jefferson C. In 1871 Mr. Massey emigrated from Georgia to Arkansas, and located in Nichols Township, Conway County, where he now resides in the quiet possession of a good farm of 160 acres of land, with 70 under cultivation, well improved and stocked. He is a member of the Masonic fraternity, Cleveland Lodge, No. 473. He and wife are members of the Cumberland Presbyterian Church, in which he holds the office of Elder. Mr. Massey is one of the active and enterprising citizens of the vicinity of Cleveland, where he has seen many changes since his arrival here in 1871.

Source: *Biographical and Historical Memoirs of Western Arkansas,* 1891.

Note: James J. Massey was residing in the Second District of Carroll County (P.O. Villa Rica) in 1860. His occupation was listed as distiller and he was residing with Angeline B. Perkins. He married her on March 15, 1863 in Carroll County, Georgia. In 1870 they were residing in the Villa Rica District of Carroll County. James was listed as a farmer.

JAMES A. MAXWELL

Captain James A. Maxwell, a farmer of Texas, is of Scotch descent. His great-grandfather Maxwell was the first one of the name who settled in this country, and that settlement was in Mecklenburgh county, North Carolina. There James, the grandfather of the subject of this sketch, was born. James moved to Morgan county, Georgia, where the subject's father, Thomas Maxwell, was born, and afterward moved to the west line of the State, where he died. The subject's father, Thomas, was born in Morgan county, Georgia, in 1818, was reared in Polk county, that State, and Calhoun, now Cleburne county, Alabama. He served in the Confederate army a short time, but was released on account of his age. When the war was over he came to Texas and died in Lamar county in 1881. He was a planter and a man of great energy; although not a sporting character, he was a lover of good horse flesh and hunting, and was of a lively disposition. Thomas married Mary, daughter of Arthur Alexander, and a descendant of an old Georgia family, and had born to him the following children – James A., William C., John W., Albert A., Marshall, Thomas, Eliza Rachel, wife of J. M. Smith; George Ann, wife of R. C. Lyon, and Exa, wife of Thomas Griffin.

James A. Maxwell was born in Polk county, Georgia, in January, 1842. He enlisted in the Confederate army in 1861, in Company D, First Alabama regiment of cavalry; was afterward transferred to Company G, Twelfth Alabama regiment, and served with the Army of the Tennessee as part of Wheeler's cavalry, and was in the battle of Corinth, Mississippi, also on the raid into Kentucky under General Bragg, in the battle at Chickamauga and the continuous line of battles from there down to Jonesboro. His command followed Sherman to the sea and up into North Carolina, and surrendered at Bentonville. He entered as a private, but rose to be captain of his company. He came to Texas in January, 1869, and began farming on nothing. He now owns 629 acres of first class land, 400 acres of which he has in cultivation, and is one of the largest and most substantial farmers of his county.

Mr. Maxwell married January 9, 1873, Dorothy E., daughter of Frank Smith, a native of Georgia, born in Oglethorpe county, and now the mother of three children – James P., Mary Maud and Julia Erbanus. Mr. Maxwell is a thoroughly go-ahead farmer, and is recognized by all his neighbors as a wide-awake and progressive citizen, who is alert not only to his own interests, but to those of his country and his fellow-citizens.

Source: *Biographical Souvenir of the State of Texas,* 1889.

Note: Arthur Alexander was an early settler of Carroll County.

MALCOMB McALLISTER

Malcomb McAllister, farmer, Eagle Hill, Ark. Mr. McAllister was born in Blount County, Tenn., on April 3, 1831, and is a son of James B. and Margaret (McRae) McAllister, natives of Tennessee and North Carolina, respectively. The parents were married in the former State, and when Malcomb was eighteen months old they moved to Carroll County, Ga., where they passed the remainder of their days. The father was a farmer all his life and in 1836 and 1837 was a soldier, assisting in removing the Indians west of the Mississippi. He died in 1860, at the age of about sixty years, and his widow followed him to the grave in 1870 at about the same age. Her death occurred in Carroll County, Ga. Both were members of the Methodist Episcopal Church South, and he was an exhorter and class leader for many years, also superintendent of the Sunday-school. As a farmer he was practical, industrious and successful. In politics he was a Democrat. Of the ten children born to this marriage, Malcomb was the fifth in order of birth. He was educated in Georgia, and when twenty-one years of age commenced for himself as a tiller of the soil. This he has since continued. He then read medicine from 1857 to 1859 under Dr. J. G. W. Brown, and in 1859 and 1860 he attended the medical college at Macon, Ga. Later he commenced practicing in Benton County, Ala., and in 1861 returned to Georgia. He enlisted in the Seventh Georgia Cavalry, Confederate Army, and remained with the same all through the war, serving principally in Virginia, and being at all times in the thickest of the fight. He was in quite a number of battles, and in numerous skirmishes and raids from Cape Fear to James River. He was on the raid when his command captured 2,700 head of cattle at Petersburg, on the James River, from the rear of the Union Army. He was one of the forty detailed to go home after horses, and while there the army surrendered. After the war Mr. McAllister went to Hunt County, Tex., and after residing there one year went to Polk County, Ark., locating on the head of Mountain Fork. There he remained for nearly two years, and then moved to Scott County, Boles, where he remained for another year. He subsequently moved back to this county and located on the head of Mountain Fork in 1875. He there has 160 acres of land, and has about 40 acres under cultivation. He abandoned the practice of medicine about ten years ago, and now gives his attention strictly to agricultural pursuits. In 1884 he was elected justice of the peace, and re-elected in 1890. When about thirteen years of age he joined the Methodist Episcopal Church South, and has been a great church worker ever since. He was married on May 5, 1851, to Miss Nancy J. Chance of Georgia, and she died at this place on December 4, 1884. To this union six children have been born: Martha H. (wife of James Watson, a farmer of this county), J. D. (now in Texas), Mollie (wife of William McBride now, in Texas), Sarah Alice (wife of John Coffman, a farmer of this county), Willie (at home), and Patty (also at home). Mr. McAllister was married again on November 8, 1885, to Mrs. Sarah C. Tyson of Rush County, Tex. She is also a member of the Methodist Episcopal Church South. Mr. McAllister is a Democrat in politics.

Source: *Biographical and Historical Memoirs of Western Arkansas,* 1891.

JAMES McBRAYER

James M'Brayer, farmer, Oval, Paulding Co., Ga., son of Andrew and Nancy (Leathers) McBrayer, was born in Paulding county in 1835. Mr. McBrayer's father – son of John McBrayer, who was a revolutionary soldier – was born in Buncombe county, N. C., in 1807, whence the family migrated to Georgia in 1817, making the journey in an ox-cart, and settled in what is now Campbell and Douglas counties – living in a tent until land could be cleared and a house built. Three months' schooling, under serious disadvantages, was all he received, but by reading and studying by a pine-knot light he acquired a fair practical education at home. In 1831 he moved to what is now Paulding county, where he accumulated a fortune, and died in 1891. Mr. McBrayer's

JAMES McBRAYER

mother, who is still living, was born in 1813, in South Carolina. Her parents were Samuel and Mary (Swanford) Leathers, an old family of revolutionary war times, who came to Georgia and settled in what is now Paulding county. In 1831 she was married to Mr. McBrayer, and of the children which blessed their union, nine are now living: James M., the subject of this sketch; Peter T.; Samuel M.; Andrew J.; George W.; Wm. C.; Joseph C.; Mrs. Mary A. Walker, and Mrs. Susannah Waldrop. Mr. McBrayer was raised a farmer, and received such education as could be obtained in the country common schools at the time. In 1857 he began life as a farmer, and had gotten a good start when the unpleasantness occurred. In 1862 he enlisted in Company I, Nineteenth Georgia regiment, with which he was engaged in the battles of the Wilderness, Fredericksburg, and others. In 1862 he was taken prisoner, but was soon exchanged, rejoined his command, and remained with it until the surrender of Gen. Johnston, April 26, 1865. Like thousands of his comrades, he returned to his home to find it a desolate waste. By well-directed labor and close management he has restored it, and has now as good a farm and is as prosperous as the most favored of his fellow-citizens. Mr. McBrayer was married in 1857 to Miss Martha, daughter of Henry and Matilda (Jackson) Cleckler, who has borne him seven children: Joseph B., Mrs. Nancy V. McLarty, Andrew E., Mrs. Elizabeth Cornet, James, Robert L., and Etta E.

Source: *Memoirs of Georgia*, 1895. Volume 2.

Note: Andrew E. McBrayer and Nancy Leathers were married in Carroll County January 27, 1833. Nancy was a daughter of Samuel and Mary (Swafford) Leathers.

PETER T. McBRAYER

Peter M'Brayer, farmer, Oval, Paulding Co., Ga., son of Andrew and Nancy (Leathers) McBrayer, was born in Paulding county in 1837. Like his brother, James, a sketch of whom will be found elsewhere, he was raised on the farm, and was educated in the old-time log schoolhouse. In 1862 he enlisted in Company I, Fifth Georgia regiment, Col. Wadkins commanding. With his command, he participated in the battles of Baker's Creek, Missionary Ridge, Dalton, Resaca, and numerous less important engagements. In April, 1864, he was captured and sent to Indianapolis, Ind., where he was detained as a prisoner nine months. While there he suffered for want of food, from insufficiency of clothing, and frozen feet. From Indianapolis he was sent to Baltimore, Md., and thence to Richmond, where he was paroled. On his return home he walked all the distance from North Carolina, and reached home three weeks before the surrender. He went to work at once to restore his farm to its antebellum condition, which he has accomplished, and by adopting improved machinery and methods, increased its productiveness and his resources. No neighboring farmer excels him in management or harvest. Mr. McBrayer was married Dec. 5, 1866, to Miss Mary F., daughter of Bennett and Jane (Ingram) Cooper, who has borne him nine children: William A., Mrs. Vilula Ellis, Andrew E., Ida D., Mary E., Peter I., Warner J., Fannie F., and Robert L.

Source: *Memoirs of Georgia*, 1895. Volume 2.

Note: Andrew E. McBrayer and Nancy Leathers were married in Carroll County January 27, 1833. Nancy was a daughter of Samuel and Mary (Swafford) Leathers.

B. J. McCAIN

B. J. McCain, merchant, Temple, Carroll Co., Ga., son of William B. and Margaret N. (McCain) McCain, was born in Troup county in 1843. His grandfather, Hugh McCain, was a native of North Carolina, and was a soldier in the revolutionary war. His parents were born in North Carolina, came to Georgia and settled in Troup county in 1840, where his father cleared a farm and built for himself two mills, merchant and saw mill. His maternal grandparents, Joe and Margaret (Moore) McCain, were also born in North Carolina. Mr. McCain was reared on the farm and his early education was obtained at a country school. In 1863 he enlisted in Company F (Capt. B. F. Long), cavalry, with which he served six months. He then enlisted in Company F (Capt. George Austin), Georgia State troops, with which he remained until the close of the war, and of which he was a corporal. He was in two battles, both fought at Coosahatchie, and at the surrender he stacked arms at Albany, Ga. After the war he returned to the farm, but in 1868 he attended school in Carrollton. The next year he worked on the farm, and the one following he attended a private school four months. In 1871 he finished his preparatory commercial education by attending Moore's business university at Atlanta. In August, 1872, he engaged as a clerk with J. C. Carter, with whom he remained four years. After that he entered into partnership with Gus Smythe, but at the end of fifteen months he sold out to his partner and formed a new partnership with L. P. Barnes. Twelve months after he retired from his business, and with George and John McGahee and I. Y. Sawtell organized the Atlanta Wild Land company. He remained in this company ten months, and then, in the fall of 1878, located in Simsville, Ga., and engaged in a general merchandise business in which he was satisfactorily successful. In 1882 he closed out in Simsville and permanently settled in Temple, where he is now, and where he has built a large and profitable trade, and is a leading business man and citizen of that part of the county. In 1875 Mr. McCain was married to Miss Tallulah V., daughter of Maj. D. A. and Nancy W. (Collier) Cook, of Atlanta, by whom he has one child surviving, Ida Tallulah. They have an adopted son, William B. Mr. McCain is a master Mason and he and his family are members of the Methodist church. He exerts a well-earned influence in the community and county.

Source: *Memoirs of Georgia*, 1895. Volume 1.

JOSEPH A. McCORD

Joseph A. McCord, merchant, Carrollton, Ga., was born in Newton County, that State, October 6, 1857. His father, William S. McCord, was one of the pioneers of Georgia, having cleared the first ground around Covington, Newton County. He had acted as sheriff of Abbeville District, S. C., where he was born in 1794. He lived to the age of seventy-four years. His wife, mother of the subject, was Miss Mary A. Moore before marriage. She is a daughter of Alexander Moore, a planter and miller, was born in 1818 in Clark County, Ga., and is still living.

Joseph A. McCord is the only child born to his parents. He began his business life at the early age of twelve years by clerking in a store in Conyers, Rockdale County, Ga., and was a bookkeeper in that place for seven years. He also acted as deputy clerk of the superior court of Rockdale County, while there.

August 27, 1883, he entered into a partnership with C. J. Almand & Bro., the style of the firm being Almand, McCord & Co. This firm continued for two years, until September 25, 1885, when it was changed to McCord & Shaw. This is one of the most prosperous firms in the city and carries a full stock of general merchandise.

Mr. McCord is an active member of the I. O. O. F., being past grand in the lodge and deputy grand master of the State of Georgia. He is identified with the Methodist Episcopal Church, South.

Source: *Biographical Souvenir of the States of Georgia and Florida*, 1889.

JOSEPH A. McCORD

Joseph A. McCord, cashier, Atlanta, Ga., son of Stewart McCord, was born in Newton county, Ga., Oct. 6, 1857. His father, who was of Scotch descent, the family having come to this country before the revolutionary war, was born in Abbeville district, S. C., in 1794, and died Aug. 31, 1868. he was a farmer, was a soldier in the war of 1812, was sheriff of Abbeville district, S. C., and came to Georgia in 1824. Mr. McCord was reared on the farm, and was educated in the country schools in Newton and Rockdale counties. When twelve years old he commenced clerking in a store at Conyers, Ga., and clerked a number of years. In 1874 he was appointed deputy clerk under T. J. Treadwell, clerk of the superior court of Rockdale county, retaining the position about four years. He then went to Carrollton, Ga., and engaged in a general merchandise business, conducting it with success and profit until 1890. In 1887 he was elected a member of the city council of Carrollton, was re-elected, and served three years. At the same time he was elected a school commissioner of Carrollton by the general assembly and served two years. In 1890 he came to Atlanta and entered the employ of the Western & Atlantic railway in the general freight office, having charge of the adjustment of all city claims for damages, etc. He remained in this office until November, 1892, when he was elected assistant cashier of the Atlanta Trust and Banking company, and on May 11, 1893, was elected cashier, a position he now holds, discharging its responsible duties with conspicuous ability. Mr. McCord was married in Carrollton, April 24, 1889, to Miss Lillie, daughter of Capt. David Croft. His wife died, leaving no issue, June 21, 1890. He is a member of the Capital City club, of the I. O. O. F., and of the Methodist church, south. Mr. McCord has the entire confidence of the commercial element of Atlanta, ranks well in financial circles, and, being a young man, may be regarded as having a bright future before him.

Source: *Memoirs of Georgia*, 1895. Volume 1.

G. A. McDANIEL

G. A. McDaniel, farmer and miller, Victory, Carroll Co., Ga., son of John and Sarah I. (Terry) McDaniel, was born in Elbert county, Ga., in 1820. His grandparents, Henry and Mary (Rucker) McDaniel, were natives of Virginia, whence they migrated to South Carolina. They afterward came to Georgia, but in a few years returned to South Carolina, where they died. Mr. McDaniel's father was born in Virginia in 1781, came to Georgia in 1810, and settled in Elbert county, where he remained until 1822, when he moved to Henry (now De Kalb) county. The only property he had was a horse, that ran away, and he had to make his crop with a grubbing hoe. He walked to South Carolina to get another horse. He lived in a tent until he could build a log cabin (dirt floor), had to go twenty miles to mill, and lived principally on corn pone and wild game. His mother was the daughter of Henry and Mary (Baldwin) Terry, native South Carolinians. Her father was a Methodist Episcopal minister and devoted his life to church work. Mr. McDaniel was reared in De Kalb county, and educated at schools taught in the old-time dirt-floor log house. About 1847 he went to Atlanta, but staid there but a short time. He then went to Spalding county, where he remained until 1854, when he removed to Bowdon, where he farmed until the war began, then he engaged in merchandising, and continued it for twenty years. He then moved to the farm where he now lives, on which he had years before built a mill. Beginning without anything, he now owns 2,000 acres of excellent land, including one of the best improved farms in the county and a mill site, and is one of the richest men in Carroll. Mr. McDaniel was married Dec. 25, 1850, in Spalding county, to Miss Martha J. Lavender – born in Henry county – daughter of James and Malinda (Ansley) Lavender, native Georgians. This union has been blessed with ten children: Sarah A., Mary M., deceased; Eliza A., Ella J., John L., Martha J., Ida B., T. Henry, Lula B. and Emma B. Mr. and Mrs. McDaniel are members of the Methodist Protestant church and he is regarded as one of Carroll's very best and worthiest citizens.

Source: *Memoirs of Georgia*, 1895. Volume 1.

SAMUEL W. McDONALD

Samuel W. McDonald, a progressive farmer and stock raiser, and one who has kept thoroughly apace with the times, was born in Randolph County, Ala., in December, 1844, being the son of Sebbon McDonald, who was born and reared in Georgia, but who was married in Alabama to Miss Rhoda Blackston, a native of the last mentioned

SAMUEL W. McDONALD

State. Mr. McDonald served in one of the old Indian wars. He was a farmer, and followed this occupation in Alabama until his death, which occurred about 1864. Samuel W. McDonald attained his growth in Alabama, remained with his father until grown, and in 1862 enlisted in the Confederate army, Seventeenth Alabama Infantry, serving until the final surrender of the Confederacy. He participated in the fight near Dalton, and was stationed nearly all the time at Mobile. He surrendered in 1865, and after being paroled returned to Alabama, where he engaged in farming in Randolph County. He moved to Arkansas in 1876, located in Clay County, remained there two years, and then moved to Boone County, Ark., whence after a residence of two years he returned to Clay County, and settled on his present farm in 1881. He has 120 acres of land, with about seventy-five fenced, and some forty under cultivation. Mr. McDonald has been married twice; first, in Clay County, in 1874, to Miss Elizabeth Sexton, a native of Illinois, who was reared in Arkansas. She died in 1885, and was the mother of four children, who are named as follows: William B., Riley S., Samuel W. and Ollie B. Mr. McDonald took for his second wife Mrs. Adaline Melton, in September, 1886, and the results of this union are two children: John E. and Reuben H. Mrs. McDonald is a native of Clay County, Ark., where she grew to womanhood. She is a member of the Methodist Episcopal Church. Mr. McDonald is a member of the Baptist Church.

Source: *Biographical and Historical Memoirs of Northeast Arkansas,* 1889.

Note: Seaborn McDonald was residing in District 713, Carroll County, Georgia in 1840. See 1840 Census.

JOHN C. McGARITY

John C. McGarity, farmer, Victory, Carroll Co., Ga., son of Jones and Mary (Embry) McGarity, was born near Atlanta in 1848. His paternal grandfather was a native of Ireland and came to America before the revolutionary war and was a soldier in the army. His grandfather, Abner McGarity, was a native of South Carolina and came to Georgia in an ox cart and settled in the woods in Elbert county in 1795 and cleared a farm. Here Mr. McGarity's father was born and reared on a farm. Starting out in life for himself, he came to De Kalb county, where he lived until 1848, when he removed to Carroll county, settled in the woods, and cleared a farm, where Mr. McGarity now lives. Mr. McGarity's mother was a daughter of John Embry, and his mother was a distant relative of Thomas Jefferson. Mr. McGarity was reared on the farm and was educated at the common county school. When the war began he was too young to enter the army, but he served a short time before the war closed. He supplemented his farm work by teaching school, and taught from 1871 to 1892. In the meantime he was elected justice of the peace, and served eight years. In 1892 he was elected to represent the county in the general assembly. Mr. McGarity was married in 1875 to Miss Martha J. Darden – born and reared in Coweta county – daughter of Elzie and Susan (Upshaw) Darden. Her father was a soldier in the Confederate army. This union has been blessed with six children: Pearl, Ruth, David, John, Joseph and Katie. Mr. and Mrs. McGarity are members of the Baptist church. Mr. McGarity is an acknowledged leader in Carroll county and no citizen commands more respect.

Source: *Memoirs of Georgia*, 1895. Volume 1.

THOMAS A. McLARTY

Dr. Thomas A. McLarty, physician and surgeon, Hope, Ark. Alexander McLarty, the great-grandfather of our subject, was a native of Scotland, who, with his third wife, Barbara (McNaught) McLarty, emigrated to the American continent in the year 1774. He was the youngest of twelve brothers, all the others being sailors, and it is supposed were lost at sea. He settled in the Old Dominion. His son, John McLarty (grandfather of subject), was born in Virginia, and his two half brothers, Alexander and Archibald, were soldiers in the war for independence, from 1778 until the close of the war. The McLartys were prominent people in Scotland, and Dr. T. A. McLarty has in his possession the church letter brought to this country by Alexander McLarty, which was given to him by one David Campbell, moderator, Presbyterian session, who was supposed to have been a descendant of the Campbell's chief of Scotland. The family was closely allied to the Wallaces of Scotland. The McLartys, like their ancestors on both sides, were soldiers and sailors, and were noted for their daring. The church letter spoken of above was written and given to Alexander McLarty on July 29, 1773. The Doctor has it well preserved, and it is an object of great interest and well worth seeing. He also has a deed to 160 acres of land that was made to Alexander McLarty, in Mecklenburg County, N. C., in 1783, described by running the lines to different trees, the kind of tree at each corner being named, viz., two oak and two hickory trees being the four corner-stones. This also is a very peculiar paper and one well worth seeing. The McLarty family are also allied to the Polk family by marriage. The parents of our subject, George W. and Charity (Bates) McLarty, had born to their union eleven children, the Doctor being sixth in order of birth. George McLarty was a farmer by occupation, and served his county and township in various offices of trust and responsibility. He held the office of postmaster for twenty years at Dark Corner, Ga., before and during the late war. He died in January, 1885. The mother of the Doctor was the daughter of Mathias Bates, who was the father of Anthony Bates, killed at the battle of the Alamo, during the war between Texas and Mexico, in 1836. The Bates family are among the Georgia settlers and among the prominent families of that State. The mother of our subject died in 1882, and of the eleven children born to her marriage, only five are now living: Julia (wife of Charles Douthit, of Stephens, Ark.), Josie (wife of John Mable, of Embry, Ga.), Jennie (wife of George M. Roberts, of Buchanan, Ga.), and Emma (wife of R. P. Gann, of Dallas, Ga.) Dr. T. A. McLarty was reared in Campbell (now Douglas) County, was early initiated into the duties of farm life, and received his education in the subscription schools of his native county. When eighteen years of age he entered the Confederate army in Company C, Thirtieth Georgia Regiment Infantry, was attached to Gen. Joseph E. Johnston's army, and was in the battle of Jackson, Miss. He was from Dalton to Atlanta, Ga., and was captured at Dallas, a short time before the Battle of Atlanta, was sent to Camp Chase, Ohio, and there remained until March, 1865, when he was paroled. He returned to Georgia, attended school during 1865, then farmed for the next year, and in 1867 again attended school. In 1868 he married Miss Emma Blanchard, daughter of T. J. and Mary A. (Taylor) Blanchard, natives of Georgia. The Taylor family were originally from Maryland, and the maternal grandmother was a Crawford, and cousin to Gov. Crawford, who fought the duel with and killed Burnside. Mrs. McLarty's family on the maternal side was among the most prominent early settlers of Georgia, and she was one of seven children, five of whom are now living: Isabella (wife of J. M. Garner, of this county), Eugenia C. (wife of H. P. Wowell, of Georgia), Luvenia A. (wife of A. G. Weddington, of Douglasville, Ga.), Emma, and Mary O. (wife of J.

THOMAS A. McLARTY

M. McElreath, of Douglasville, Ga.) Mrs. McLarty's father died on January 5, 1881, and the mother on February 14, 1884. Both were members of the Baptist Church. Mrs. McLarty had two brothers who died during the war: James T. died while a prisoner on his way to Vicksburg to be exchanged, and Lucius, in Savannah, Ga. Both were in the Confederate service. Mr. McLarty tilled the soil in Georgia until 1870, when he came to this State and county, and here continued his former occupation until 1872. He then returned to Douglas County, Ga., where he farmed until 1876, when he commenced the study of medicine under his brother, W. A., and in the fall of 1877 attended the Atlanta Medical College, from which institution he graduated in the spring of 1879. He located then at Villa Rica, Ga., and there practiced for three years. Later he moved to Hamlet, Polk County, Ga., practiced there four years, and in 1885 he came to this county, locating on his present property, which consists of eighty acres of land. Here in connection with farming he is engaged in an extensive practice. To his marriage have been born three children: Lola (wife of S. R. Aubrey, of Spring Hill), Lonnie and Ezra. The Doctor and wife are members of the Methodist Episcopal Church, and the Doctor is a member of the school board of his district, and also a member of the State and county medical societies.

Source: *Biographical and Historical Memoirs of Southern Arkansas,* 1890.

C. L. McPHERSON

C. L. McPherson, farmer, Bremen, Haralson Co., Ga., son of Elijah and Sarah (Small) McPherson, was born in Carroll county, Ga., April 4, 1844. His father was born in Pennsylvania, July 13, 1789, migrated from there to Tennessee, where he married, and in 1830 moved in an ox-cart from Tennessee to Georgia and settled in Carroll county. He was a farmer and saw-mill man, but had no property. His mother was born in Tennessee in 1809. Mr. McPherson was reared on the farm and received very little schooling. He began life on 100 acres of land, with one ox and a wagon. He enlisted in 1864 in a company belonging to the Seventh Georgia regiment, state troops, and subsequently entered the Confederate service, and was sent to Virginia. He was captured Aug. 19, 1864, and sent to Point Lookout, Md., where he remained until Sept. 29, 1864, when he was released, and Oct. 6

following rejoined his command in Virginia, with which he remained until the surrender. Mr. McPherson is considered one of the best and most successful farmers in the county, perfectly reliable, and in the highest degree responsible. Mr. McPherson was married in 1867 to Miss Lucinda, daughter of John L. and Marguerite Hamilton, of Haralson county, who has borne him five children: A. P., N. C., L. D., H. R. and J. H.

Source: *Memoirs of Georgia*, 1895. Volume 1.

FRANKLIN T. McRAE

Franklin T. McRae was born in Georgia, and came to Texas, with his father and his family, in 1856. His father is Malcolm A. McRae.

Franklin T. McRae married Miss Flora A. McDougal, daughter of Daniel McDougal, of Tennessee. The latter moved to Missouri, and in that State Flora was born. Mrs. McRae has borne her husband five children, named as follows – Clarence M., Rosilla, Corilla (who died at the age of four years), James N. and Matilda C. Mr. McRae is the owner of 300 acres of good land, 100 acres of which are under cultivation.

Source: *Biographical Souvenir of the State of Texas*, 1889.

MALCOLM A. McRAE

Malcolm A. McRae was born in South Carolina May 15, 1810; at the age of four years he was taken by his parents to North Carolina; at ten he went to the Hiawatha [Hiawassee] purchase, and at twenty went to Georgia, in which State he married in 1832, February 22, the widow of John Steward, whose maiden name was Mary Whisenhunt. After fourteen years' residence in Georgia he went to Missouri; then, three years later, returned to Georgia, remained there five years longer, and then moved to Arkansas, where he stayed until 1856, when he came to Texas. He arrived in Georgia the 31st day of July, 1830, was elected constable before he was twenty-one years old, and served ten years under a military commission from the governor of the State; he also served as justice of the peace in Georgia, Arkansas and Texas, and no appeal was ever taken from his docket. His father, Hugh B. McRae, was born in Scotland, came to America at the age of eight years, settled in South Carolina and married Nancy McDuffey; they reared five children, named – Daniel, Margaret, William J., Malcolm A., and Hugh J. Of these, Malcolm A., the subject of this sketch, purchased, on his settlement in Texas, 444 acres on which he has since lived.

The children born to Malcolm A. McRae are ten in number and named as follows – Hugh J., Adam R., Barbara A., Nancy J. E., Eliza M., Adam B., Franklin T., Malcolm N., Mary A. and Thursey C.

In 1880, at the age of seventy, Mr. McRae withdrew from business affairs of life and is now living in retirement, having administered his estate, making his heirs happy and prosperous, but retaining for himself sufficient to carry him through life. Indeed, he has done more than that, for since his retirement he has accumulated over $2,000 above his absolute expenses, and owns, besides, 198 shares in the Atlantic and Pacific Mining and Tunnel Company, of Colorado. He is of a long-lived family, all of his grandparents having lived to be over one hundred years of age.

Source: *Biographical Souvenir of the State of Texas*, 1889.

Note: Malcolm A. McRae married Mary Magdalene (Whisenhunt) Stewart in Carroll County, Georgia February 21, 1832. In 1840 the Malcolm McRae family was living in Carroll County, Georgia. See 1840 Census. His son Adam Riley McRae married Mary F. Lynch in Carroll County, Georgia December 2, 1853.

HORACE P. McWHORTER

Dr. Horace P. McWhorter, an eminent young practitioner of Collinsville, DeKalb county, Ala., is a native of Gaylesville, Cherokee county, Ala., and was born September 6, 1859. His grandfather, Allen M. McWhorter, came of an old South Carolina family and was born in Anderson district, that state, whence he removed, when a young man, to Carroll county, Ga., where he reared a family and where he passed the remainder of his years. His son, Dr. A. M. McWhorter, was there married about 1852, and in 1857 came to Alabama, stopped for a short period of time in Lebanon, DeKalb county, and then located in Gaylesville, Cherokee county, where he resided until 1890, when he removed to Collinsville for the purpose of making his home with his son, Dr. Horace P. In January, 1892, however, he made a trip to Selma,

HORACE P. McWHORTER

Cal., to visit a son, and while there sickened and died. He was a graduate of Atlanta Medical college and always enjoyed a lucrative practice; in politics he was a democrat; he was also a royal arch Mason, but not a member of any church, although he died a Christian. His wife bore the maiden name of Mahala J. Davis, and she bore her husband nine children, who were named, in order of birth, as follows: Milton, who is a Methodist Episcopal minister of Selma, Cal.; Dora, the wife of Col. Charles Rattrey, of Gaylesville, Ala.; Della E., now Mrs. Joe R. Roberts, of Collinsville; Horace P., the physician whith whose name this sketch opens; Zachariah D., president of the high school at Greenville, N. C.; Robert L., a physician of Gaylesville, Ala.; Jessie L., married to T. C. Banks, cashier of Attala bank, Attala, Ala.; E. H. McWhorter, a Methodist Episcopal clergyman at Gadsden, Ala.; and Bershie F., deceased. Mrs. Mahala J. (Davis) McWhorter now resides with her son, Dr. Horace P. She was born in Anderson district, S. C., and was taken, when a girl of fourteen, to Carroll county, where her parents made settlement. Dr. Horace P. McWhorter received his literary education at the high school in Gaylesville and read medicine in the office of his father, and after this course of preparatory study passed the session of 1879-80 at the Atlanta Medical college, and then attended the Vanderbilt university at Nashville, Tenn., from which he graduated in the spring of 1881, having devoted his special attention to chemistry. He at once located at Collinsville for the practice of his profession, and has met with an abundant success. He stands high in the estimation of his fellow practitioners in his section as well as in that of the general public, being a member of the State Medical society and member of its examining board. In politics, the doctor is a democrat, and under the auspices of that party holds the position of county health officer. In religion he is a Methodist and is a trustee of the church. The first marriage of the doctor took place in January, 1882, to Miss Fannie C. Newman, at Collinsville; this lady bore one child, Thomas E., now deceased, and on June 6, 1885, she herself passed away. On June 24, 1886, Dr. McWhorter married, for his second wife, Miss Naomi J. Beeson, and this union has been crowned by the birth of three children: Marcus B., deceased, Horace L. and Jerome Cochran.

Source: *Memorial Record of Alabama*, 1893. Volume 1.

JAMES D. MEAD

James D. Mead, an energetic and successful agriculturalist of Lake City Township, was born in Madison County, Ga., in 1822, and is the son of John and Elizabeth (Hall) Mead, the former a native of Georgia, the latter of South Carolina. His grandfather, Miner M. Mead, was of English descent, and was born in Virginia, where his parents had settled a few years previous. He served in the Revolutionary War, and was afterward a pensioner for services rendered. His wife, Mary Mead, lived to be one hundred and five years of age, and drew a pension after her husband's death. She died in Carroll County, Ga., having lived a devoted Christian life as a member of the Baptist Church. They were the parents of thirteen children, John, the father of our subject, being the oldest child. John Mead served in the War of 1812, and after a life of success and usefulness, died in Georgia, when fifty-seven years of age. The mother died in Craighead County, at the home of her son, James, in 1867. To them were born nine children, James D. being the third child, and he and two sisters, Mary and Sarah, are the only survivors, and all live in this county.

Mr. Mead was reared and educated in Georgia, where he resided until the spring of 1857, when, with his family, consisting of his wife and five children, he came to Arkansas, locating on what is now Bay Siding. There he followed farming for sixteen years, and in 1872 moved to his present location. Since coming to Arkansas he has put in cultivation over 200 acres of land, and now owns 480 acres, and has under good cultivation 125 acres. April 6, 1848, he was united in marriage with Miss Thessa Moon, born in Georgia, in 1829, who died in this county, in 1867. Their union was blessed by nine children, only two of whom are now living: Mrs. Nancy S. McLean and James W. Mr. Mead was married a second time, in 1872, this time selecting Mrs. Elizabeth Farmer, *nee* Lewis, who, by her former marriage was the mother of three children: Mrs. Mary Gatlin, Mrs. Sarah Bagwell and Mrs. Nellie Wilson. Mr. Mead's family have always been Whigs, and he is now a stanch Republican.

Source: *Biographical and Historical Memoirs of Northeast Arkansas,* 1889.

JAMES W. MEAD

James W. Mead, a leading planter of the county and also mail contractor, is a native of Georgia, born in Madison County, January 22, 1850. His parents were James D. and Thessa (Moon) Mead [see sketch], both natives of Georgia. He came with his father to this State and county when a boy seven years of age, and was reared on his father's farm, receiving his education at the county schools. He chose as his life companion, Jane Beaty, a native of Arkansas, reared in this county, and December 24, 1868, they were united in marriage. He engaged in farming for several years after this event, and in 1880 opened a saloon at Lake City, and was engaged in the saloon business for six years. In 1883 he was appointed deputy sheriff, and served in that capacity until November, 1888. Since that time he has been farming. Mr. and Mrs. Mead have two children, Nora and Otto, and lost three in early childhood. Mr. Mead has been quite prominent in local affairs, is a Republican in politics, and has been postmaster, serving in that capacity for several years. He is a Knight of Honor and also a Mason.

Source: *Biographical and Historical Memoirs of Northeast Arkansas,* 1889.

Note: See preceding sketch of his father for connection to Carroll County.

J. B. MERRILL

J. B. Merrill, attorney of Edwardsville, was born in Georgia in 1843, a son of Joseph and Susan (Lamberth) Merrill, both natives of Georgia. The father was a son of Joseph and Maria (Bell) Merrill, both natives of South Carolina. The mother was a daughter of John and Permelia (Garrison) Lamberth. The grandfather was one of the pioneer settlers of Tallapoosa county, Ala., and served as tax collector of that county for many years. J. B. Merrill was raised on the farm and attended the common schools of his county, and in the winter of 1860 he entered Irwin college, Tenn., but when the war came on he, in company with about sixty other students, in May, 1861, enlisted in company B, cavalry, under Capt. Wilcoxon. He served as a private until 1862, when he was elected second lieutenant and as such served about one year, when he was made first lieutenant and served eight months, when he became captain of the company and served in that capacity till the close of the war. The first fight of the company was at Cotton Hill, and he also took part in several others among which may be mentioned Sharpsburg, Wilderness, Yellow Tavern, Jack Shop and Gettysburg; he was also with Stuart at the time he went around the

J. B. MERRILL

Federal forces. After the war he returned home to Georgia and followed the plow for two or three years; in 1866 he began reading law, was admitted to the bar in 1872 and began practice at his old home, where his ability was at once recognized, and where he built up a large practice; in 1886, having by this time large interests in mineral lands in Alabama, he came here to look after the same and settled in Edwardsville, where he now stands at the head of his profession. In 1867 he married Mary Faver, daughter of Sanders and Caroline (Davis) Faver, both of French descent. This union has been blessed with five children: Walter B., a graduate of Oxford college and now a practicing attorney with his father; Rosa, wife of John W. Abercrombie, and the mother of one child, Myrl; Hugh, Myrtle and Clyde. The mother was born in Georgia. She is a member of the Baptist church and he is a member of the Masonic order. Mr. Merrill has served three times as mayor of Edwardsville, having been elected without any solicitation on his part. He has largely prepared, at a cost of $13,000, to mine gold, owning a large tract of land which is underlaid with a rich vein of the precious metal.

Source: *Memorial Record of Alabama*, 1893. Volume 1.

Note: J. B. Merrill's parents were married in Carroll County, Georgia September 20, 1842. His father resided in Carroll County in 1850, 1860, and 1870. See Census records for those years. Based on the fact that his parents were married in Carroll County and that his family lived here in 1850, it is probable that J. B. Merrill was born in Carroll County.

JAMES D. MOORE

James D. Moore, farmer, Whitesburg, Carroll Co., Ga., son of Abraham and Ann (Dismukes) Moore, was born near Raleigh, N. C., in 1814. His paternal grandfather was Abraham Moore, who was a soldier in the revolutionary army. His maternal grandparents, George and Elizabeth (Thompson) Dismukes, were North Carolinians, and his grandfather Dismukes served through the revolutionary war as a major in the patriot army. Mr. Moore's father was born and reared in North Carolina, but his father and mother died, and he was left an orphan when a very small child and was reared in Pittsboro, N. C., in the home of his grandfather Dismukes. He learned but little from his books, but was taught to work, and thanks to his inborn will-power and energy has made a success. In 1834, when twenty years of age, he came to Georgia and settled in Carroll county. The following fall he located where he now lives, where for many miles around the clearings were few and far between. He came to Georgia with a horse and a pair of saddle-bags; now he has 1,800 acres of good land lying on the Chattahoochee river, on which he has one of the most productive and best improved farms in all that section, and ranks as one of the most substantial and reliable citizens, as well as one of the best farmers in Carroll county. During the war a small battle was fought on his farm, during which shot and shell flew thick and fast all about. All the windows in his house were shattered, and there remains a hole in the wall of his house where one shell, coming into a window, passed out on the opposite side. Fortunately no one about the premises was hurt. Mr. Moore has owned a ferry across the Chattahoochee river at this place from the time he first settled there. On one occasion he was getting some parties across the river who were fleeing before the Federal army, among them Mr. William Amos, when the skirmish began. Before the boat reached the opposite shore the troops reached the river and fired upon the passengers. Mr. Amos fell by his side, but he stood by them and the boat, and at the risk of his own life saved them. In 1837 Mr. Moore was married to Mrs. Caroline (nee Martin) Malone, daughter of Benjamin Martin, of Jones county, granddaughter of Mr. Lester, of the same county. Mr. and Mrs. Moore were the parents of seven children, five of whom are living: Mrs. W. A. Parks; Mrs. Robert Early; Mrs. W. W. Kelly; George W., deceased; James D., Jr.; Dr. John F., deceased, and Benjamin F. The two surviving sons, J. D. and B. F. Moore, are hardware merchants of the Moore & Handley Hardware company, Birmingham, Ala.

Source: *Memoirs of Georgia*, 1895. Volume 1.

JAMES P. MOORE

James P. Moore, capitalist, Carrollton, Carroll Co., Ga., son of John and Levisa (Petty) Moore, was born in Spartanburg district, S. C., in 1839. His paternal grandparents, Hugh and Elizabeth (Thomas) Moore, were natives of South Carolina. His grandfather was a soldier in the revolutionary war and his grandson – the subject of this sketch,

JAMES P. MOORE

is "a chip of the old block" – has the musket he "toted" all through that memorable struggle. His maternal grandfather, Charles Petty, was also a soldier in the patriot army. Mr. Moore was reared in South Carolina and received a limited education, and when a mere child had to walk three miles daily to obtain it. April 1, 1861, he enlisted in Company H (Capt. Joe Walker), Fifth South Carolina regiment (Col. Jenkins), which was assigned to the command of Gen. Beauregard. He served in this company nearly a year, when another company was formed known as the First Palmetto Sharpshooters, which caused some changes, and in the reorganization of Company H Mr. Moore was made captain, which he continued to be until the surrender. He was present at the firing on Fort Sumter. When it fell he went to Virginia, and beginning with First Manassas, participated in many of the bloodiest and most fiercely contested battles during the entire war – including every battle in which Jenkins' brigade was engaged. That he was in the foremost on every battlefield it is needless to say, for with a double strain of revolutionary blood in his veins, and South Carolina blood at that, nothing else could be expected. It has been stated above that he had in his possession the musket which his Grandfather Moore carried during the war for independence. The following incident will show why he should be doubly proud of it – first, its family and historic interest; second, the circumstances attending its retention. After the war, in pursuance of a military order, the union soldiers proceeded to gather up all the arms in private hands in the south. When this old musket was demanded Mr. Moore refused to give it up, and when the soldiers attempted to take it by force he foiled them and made his escape with it. It is asserted that many a Federal soldier "bit the dust" in after attempts to capture him, and on roll call was reported "missing." Although he escaped capture, the continual danger he was in determined him to leave the state; so, in 1873, he came to Georgia and settled in Carroll county. He was brick-mason, and worked at his trade, but he has done so well and managed and invested his gains so judiciously that he now ranks as one of the moneyed men of the county. In 1867 Mr. Moore was married to Miss Honora Elkin, daughter of Elbert and Mary Elkin. Mr. Moore stands well in Carroll county and is very much esteemed by all privileged with his intimate friendship.

Source: *Memoirs of Georgia*, 1895. Volume 1.

C. C. MORRIS

C. C. Morris, farmer, Bowdon, Carroll Co., Ga., son of J. L. and Elizabeth (Almond) Morris, was born in Carroll county in 1856. His paternal grandparents, William and Hannah (Biggars) Morris, were natives of South Carolina, came to Georgia early in this century, and settled in what is now De Kalb county. He was a farmer, and, also, a Missionary Baptist minister and preached in the old log churches. He was a soldier in the revolutionary army. Mr. Morris' father was born in De Kalb county in 1826, and was a farmer. He enlisted in 1861, was a lieutenant in his company and remained in the army through the conflict. His maternal grandparents, Asbern and Jane (Biggars) Almond, were early settlers, and the grandfather was a revolutionary soldier. Mr. Morris was reared on a farm in Carroll county, and received a fair common school education. Adopting farming as a pursuit, but without means, he acquired a good farm, and is among those at the head of the list as progressive farmers, manages well, is much esteemed and is prosperous. He has a tract of more than 200 acres of choice land, productive, with good improvements. In 1882 Mr. Morris married Miss Rebecca Lovvorn, daughter of W. D. Lovvorn, an old and influential settler, who has borne him six children: Eva, Mattie, Joseph and Otto, living; and Lillian and Anna, deceased. Himself and wife are members of the Baptist church.

Sources: *Memoirs of Georgia*, 1895. Volume 1.

H. L. MORROW

H. L. Morrow, farmer and miller, Whitesburg, Carroll Co., Ga., son of William H. and Nancy (Elliott) Morrow, was born in Newton county, Ga., March 15, 1823. His grandparents on his father's side, Robert and Nancy (Herly) Morrow, were Virginians, and came to Georgia in 1795. His grandfather was a soldier in the revolutionary war. His grandparents on his mother's side, George and Mary (Cloud) Elliott, were natives of Virginia, and the grandfather was a soldier in the patriot army during the revolutionary war. Mrs. Morrow's grand-uncle, Zeke Cloud, joined the patriot army when but fourteen years of age, and remained with it until independence was achieved. Mr. Morrow's father was born May 12, 1788, in what is now Morgan county, Ga., and his mother was born Dec. 12, 1790, in what is now Jasper county, Ga. He was a soldier in the war of 1812, in which he served as

H. L. MORROW

quartermaster. He also served as sheriff of Newton county for many years. Mr. Morrow was reared in Newton county until he was twelve years old, when the family moved to Henry county. His father died when he was only seventeen months old, and from that time until he became of age he had a hard time of it. When he first went to school it was under an old tent, then in the old-time dirt floor log school house, with puncheon seats and stick and mud chimney, etc. But such was the necessity for work to help his widowed mother that he received very little schooling – he couldn't be spared from the field. In 1863, he enlisted in Company E (Capt. Mann), Seventh Georgia regiment, was at one time acting lieutenant, and most of the time was on guard duty in and around Atlanta. Mr. Morrow was married Dec. 17, 1844, to Miss Mary A. Gilbert – born in Henry county, Ga., Nov. 15, 1826 – daughter of Matthew and Tabitha (Mathews) Gilbert, North Carolinians, who came to Georgia, and settled in the woods in Henry county in 1820. Eleven children have blessed this union, of whom eight are now living: James R., born Sept. 12, 1845; Jane T., Jan. 19, 1847; Zachary T., Feb. 19, 1849; Nancy T., Dec. 3, 1850; Polly Ann, Feb. 4, 1853; William D., Jan. 30, 1855; Millard F., Dec. 25, 1856; Mary J., Dec. 24, 1859; Lizzie O., Sept. 12, 1862; Roberta L., June 7, 1865; Joe J., July 30, 1870. When he was married he had nothing but good health and habits, a robust constitution and sturdy manhood trained to labor and self-reliance. The first year after his marriage he rented land, afterward bought some land and settled on it. In 1848 he commenced milling in a small way, and as he prospered added more and improved machinery. It is, however, what is known as a "custom mill," grinding for toll, and makes meal and flour as good as the best. Mr. Morrow has a splendid mill property on a well-improved and productive 800-acre plantation, besides a pleasant residence and "home place" in Whitesburg. His success is a striking and instructive illustration of what is possible in Georgia, with industry, economy and integrity, when coupled with a determined will. Though not a millionaire in the popular sense he is wealthy, as are many thousands just like him, beyond computation. No citizen of Carroll county is more highly esteemed. Fifty years a master Mason he has exemplified its teachings in his life. Himself and wife are members of the United Congregational church.

Source: *Memoirs of Georgia*, 1895. Volume 1.

G. W. C. MUNRO

G. W. C. Munro, planter, Putnam, Marion Co., Ga., son of Edward and Harriett (De Lespire) Munro, was born in 1825, on Danfuski island, S. C. His paternal grandparents, Edward and Ann Munro, natives of Scotland, on coming to America, settled in Nova Scotia, and afterward in New Jersey. On attaining manhood, Edward Munro, the father, left his birthplace, Newark, N. J., for the Bahama islands, where he married Harriett De Lespire, of Charleston, S. C. The family lived some years on the Bahama islands; then on Danfuski island, S. C.; a short time in Savannah, Ga.; then in Twiggs county, and finally settled in Dooly county, Ga. The maternal grandfather, Dr. Joseph De Lespire, was a native of France, and the maternal grandmother was a native of England. Dr. Jospeh De Lespire, a surgeon in the French army, who came to America with the French admiral, Count d'Estaing. At the close of the revolutionary war he settled in Charleston, where he practiced his profession during the remainder of his life. G. W. C. Munro was reared on a plantation, and received a good common school education. Conducting and supervising his planting interests has been the occupation of his life. Since 1857 he has lived at his present home in Marion county. In 1863 he enlisted in Company G of the Twenty-ninth Georgia battalion, in which he served until the close of the war. In 1855 he married Martha A. Stevens, daughter of Hampton and Attalissa (Sparks) Stevens, of Marion county, Ga. The children of G. W. C. Munro are: Ida Munro, Mrs. Ola M. Evans, Mrs. Mattie M. Simpson, George P. Munro, Dr. Henry S. Munro and Horace N. Munro.

Source: *Memoirs of Georgia*, 1895. Volume 2.

Note: The George P. Munro mentioned in this sketch was the father of Martha Munro, wife of Irvine Sullivan Ingram, and Ida Munro, wife of James C. Bonner. The Munros never resided in Carroll County, but George P. Munro was chairman of the Board of Trustees of the Fourth District A&M School at its creation and acting on behalf of the trustees and the state of Georgia signed the deed for the purchase of the original tract of property on which the University of West Georgia now stands.

M. E. MURPHEY

M. E. Murphey, farmer, Carrollton, Carroll Co., Ga., son of William and Martha (Murphey) Murphey, was born in Talbot county, Ga., in 1827. His father was born in South Carolina, in 1798, came to

Georgia when a young man on pack horses, and settled in the woods in Wilkes county, where he cleared a farm. A few years afterward he removed to Talbot county, and thence to Sumter county, in 1836. He was a soldier in the Indian war of that date, and lived to be seventy-six years of age. Mr. Murphey's mother was a Murphey, who first married James Willis, who died, and then she married Mr. Murphey. M. E. Murphey was reared in Sumter county and educated in the historic dirt floor log school house, split log seats and mud and dirt chimney, etc., and walked three miles, generally barefooted, to school. In 1861, he enlisted in what was known as the "Nelson Rangers," under Capt. Nelson, who was killed at Tupelo, Miss., and was succeeded by Capt. Ragland. He experienced some very hard and trying service, and was engaged in many very hot skirmishes, but although he kept in the field until the war ended, he escaped both wounds and capture. When he came out of the war all he had, he says, "was a spell of chills and fever and a horse." He first went to Coweta county and went to work on a farm with a vim, and remained there until 1883, when he moved into Carroll county, where he now owns a 600-acre well-improved farm, a beautiful home in Carrollton, and "cash in advance." Mr. Murphey was married in 1860 to Miss Sarah Kampson – born in South Carolina – daughter of Peter and Mary (Long) Kampson, natives of South Carolina who came to Georgia from that state in 1844. This union has been blessed with six children: Peter, Beulah, Jeffy, Katie, William J. and Lizzie. Mrs. Murphey, who was a member of the Lutheran church, died in 1892.

Source: *Memoirs of Georgia*, 1895. Volume 1.

JOHN M. MUSE

Rev. J. M. Muse was born in Wilkes county, Georgia, October 16th, 1818. His parents died during his infancy, and he was reared by his grandmother, Elizabeth, and his step-grandfather, Daniel Stalker. Little interest being manifested on the subject of education in his early life, he was largely deprived of its advantages; going to school only a few years, and only from one to three months each year. As he grew toward manhood, however, his thirst for knowledge increased, and he became a great reader. From his youth, the Bible has been his most frequent companion in hours of study, and now he is willing to endorse other religious works just so far as they are in accordance with it, and no farther. In his boyhood his mind was profoundly im-

pressed on the subject of religion during a prayer offered up in Scotch brogue by his grandfather, one night when his grandmother was absent from home. There were but those two present, and yet, as usual, they knelt at the family altar. The old man after praying for his companion and himself, prayed for the stripling, simply, fervently, asking that he might be kept from the temptations of youth, made a true follower of Christ, and put into the ministry of reconciliation.

At the age of nineteen he was baptized by Rev. P. Matthews, at Friendship church, Wilkes county. He removed, in 1852, to Carroll county, joined the church at Carrollton, and was a constituent member of Bethel church at its organization. In 1855 he was made a deacon and was licensed to preach. He was ordained, January, 1858, by Revs. J. Reeves, T. Burke and J. Riggs, and took charge of Macedonia church, which he served continuously for twenty years, except one year spent in the army as missionary of the Tallapoosa Association. He has served other churches in Carroll and adjacent counties, with great success, baptizing as many as 165 persons in one church, as in the army he baptized over 200 soldiers. For five years he has been constrained, by feeble health, to restrict his labors, and is pastor at present only of Ephesus church, Douglas county. He was elected Moderator of Tallapoosa Association in 1865, and filled the chair for nine years, and, on the constitution of Carrollton Association, in 1874, held the same position in it for two years. During all this time there was but a single appeal from his decision, and in that case he was overwhelmingly sustained by the body.

He has been twice married, first, to Miss Martha E. Howard, and afterward to Miss Cynthia J. Turner, both of Wilkes county, and has eleven living children. He is strictly speaking, a doctrinal preacher, recognizing God as the author of all good, this good as wrought according to His own eternal purpose, and this purpose as displayed in keeping His chosen ones, by *His* power, through faith, unto salvation. He is widely known as a Landmark Baptist, and endeavors to practice what he preaches.

Source: *History of the Baptist Denomination in Georgia,* 1881.

J. T. MUSICK

J. T. Musick, M. D., Pittsburgh, Camp county, Texas, was born in Chambers county, Alabama, September 23, 1846, a son of George W. and Margaret E. (Christian) Musick, the former a native of Tennessee, and the latter of Edgefield district, South Carolina, and a daughter of Thomas E. Christian. In 1852 they moved to Texas and settled in Upshur county, and became well-to-do farmers, making this their home the rest of their lives. The father died in 1883, and the mother in 1886. They had a family of ten children – J. T., Louis S., Dr. G. F., Dr. Jas. A., George W., William R., Dixie Young, Walter J., Edgar and Leta.

J. T. Musick was six years old when his parents moved to Texas, and was reared and educated at Gilmer, Upshur county. When a young man he chose the profession of medicine as his life work and began its study, and in 1869 graduated from the Medical University of New Orleans. He has been a successful practitioner for twenty years, and in 1889 took a post-graduate course in the New York Polyclinic College. Dr. Musick is a close student of his profession, is a hard worker, and has been a popular physician wherever he has made his residence. He is well thought of in the medical fraternity, and has many friends who value his friendship aside from the fact of his being a successful physician. The doctor was married January 2, 1870, to Miss S. C. Willis, daughter of Owen J. Willis, of Barnesville, Georgia. He is a member of the State Medical Association, and vice-president of the Northeast Texas Medical Association.

Source: *Biographical Souvenir of the State of Texas*, 1889.

Note: J. T. Musick was the grandson of Jonathan Musick, who resided in Carroll County in 1830 and in Chambers County, Alabama in 1840. See 1830 and 1840 Censuses.

JOSEPH J. NIXON

Joseph J. Nixon, planter, Palmetto, Campbell county, Ga., is the son of Francis and Anna (Ray) Nixon, and was born in Meriwether county, Ga., Oct. 12, 1839. The grandfather of this gentleman, Joseph Nixon, was a native of Ireland, and came to Georgia a young man in the latter part of the last century, settling in Oglethorpe county, where he married. He subsequently moved to Walton county, thence to Coweta, where he lived till his death, which occurred in 1830. The father of Mr. Nixon was reared in Coweta county, but was married in Meriwether county, where he lived until 1853, when he settled in the southern part of Campbell county, near where his son now lives. In

1872 he moved to Heard county, where he died in 1881. In disposition he was a quiet, retired man, a member of the Baptist church, a planter by occupation. He was twice married. Of the six children born to the first marriage, five are living: Joseph J., the subject of this sketch; Martha J., widow of M. M. Smith, Campbell county; Rebecca, wife of J. M. Windom, Carroll county; George, Cass county, Tex.; Wiley, Coweta county, and Thomas, who was a private in Company C, Nineteenth Georgia regiment, was killed at second Manassas. The mother died in 1852 and the father subsequently married Miss Ann Grantham of Meriwether county, who bore him eight children. Joseph J. Nixon was reared in the neighborhood where he now lives. At the opening of the war he was just of age and ready to serve his country. He enlisted as a private in Company C, Nineteenth Georgia regiment, and served in the army of Virginia. He was engaged in the battles of Seven Pines, seven days' fight around Richmond, Fredericksburg, Chancellorsville, Kingston and Bentonville. N. C., the last battle of the war. In the latter fight he was slightly wounded, having gone through the entire war up to that time without a scratch. He was paroled at Salisbury, N. C., after which he settled down to the peaceful pursuit of farming. With nothing to invest except his own strength and perseverance, he rented land near the old homestead till 1873, when he bought 200 acres of the present location, to which have been added about 400 acres more. This plantation is three miles from Palmetto, and was nearly all covered with a dense growth of oak, pine and hickory. Mr. Nixon has cleared this land nearly all himself, and now has about 300 acres under cultivation. He married Miss Louisa M., daughter of John B. and Temperance Smith, Sept. 3, 1869, and has become the father of ten children, seven of whom are living: Moses, planter, Campbell county; Osey, John B., Arena, Thomas J., William and Millie at home. Mr. Nixon enjoys the reputation of being an excellent farmer and is a man whom the people revere for his many noble qualities of head and heart. As a democrat he does his duty quietly at the polls, not having any taste for the excitement of political life. He and his family are members of the Baptist church.

Source: *Memoirs of Georgia*, 1895. Volume 1.

WILEY NIXON

Wiley Nixon, farmer, Mandeville, Carroll Co., Ga., son of Joe and Martha (Ward) Nixon, was born in Oglethorpe county, Ga., Sept. 15, 1816. His father was born in what is now Wilkes county, Ga., about 1775. (This territory was acquired from the Indians in 1773 and Wilkes county was laid out in 1777.) He was bound out when a boy and learned the carpenter's trade; when older engaged in farming also, and was a soldier in the war of 1812. He moved to Coweta county in 1830, settled in the woods and lived in a dirt floor log cabin. Mr. Nixon's maternal grandparents, Sam and Eda (Hudson) Ward, were among the early settlers of that part of Georgia. Mr. Nixon grew to manhood on the farm and attended school at the historic log schoolhouse. The first house he lived in the boards were fastened on with wooden pins. He came to Coweta county with his father and lived in that county until 1874, when he moved and settled on a partly-cleared farm in Carroll county, afterward clearing what he wanted. He began life very poor, has worked hard on the farm all his life, and although not rich he has a competency and is rich in the possession of sincere friends, and the consciousness of a well-spent life. He owns 600 acres of good land, a farm well-improved and a good home in which to spend his declining years. Mr. Nixon was married to Miss Elizabeth Fullenlove (born in Coweta county), daughter of Lud and Alsa (Freeman) Fullenlove. To them nine children have been born: Weldin I., J. Page, Fannie, Rebecca, Meda, Ludwell, Nanna, William and Ada. Mr. Nixon has been a member of the masonic fraternity more than forty years, and is regarded as one of the most substantial, and is among the most respected of the county's citizens.

Source: *Memoirs of Georgia*, 1895. Volume 1.

JAMES P. M. NORMAN

James P. M. Norman. One of the most popular and widely known of Douglas County's county officers is James P. M. Norman, who has been identified with the growth and the interests of the county for many years. Mr. Norman was born in Carroll County, Ga., April 27, 1847, and is a son of Abner S. and Charlotte (Orr) Norman, natives respectively of Alabama and South Carolina. George Norman, grandfather of our subject, came from Scotland to this country, and brought with him the sturdy habits so characteristic of those of that nationality. Settling in Alabama, he there reared his family, and after a long and useful life passed to that bourne from whence no traveler returns. Abner S. Norman came to Douglas County, Mo., in 1863, and the following year was killed by bushwhackers near Yellville, Ark. He was with the army, but was not a soldier. Mrs. Norman died in 1881. Both were worthy members of the Methodist Episcopal Church South. The father and mother had emigrated from Georgia to Arkansas, and settled in what is now Baxter county in 1853. In 1863 they came to this county, as above stated, being obliged to leave Arkansas on account of sympathizing with the Union. There was a family of eleven children born to this worthy couple: Nancy C.; Sarah A., deceased, was the wife of W. J. Cooley, of Arkansas; George L., lost his life in the late war, dying in 1863; William C. died in the army in 1862; Abner J. was a soldier in the same regiment, and was killed by accident at the close of the war; Eliza V. is the wife of Jacob A. Sagerser, a farmer of this county; James P. M. (subject); Mary J., wife of John Hickman, of Baxter County, Ark.; Robert F. is engaged in the lumber business in Greene County, Mo.; Jason F., a merchant, of Romance; and Charlotte A., the wife of Taylor Lutts, of Howell County, Mo. The father was at one time a Whig, but later he espoused the principles of the Republican party. He was well and favorably known in the county, and while a resident of Arkansas held the office of justice of the peace. He was one of the good old pioneers, so many of whom have passed away, and was a noted deer hunter. The early life of our subject was passed on a farm, and his early or rudimentary education was received in the common schools of the county. Later he attended school in Christian county, and after reaching his twenty-first year entered the Mountain Home College, where he remained for three years. In 1869 he came to Douglas county, and for eleven years followed teaching in that and other counties. As a successful and thorough educator he became well known, and followed that profession until 1878 or 1879. Early in life he began farming, and carried this on in connection with school teaching. He now resides near Arden, and has a farm of 167 acres, besides 40 acres near Ava, eighty acres in Webster County, and a third interest in eighty acres of mining lands in this county. Mr. Norman has been unusually successful as an agriculturalist and stockman, and is one of the leading farmers of the county. He is with the Populist party, and in 1880 was elected to the office of county assessor, to which position he was reelected in 1882. In the year 1890 he was elec-

JAMES P. M. NORMAN

ted to the office of county collector of Douglas County, and while discharging the duties of this office made his home in Ava. He is a member of the Methodist Episcopal Church, and is a Mason, a member of Ava Lodge. Mr. Norman was married first in 1869 to Miss Mary F. Ellison, daughter of A. M. and Frances Ellison, of this county. The father is deceased, but the mother is still living. Mrs. Norman was born in 1846, in Webster County, and died in 1886, leaving four children: Lucy J., wife of William E. Banks; Minnie B. is a prominent teacher; Ada F. married Fred J. Hartin, of Dallas, Tex.; and Robert M. Mr. Norman's second marriage was with Miss Mary O. Carrick, daughter of James and Ruth (Skein) Carrick, who came to this country at an early day, and are now living near Cedar Gap, Webster County. Mr. and Mrs. Norman have three children: Homer J., Clyde E., and Quincy E. Mr. Norman has a fine farm, and is one of the most successful tillers of the soil in the county. He is a leading man in his section, and not only takes a deep interest in educational matters, but in all other worthy enterprises.

Source: *A Reminiscent History of the Ozark Region*, 1894.

JASON F. NORMAN

Jason F. Norman. Special adaptability to any particular calling in life is the one necessary adjunct to success of a permanent kind. No matter what the vim and determination characterizing a man's start in business, unless he is to the manner born, he will find to his sorrow that his line has been falsely cast, and the quicker he draws aside and takes up another, the better it will be for him. It has often been the case that a man will make a success of several different occupations, and this has been the experience of Jason F. Norman, who is not only engaged in general merchandising, but also in job printing and bookbinding at Romance, Mo. He was born in Fulton County, Ark., in 1854, a son of Abner S. and Charlotte (Orr) Norman, the former of whom was born in Georgia in 1811, and the latter in South Carolina in 1815, their marriage occurring in the former State in 1834. Their first removal was to Arkansas about 1852, and after a short residence in Conway County they removed to Fulton County in 1862, and later to Douglas County, Mo. April 9, 1864, Mr. Norman was killed in Marion County, Ark., while with the Federal Army, but of which he was not a member, being a cripple. He was a farmer and school teacher, was a justice of the peace for many years in different counties, and led an active, industrious and honest life. He was a recognized leader in social and business circles, took an active interest in all public matters, and he was ever a loyal citizen of the United States. His father, George Norman, is supposed to have been a native of Georgia, in which State he spent his entire life, dying when Abner was a lad. He was of French extraction. His eldest son, Charles, was a prominent lawyer and died in Alabama, when about ninety years of age. The maternal grandfather, Lodowick Orr, was of English and Scotch ancestry and by occupation was a Methodist minister and a school teacher. He was finely educated, was a man of much force of character, and was a leader in all enterprises pertaining to the advancement of the section in which he resided. His wife, Nancy Orr, died in Alabama. The mother of the subject of this sketch died in Polk County, Mo., in 1880, having been a member of the Methodist Church since 1822. She became the mother of eleven children: George L., who died at Ozark, Mo.; William Clark, who died at Rome, Mo.; Abner J., who was killed at Ozark, Mo., near the close of the war, having been a Federal soldier throughout the struggle; J. P. M., a teacher and farmer of Ava, Mo., was at one time the tax collector of Douglas County, and also served two terms as tax assessor; Robert F., who has been engaged in farming and teaching, is at present a lumber dealer at Republic, Mo.; Jason F.; Nancy C. (Clements) of Cincinnati, Ark.; Sarah A., who died in 1865, the wife of William Cooley; Eliza V., wife of J. A. Sagerser of John's Mills, Mo.; Mary J., wife of John Hickman of Mt. Home, Ark.; and C. Ann, wife of Taylor Lutts of Pottersville, Mo. Jason F. Norman made his home with his mother until he reached man's estate, and received the principal part of his literary education at Mt. Home, Ark., after which he was engaged in teaching in Missouri and Arkansas for some ten years. In 1879 he was married in Ozark County, Mo., to Sallie C., daughter of Barton and Mary J. Barnett, whose entire lives were spent in their native State of Tennessee. Mrs. Norman came to Missouri with her grandfather McGee, and here met and married Mr. Norman, by whom she has one daughter, Daisy. In 1880 Mr. Norman located in Romance and engaged in general merchandising, in which he has since done a prosperous business. He handles cotton and produce, and also does a binding and job printing business, which he has found to be profitable. He is a member of the Methodist Church, is an active worker in the Sunday-school, and is now president of the Ozark County Sunday-school Association. The first church that was ever dedicated in Ozark County was built on his land at Romance at a cost of $650, nearly half of which Mr. Norman gave. He has always been a staunch Republican in politics, and cast his first presidential vote for Hayes in 1876. In August, 1894, he removed to Seymour, Mo., and established a job printing office and bindery, having leased his mercantile business at Romance to another party, who continues there.

Source: *A Reminiscent History of the Ozark Region*, 1894.

Note: Jason F. Norman is a brother of James P. M. Norman, subject of the previous sketch. His brother was born in Carroll County, Georgia in 1847, but Jason was born in Arkansas in 1854 shortly after the family's removal to that state.

WILLIAM T. OGLETREE

William T. Ogletree, farmer, Carrollton, Carroll Co., Ga., son of Absalom and Matilda (Stewart) Ogletree, was born in Monroe county, Ga., in 1834. His paternal grandparents were William and Martha (Bird) Ogletree. His grandfather was born in Virginia in 1764, and came to Georgia and settled in Wilkes county about 1784, and was married in 1785. When he came to the county it was a wooded wilderness, and he suffered all the trials, hardships and privations incident to pioneer life. He was the Daniel Boone of Wilkes county. Mr. Ogletree's father was born in Wilkes county in 1811, where he was reared on a farm, but at the age of twenty he entered the ministry and continued in it through life. His mother was born in Oglethorpe county, Ga., and was the daughter of Thomas and Nancy (Russell) Stewart, early settlers of the county. Her father was a farmer and lived to a good old age. Mr. Ogletree's mother, eighty years old, is still living. Mr. Ogletree was reared on the farm in Oglethorpe county and received a good common-school education in Monroe county, Ga. After receiving his education he taught school awhile. In 1861 he enlisted in Company F (Capt. D. J. Bailey, afterward Capt. Andrews, Capt. Bailey having been elected colonel), Thirtieth Georgia regiment, which was assigned to Gen. Mercer's command. He participated in some of the most hotly-contested battles of the conflict. Among them: Jackson, Miss., and Chickamauga, where his brigade opened the fight; Lookout Mountain, Missionary Ridge, Resaca, New Hope church and in nearly every engagement from Resaca to Atlanta. He was wounded at Peachtree creek, Atlanta, which compelled him to retire for two months. On his recovery he hastened to rejoin his command with which he remained until Dec. 16, 1864, when he was captured at Nashville and sent to Johnson's Island and held until the close of the war. On his release he came to Spalding county, Ga., where he remained until 1881, when he removed to Carroll county and settled where he now lives. He had to begin anew after the war, and in the battle of life has been as courageous and true as he was on the tented field, and has done well. Mr. Ogletree was married in 1859 to Miss Cordelia Colbert (born in Spalding county), daughter of Albert G. Colbert, descendant from the early emigrants from Ireland to this country. One child only, Wilbur S., has blessed this union. Mr. Ogletree is a member of the Christian church, and his wife is a member of the Methodist church. While living in Spalding county before the war he served as a justice of the peace. Mr. Ogletree is one of Carroll's most substantial, as well as one of its most highly esteemed citizens, to whom his neighbors are attached because of his kindly nature.

Sources: *Memoirs of Georgia*, 1895. Volume 1.

GEORGE A. OWEN

George A. Owen, farmer and miller, Dallas, Paulding Co., Ga., son of Arnold and Polly (Brown) Owen, was born near Providence, R. I., in 1822. His paternal grandfather, Thomas Owen, was a soldier in the patriot army during the revolutionary war. Mr. Owen's father was born in Rhode Island in 1797, was a successful farmer, and died in his native state in 1878. His mother was born in 1802, daughter of Esic Brown, her father also being a revolutionary soldier. She died in her seventy-sixth year. Mr. Owen was reared on his father's farm and received a good English education in the common schools of the state. After leaving school he served a four years' apprenticeship with a millwright, and in 1848 came to Georgia to work at his trade. He finally permanently established himself in Paulding county, and engaged in farming and milling, succeeding at both. Being a miller he was exempt from military service during the war, but was compelled to grind the tithes exacted from the farmers for the support of the soldiers in the Confederate army. During the war his house was made headquarters for Gen. Veach, of Illinois, of the Union army, and his houses and mills were spared, but his five slaves, his stock and crops were run off or destroyed. He has been a successful farmer and miller and has placed himself in comfortable circumstances. In 1882 he was elected judge of the probate court of the county, and served one term. Mr. Owen was married in 1862 to Miss Nancy, daughter of Bailey and Nancy (Evans) Bone. Of six children, the fruit of this union, four are living: Mrs. Mollie Williams; Nellie G., single; Felton and Benjamin A.

Source: *Memoirs of Georgia*, 1895. Volume 2.

Note: Bailey Bone was residing in District 642 of Carroll County, Georgia in 1840. See 1840 Census.

HENRY G. PARKER

Henry G. Parker, farmer, Mamdeville, Carroll Co., Ga., son of John and Margaret (Byrum) Parker, was born in Pike county, Ga., in 1841. His paternal grandfather, Enoch Parker, came from North Carolina to Georgia in 1795, and settled in the woods in Lincoln county, where his father was born in 1800. His maternal grandfather, Beverly Byrum, was a native of North Carolina, came from there to Georgia in an ox-cart early in this century, and cleared himself a farm and a home in the virgin forest. Mr. Parker was reared in Pike county, worked on the farm, and went to school only four days. In 1862, he enlisted in Company H (Capt. Redman), Forty-fourth Georgia regiment, and remained in the service until May, 1863. He was in two hard fought battles – Gainesville and Sharpsburg, in which last his company had twenty-six killed. He lost his right leg, and being thereby disabled for further service, came home. He went to Coweta county and lived there and farmed until 1875, when he removed to Carroll county and bought a nice 300-acre farm, which he has paid for and so improved as to make him a comfortable home. He came out of the war a very poor and a disabled man, yet has secured a good home by his own industry and economy, and reared a not small family of children. Mr. Parker was married in 1868 to Miss Sarah Cannon – born in Pike county –

daughter of George and Mary (Elliott) Cannon, who were among the early settlers of Pike county. This union has been blessed with eight children: Jennie, Mary, Henry S., George, Lizzie, Ella, Harriet and Leila. Mrs. Parker is a member of the Protestant Methodist church, and Mr. Parker is worthily held in esteem by the community in which he lives.

Source: *Memoirs of Georgia*, 1895. Volume 1.

TRUSTIN PHILLIPS

This aged servant of God, living in the vicinity of Jonesboro, was born April 1st, 1804, in Darlington district, South Carolina. His mother dying when he was an infant, he was reared by a kind stepmother. He was the youngest of twelve children, three of whom were ministers, and lived to a good old age preaching "the glorious Gospel of the blessed God." His opportunities for receiving an education were poor, having gone to school only a few weeks; but by close application at a pine-knot fire by night, when the labors of the day were over, he greatly improved himself. He was a moral young man, and always shunned bad company. He was married in 1823 to Miss Piety Parnal, of Newton county, and reared four children, all of whom were Baptists, and one, now deceased, a licensed preacher.

Rev. Trustin Phillips was converted in 1826, and baptized in 1827, by Rev. Benjamin Wilson, at Liberty church, Newton county. He was called to ordination by that church, and ordained at Long Shoal church, October 12th, 1838. He has been pastor of the following churches: Liberty, Long Shoal, Zion, New Bethel and Rockdale, in Newton county; Liberty and Salem, in Henry; Tanner's, Mt. Zion and Forest Grove, in Clayton; Flat Creek, Fayetteville, Antioch, White Water and Salem, in Fayette; Bethlehem, Holly Spring, New Hope and Sardis, in Coweta; Bethsaida and Deep Creek, in Campbell; Yellow Dirt, Central Hatchie, Pleasant Hill, Enon and Franklin, in Heard; and Mt. Zion and Bethesda, in Carroll.

He is a man of studious habits, and a constant and appreciative reader of good books. He has been very successful as a pastor, punctual to all his appointments, and prompt in all business engagements. He is a good, faithful preacher, of fair common abilities as a speaker, has a strong, clear voice, and is powerful in exhortation at the close of his sermons. He has been, and is yet, a splendid singer, and was chosen as chorister soon after he joined the church. He is a warm friend of the temperance cause, strongly advocating it in the pulpit, and practicing what he preaches. He has always opposed the use of tobacco. His discipline in his family is firm, and he urges the necessity of it in the churches. His wife is a devotedly pious woman, and has been a strong helper to him in his ministerial labors. Although his remuneration has been small, she has always said, "Go, and I will take care of the stuff." She has greatly aided him in raising missionary funds.

He and Rev. C. D. Mallary and Rev. J. S. Callaway were the presbytery that constituted the Stone Mountain Association, October, 1839. He has also aided in the constitution of a goodly number of churches in the region over which his labors were extended. He is of medium height, heavily built, with fair complexion, enjoys good health, and having a good constitution and being of temperate habits, is likely to live many years longer. He is firm in his convictions of right, and yet social and agreeable in his intercourse with his fellow-men. He is a man of unblemished character, and an honor to his friends and to the cause of his Master.

Source: *History of the Baptist Denomination in Georgia*, 1881.

RICHARD PHILPOT

Richard Philpot, farmer, Cedartown, Polk Co., Ga., son of William and Elizabeth (York) Philpot, was born in Carroll county, Ga., Nov. 15, 1827. His parents, who had some means, not large, migrated from Tennessee to Georgia and settled in Paulding county, making the trip in wagons drawn by oxen. His father died in Paulding county in 1844, and his mother in 1850. Mr. Philpot's educational advantages were very limited, and what schooling he had was obtained in the old-time dirt floor log school house, with puncheon seats, etc. When the late war was precipitated he enlisted in the Confederate service, but after a few months' experience provided a substitute and was released. Starting with nothing after the war, he has acquired a fine estate, a competency, is a progressive and prosperous farmer, and is a most highly esteemed citizen. Mr. Philpot was married in 1859 to Miss Elizabeth, daughter of John and Sarah Blackburn, of Haralson county, Ga., and to them fourteen children have been born: Alexander B., Charles C., Mary, William, Joseph H., Augustus V., Minerva, Elizabeth, Fannie, Annie, David, Thomas, Seaborn and Jasper. His wife, born in 1844, died in 1888. He is an exemplary member of the Baptist church.

Source: *Memoirs of Georgia*, 1895. Volume 2.

Note: Benjamin McFarland Long, whom tradition says was the first white child born in Carroll County, was born on November 5, 1827, ten days before Richard Philpot.

W. H. POOLE

W. H. Poole, physician and surgeon, Douglasville, Douglas Co., Ga., son of T. J. and Sarah (Brown) Poole, was born in South Carolina in 1833. His grandfather, Benjamin Poole, of English lineage, was born in South Carolina in 1780, served as a soldier in the last war with Great Britain in 1812, in the Seminole war of 1836, and died in 1850. Dr. Poole's father was born in South Carolina in 1810, was raised a farmer in that state, whence he migrated to Georgia, making the trip in ox-carts, and settled in Carroll county. He farmed in that county until 1850, when he moved to Cass (now Bartow) county, where he engaged in mining. From there he went to Iron Mountain, Ala., and thence to the famous Shelby mines, in the same state. He pursued his mining operations there until about 1870, when he returned to his old home in Georgia. There he conducted a farm until 1874, when he was killed by his horse running away. Dr. Poole's mother, daughter of William Brown, who distinguished himself in the war of 1812, and in the Indian war of 1836, was born in South Carolina in 1812. She was married in 1832 and is still living. Dr. Poole was raised on the farm and received his primary education at the near by country schools, and when eighteen years old was sent to Hiwassee college. After being there three and a half years he had to leave on account of failing health, and did not graduate. A short time after that he began the study of medicine in the office of Dr. M. F. La Dell, an eminent physician of Cedartown, Ga., under whose instruction he remained two years. He then entered the Savannah Medical college – well known at the time as the "Old Arnold School" – where he remained two years, serving one year as interne in the Marine hospital. He graduated in 1860 with the first honors of his class. His graduating thesis – subject,

W. H. POOLE

"Modus Operandi of Medicines" – was published in the medical journals of the day and attracted the attention of the profession. During the war he was an examining surgeon for the Confederate army. Soon after the surrender he located near the present site of Douglasville. His natural ability and acquired attainments, his large experience, though yet young in the profession, and an already recognized superior physician, secured for him an extensive and profitable practice. He has been exceptionally successful in his practice, and has a well-earned, wide reputation, few, if any, physicians outranking him. He is an extensive planter and owns and operates several of the best farms in the county and two grist mills. Dr. Poole was married Oct. 3, 1861, to Miss Annie Marcella, daughter of Reuben and Flora (Price) Vansant, of an old South Carolina family. Eight children have blessed this union: Italia D., Mrs. Baxley, Carrie A., William T., Reuben H., Thomas J., Sallie, May and De Witt. Dr. Poole is a prominent member of the Masonic fraternity and of the Lutheran church.

Source: *Memoirs of Georgia*, 1895. Volume 1.

Note: T. J. Poole is buried in Carroll County, Georgia.

F. F. PRITCHETT

F. F. Pritchett, merchant, Villa Rica, Carroll Co., Ga., son of Robert and Anna Eliza (Alexander) Pritchett, was born in Virginia in 1849. His grandfather, Joshua Pritchett, was of French descent, born in Virginia, and of considerable local influence. His father was a native of Virginia and a manufacturer of tobacco, a business which he followed with success and profit until 1856, when he came to Georgia and settled on a farm, where he remained until he died. His maternal grandparents, Frank and Nancy (Bell) Alexander, were natives of Newton, S. C., whence they went to Mobile. There he engaged in business, and was also agent for the bay boats many years. Subsequently he was appointed to a position in the custom house which he held until he was seventy-five years old, when he retired and located on the bay, finishing his days there. He lived in Mobile and on the bay about fifty years, and bought his land from the French. Mr. Pritchett was reared mostly in Georgia, and received but a limited education. He was too young to enter the army during the war, but he served in what was known as the home guard. He went into business in Villa Rica and soon, by assiduous attention and energy, established a large and profitable trade. In 1882 he built one of the largest and best business houses in the little city, and in 1888 formed a partnership with W. H. and G. B. Malone, and has established the best paying business of any person or firm in that part of the state. Mr. Pritchett is a thoroughbred, thorough-going business man of the strictest integrity, possessing the unusual confidence of the people; while Mr. Malone is a young man of irreproachable character and remarkable business and financial ability. Mr. Pritchett was married in 1881 to Miss Lucy J. Malone, born and reared in Carroll county, daughter of Jerry D. and Mary (Hale) Malone, by whom he has had four children: Karl, Robert H., Florence, and Mary E. Mr. and Mrs. Pritchett are active members of the Presbyterian church.

Source: *Memoirs of Georgia*, 1895. Volume 1.

JAMES RAINWATER

This venerable father in Israel has left behind him the memory of a life stretching through seventy-six years, marked throughout by a pure morality, and hallowed for more than half a century by simple yet strong faith in Christ. In him were fulfilled those words of Scripture: "The hoary head is a crown of glory, if it be found in the way of righteousness."

"The days of the years of his pilgrimage" began in Spartanburg district, South Carolina, January 13th, 1795. No record of his early youth survives; but in the year 1820 he made a profession of faith in Christ and connected himself with the Philadelphia Baptist church, in his native district. Five years later that church granted him authority to preach, and we quote the document of licensure in full, for the sake of a notable peculiarity of phrase, which may or may not have been partially current at that time:

"STATE OF SOUTH CAROLINA, Spartanburg District:

"We, the Baptist Church of Christ at Philadelphia, believing that a dispensation of the Gospel has been committed to the charge of our beloved brother, JAMES RAINWATER, therefore *tolerate* him to preach the Gospel of our Lord Jesus Christ, in any part of the world where God, in his providence, may call him.

"Done in church conference, this 12th day of March, 1825, and signed by order of the church.   Moses H. Smith, C. C."

JAMES RAINWATER

This action was followed by his ordination, January 6th, 1826, the presbytery consisting of Revs. Thomas Bomar, Gabriel Phillips, T. P. Hernden, Miles Rainwater and Nathan Langston. He became pastor of the Philadelphia church, and held that position until November, 1835, when he removed to Georgia and settled in Coweta county. After a residence there of ten or twelve years, he transferred his home to Campbell county, where the rest of his life was passed in simplicity of spirit and in useful toil. He served Macedonia church, Coweta county, twenty-two years, and Antioch, Meriwether county, twenty-five years; besides ministering for a number of years to Ramah, Providence, Enon and Bethlehem churches, Campbell county, Carrollton and Pleasant Grove churches, Carroll county, and still others.

Deprived in a large degree of the advantages of early education, he was possessed of a vigorous, well-balanced mind, which, united with his deep piety and untiring energy, made him a power among the churches of his day. Endowed with a sound constitution and a full, strong voice, his love for the name and the cause of Christ led him to undergo physical labors that would have shattered the health of ordinary men. He feared not to attack error and sin in any of their Protean forms; and he discharged this usually unwelcome task with such earnestness of purpose and meekness of manner as to secure the respect and confidence of all classes. This was exemplified by his bold advocacy of temperance when its friends were few and its enemies numerous and powerful, and by the success which crowned that advocacy. But that which is first in importance was always first in his affection; he found his chief delight in "preaching Jesus and the resurrection," and few men have been more effective in winning souls to the Redeemer.

Mr. Rainwater continued in charge of his churches until a few years before his death, when the infirmities of old age compelled him to relinquish them. Even then, unlike the soldier who retires, when wounded, from the line of battle, he persisted, as often as opportunity allowed, in lifting up his voice in warning, even after disease had broken it.

It would be easy for the reader to judge what manner of death must follow such a life. But the record is pleasant, and we make it, less because it is necessary than because we love to speak of it. His last admonition to his brethren on his dying bed was, "Pray for the salvation of sinners," and "Clear as the clearest" were his ringing words of reply, when a friend asked whether he saw his way clear. In this frame of mind, the torch of mortal life went out, June 22nd, 1871. To him the tomb was the gateway to the skies; and doubtless, his enfranchised spirit "leaped with joy" out of the prison-house of clay into the heavenly temple.

He was married in the fall of 1817 to Miss Polly Mason, of Spartanburg district, South Carolina, and in the spring of 1859 to Mrs. Nancy Dobbs, near Villa Rica, Carroll county, Georgia. The first wife became the mother of twelve children, of whom four only are living.

Source: *History of the Baptist Denomination in Georgia*, 1881.

OSCAR REESE

Oscar Reese, mayor of Carrollton, Ga., was born in Coweta County, Ga., August 31, 1848. Augustus C., the father of the subject, has been a local Methodist preacher for thirty-eight years, a teacher since 1841, and is still engaged in those professions. He was born in Hillsboro, Jasper County, Ga., February 1, 1822. After graduating from Emory College, Oxford, Ga., and receiving the degree of A. M., he selected the professions above mentioned, and has since followed them assiduously.

December 28, 1841, he married Miss Celeste Dewel, a daughter of Eli Dewel; she was born in Essex County, N. Y., and received her education under the tutorship of Mrs. Emma Willard. To this union are born five children, who are now living, viz.: A. A. E., born April 29, 1844; Oscar (our subject); Joseph E., born October 19, 1849; Minnie C. D., born September 8, 1857; and Melvin B., born July 29, 1861.

Oscar Reese, our subject, after receiving a good common school education, enlisted in November, 1861, in the Confederate army, company F, First Georgia regiment, for six months, during which time he served in Georgia. Upon the expiration of his term of service, however, he was too young to re-enlist until September, 1864, when he again joined the army and served on the coast of South Carolina and Georgia until the close of the conflict. Upon his return home he began the study of law with W. W. & H. F. Merrell, and was admitted to the bar in March, 1867, in Coweta County. For the following three years he journalized in the house of representatives, but since that time he has given his whole attention to his profession in Carrollton, Ga., building up a large and lucrative practice. In 1885 he was elected mayor of Carrollton, re-elected in 1887, and also in 1888.

In January, 1875, he married Miss M. F. Reid, of LaGrange, Ga., and a daughter of Alex. Reid. They are the parents of five living children, viz.: Boss, Dave, Bill, Pat and Kate.

Source: *Biographical Souvenir of the States of Georgia and Florida*, 1889.

JAMES REEVES

Rev. Jeremiah Reeves came from England to North Carolina in Colonial times, and, with his family shared the trials and hardships of the war that achieved American independence. Early one morning during that war, while he was absent, a British officer with a squad of soldiers suddenly appeared at his house and ordered breakfast for his troops. Returning soon after, Mr. Reeves countermanded the order and reproached the intruders with the loss of his horses. When challenged as to the right by which he dared to act in that style, he answered: "By the inalienable right God has given me to protect my family and to provide for it." In response to the further inquiry who and what he was, he said: "My name is Jeremiah Reeves, and I am for my country, sir." Singularly enough, the officer bore the same name, and a little investigation showed that the two were near relatives. The raiding force was withdrawn without further molestation – a signal instance of the overruling Providence which, "out of the nettle, danger, can pluck the flower, safety," for the upright, through the very things which seem to threaten ruin.

Of the six sons of this venerable man, four, like himself, became ministers of the Gospel – Malachi, Jeremiah, John and James. These, all, with more or less prominence, wrought a useful work among Georgia Baptists in the first half of the present century. They took an efficient part in the discussions which held the great body of our people faithful to the principles of the early Baptists and of the New Testament, and led to the secession of the "Anti-Missionaries" from the communion of their less changeful brethren. With the exception of Malachi, who, up to the time of his death, a period of nearly thirty years, served as pastor the church (in Wilkes or Oglethorpe county) which called him to ordination, they performed much evangelistic labor in the sparse but growing settlements of the State.

Rev. James Reeves was born in Guilford county, North Carolina, in the year 1784. He received only such elementary education as was furnished by the private schools of the country in those times, but sought to make up the deficiency by assiduous study all through his life. During his earlier manhood, he labored hard by day and read to a late hour at night, mostly by a lightwood fire. In after years, when in easier circumstances, he was an almost constant reader and close student. While fond of history, poetry and general literature, he made the Bible his great text-book; and such was his familiarity with its pages and his mastery of its truths, that he was called a "living concordance" and a "walking body of divinity." In ripe old age, he often said that "if it were possible for the New Testament to be destroyed, he would possess an advantage over most persons, as he had very near all of it in his heart!" By many, he was accounted the best Scripturist in the Georgia Baptist Convention.

A young man, with a wife and one or two small children, Mr. Reeves settled in Jasper county, Georgia, when that portion of the State was called "the Purchase." The teams employed in moving them landed them late one afternoon on the site selected for his future home, and they passed the first night with no covering but the star-spangled canopy of heaven. At dawn next morning he felled a tree, from which he soon made boards enough to provide a temporary shelter for his family, until he could get logs together and obtain sufficient help to erect some cabins. He then addressed himself to the task of clearing away the forest and fitting fields for culture, as the only means of procuring bread. Game was so plentiful that the deer would come into his clearing and eat the buds on the timber he had felled, while, under the pressure of his work, he could not spare time to molest them. With this resolute industry he supported himself and his family through life by the labor of his hands as a farmer. He served the churches with little or no compensation, and may be said to have given his life gratuitously to the cause of the Master. Nor, during all the years, were the poor who sought his help ever sent empty away.

The date of Mr. Reeves' new birth and baptism has been lost.

JAMES REEVES

He was licensed and ordained in 1814, in the thirtieth year of his age; beginning then an active ministry which was to stretch through four decades, for he never ceased from pastoral service until the weight of three-score years and ten rendered the flesh too weak to be an instrument to the willingness of the spirit. He was ardently devoted to the duties of the sacred office and eminently successful in winning souls to Christ; but he gloried chiefly in being a pioneer preacher, searching out destitute fields and establishing churches in them. When he settled in Jasper county, it was on the frontier of civilization; and he labored there. When Butts became newly acquired territory, and white men were making their homes in it, he left his pleasant surroundings to dwell and minister among them. When the tide of emigration swept further westward, he went forward with it, planting the standard of the cross in what was then comparatively a wilderness, as far as the State line, and even beyond. With Rev. John Wood, and other zealous servants of Christ, he preached in the log cabins of the new settlers and under temporary arbors constructed for the purpose, supplied the people with Bibles and tracts, organized Sunday-schools and temperance societies, and constituted some of the churches now most flourishing in all that region. While traveling through the wild country, he would meet a man by the way, and, with that "passion for souls" which led him, in his last illness, to manifest more concern for the conversion of the physician than for his own recovery, would stop and preach to him the Lord Jesus as the only hope of salvation. When through, he would leave him to the further operation of the Holy Spirit, and perhaps would hear no more from him, until a request came to visit his neighborhood and baptize him. Compliance with this request would often lead to the organization of a church. His zeal for the work of the pioneer explains the fact that the churches of which he was pastor lay in Jasper, Butts, Henry, Campbell, Paulding, Carroll, Coweta, Heard and Troup counties, Georgia, and in eastern Alabama. It explains also the further fact, that of a great portion of these churches he was not the pastor merely, but the founder.

Mr. Reeves was twice married; first, to a Miss McElroy, of Wilkes or Jasper, who bore him ten children; and afterward to a Mrs. Phillips, of Troup, who bore him five, and is still living, venerable in years and in godliness. He reared these fifteen children of his own, with seven step-children, in the fear of the Lord; showing an impartial affection to all of them, and when school facilities were wanting, instructing them himself by night and at noon. Nearly all his children have been consistent members of Baptist churches, and one of them, James F. Reeves, is a minister of the Gospel. The interest he felt in their spiritual welfare was manifested as well in behalf of his servants, whom, at stated seasons, he assembled in the house, reading the Scriptures, and praying for them and with them. A man of prayer in all things, he was especially strict in the maintenance of family worship, allowing the absence of no member except in case of necessity. He would often rise from a sick bed, when able to sit up only a few minutes at a time, in order to lead the household devotions.

Throughout his last illness, he ceased not to exhort and counsel all who came to see him, whether saints or sinners, even after he had to be supported on the bed, in a sitting position. As the closing hour approached he arose, though greatly debilitated, and asked to be helped to his easy chair near the fire, that he might join with the family and friends in prayer. When a passage of Scripture was read, he turned to Rev. Thornton Burke, his bosom friend and co-laborer in the ministry for years, and said; "Brother Burke, I want to try to pray with and for my family one more time before I go hence; if my breath fails and I sink in death, let there be no confusion, but you just take up my prayer where I may leave off, and finish it." He then poured out his soul in prayer for those present, for the absent members of the family, for the spread of the Gospel, for the prosperity of Zion. After agonizing long and fervently in that last offering as the priest of the household, he closed with a most earnest appeal in behalf of our country, so soon, alas! To be involved in war and deluged with blood. Having given all necessary directions as to his temporal affairs, and designated I Timothy 1:15, as the text from which he wished Rev. T. Burke to preach his funeral sermon, he calmly "fell on sleep," and was "gathered, as a shock of corn fully ripe, into the garner of the Lord." Who can doubt that, as his son said to him when lying on the verge of Jordan, he "passed over the river" to sit down with Abraham, Isaac and Jacob in the kingdom of heaven?" Who can doubt that, as he said then to his son, "the theme of their conversation, the burden of their song, was, and is, and shall be, redeeming grace and dying love?"

Source: *History of the Baptist Denomination in Georgia*, 1881.

JAMES REEVES

The subject of this imperfect sketch, was the son of a Baptist minister, Jeremiah Reeves, of North Carolina, who removed to Georgia and settled in Wilkes county. He had four sons, all of whom became Baptist preachers, Malachi, Jeremiah (whose history also occurs in this volume), John and James. The oldest, Malachi, was an eminently useful man in his day, and was contemporary with Jesse Mercer, Thomas Rhodes, and other distinguished characters. John was still living at last accounts, a very old man. He has been quite useful in his day.

James Reeves was born in Wilkes county, where he was brought up, and lived successively in Jasper, Butts, and Troup. His last move was to Carroll county, where he died, April 6th, 1858, in the seventy-fourth year of his age. When converted, and by whom baptized, the writer has not been able to ascertain. It is believed he was about thirty when he commenced preaching, which was probably in Jasper county. He was twice married – first, to a Miss McElroy, and next to a Mrs. Phillips. He raised a large family of children, some of whom passed away to the better country in advance of their father. The characters of those who remain do no discredit to their parentage.

He was a *praying* man. He was never known to omit family prayer, when it was possible to attend to it; and if practicable, all his family must participate. The writer remembers an anecdote told of him in the early settlement of Troup county. The neighbors were accustomed to assist one another in building their log cabins, rolling logs, etc. Boards being in demand for covering a house, it was agreed that one party of men should meet at Mr. Reeves' for early breakfast, and another party at one of his neighbors, and thence sally forth for the day's work. Whichever party should find a suitable *board-tree* first, was to commence operations, not waiting for the other. Those who met at Mr. Reeves' were there by daylight, and were in a great hurry to get to work early. But no matter what the hurry was, *family worship* must be attended to first. The good man produced his Bible, and went through this service with due solemnity. Breakfast over, he and his party were not long in finding several *first rate board-trees*, on which they went to work with a will. It was growing late when the other party made their appearance, rather crest-fallen. "They had started out very early, (they said,) had falled several trees, but they had labored in vain, not having succeeded in making a single good board." Mr. Reeves kindly replied, "I fear you did not take time to pray before starting." Which was true, though some of them were professors of religion.

From his entrance into the ministry, he was ardently devoted to its sacred duties, and eminently successful in winning souls to Christ. He gloried in being *a pioneer preacher,* in searching out destitute fields, and in establishing and building up churches therein. It was this spirit that prompted him to leave his pleasant home in Jasper county, and settle for a time in Butts, which was then newly acquired territory. And then, when the tide of emigration swept still further westward, into Troup and adjoining counties, Mr. Reeves went forward with the emigrants, and with John Wood and other zealous and devoted servants of Christ, planted the cross in what was then comparatively a wilderness. They preached in the log cabins of the new settlers, and under temporary arbors constructed for the purpose, supplied the people with Bibles and tracts, and established Sabbath schools and temperance societies. Some of the most flourishing churches now in Troup and adjoining counties were organized by Reeves and his coadjutors. And all this work was done as a labor of love, for they had no hope or prospect of earthly reward. Their families were maintained by the labor of their own hands, or that of their servants, and they went forth, sowing the good seed of the kingdom, without cost to those who reaped the benefits thereof. It was the unrequited labors of such men that gave the Baptists the vast ground in all that region. Let none imagine that this task was accomplished without opposition. The "anti-mission" war was raged in those days with a bitterness of which the present generation have but a faint conception. Mr. Reeves stood firm as a rock and as bold as a lion in favor of the truth on this subject. Hence, he came in for his full share of persecution and reproach. Though exceedingly mild in spirit, and affable in manner, his adversaries found him ever ready to "contend earnestly for the faith once delivered to the saints."

Mr. Reeves was *a Bible preacher.* He was frequently called a *living concordance.* His familiarity with the sacred oracles was doubtless the result of a habit which prevailed among the fathers of our Baptist Israel in Georgia, much more generally than among the preachers of this generation — *the habit of daily reading and studying the Word.* They read the Bible more than any other book. Indeed, many of them read scarce anything else. The consequences were, that their sermons abounded with scripture quotations and illustrations, they were more fully established in the doctrines of grace, and they preached with an *unction which nothing but the word and spirit of God can impart.*

Our brother was remarkable for *punctuality* in all his engagements, whether secular or religious. No man enjoyed in a higher degree the confidence of those with whom he had dealings. When the time arrived for him to start off to his preaching appointments, neither rain, nor snow, nor sleet prevented his going. His benevolence knew no bounds. The poor he never turned away empty. If they had money to pay for provisions, they got them. If not, they got them any how. If there was not sufficient for the rich and poor, he invariably gave the preference to the latter.

Old age neither dampened the ardor nor restrained the zeal of Mr. Reeves in the great work to which he had so faithfully devoted his life. A friend, who visited him in March, 1858, says, in substance: "The time for his departure was drawing nigh. He was fully sensible of this, but talked as calmly about it as if he was going on a journey. His only desire to live longer was that he might preach the gospel. He manifested more concern for the conversion of his attending physician than for his own recovery. Throughout his sickness, he ceased not to exhort and counsel all who came about him, whether saints or sinners. Among his last words were, that, although he felt no great ecstacy in view of death, he had an abiding faith that all was well. As his last hour approached, he rose from his bed, though greatly debilitated, and asked to be helped to a seat near the fire, so that he might have family prayer once more. Having requested a brother Burke, who was present, to take up and complete his prayer should his breath fail, he agonized long and fervently in that last offering which he made as priest of his household. It was noticed by his friends that he made most fervent appeals for his country – that country which was so soon to be deluged with blood. Having given all necessary directions about his temporal affairs, designated the text from which he wished brother Burke to deliver his funeral discourse, (2d Timothy, chapter iv, 6, 7 and 8 verses,) he calmly fell asleep in Jesus, and was gathered, 'as a shock of corn fully ripe,' into the garner of the Lord." The author has known but few as good men as *James Reeves.*

Source: J. H. Campbell, *Georgia Baptists: Historical and Biographical,* 319-322.

JAMES REEVES

Rev, James Reeves, was born in Wilkes Co., Ga., in 1783, and died in Carroll County, April 6, 1858, in the seventy-fifth year of his age. He was most decidedly a praying man and a student of the Bible. From his entrance into the ministry he was devoted to its sacred duties, and gloried in being a pioneer preacher. He removed successively to Jasper, Butts, and Troup Counties, following the tide of immigration, and with John Wood and other zealous ministers planted the cross in what was then, comparatively speaking, a wilderness. Preaching in log cabins and under temporary arbors, they supplied the people with Bibles and tracts, and established Sunday-schools and temperance societies. Some of the most flourishing churches in Troup and the adjoining counties were established by Reeves and his coadjutors. In those days the anti mission war raged, and James Reeves was one of the firmest defenders of missions. He was benevolent and exceedingly punctual, and no one enjoyed more the confidence of those who knew him. To the very last he was faithful and devoted, old age neither dampening his ardor nor restraining his zeal, and death found him "as a shock of corn fully ripe."

Source: Cathcart, ed. *The Baptist Encyclopedia,* vol. 2, 965.

JOSEPH A. REEVES

J. A. Reeves, a member of the firm of Reeves & Son, is one [of] the pioneer merchants of Camden, Ark., and being public-spirited, liberal-minded and generous in disposition, he receives a most liberal share of public favor. His establishment is one of [the] most attractive of the kind in Southern Arkansas, and as he sells his goods at very low prices, and is honest and upright in his dealings with his patrons, he fully deserves his present success. He was born in Troup County, Ga., August 22, 1836, and is a son of James and Nancy (Harper) Reeves, the former a native of North Carolina, and the latter of Georgia. They were married in the latter State, and lived and died there, the former having been an active participant in the War of 1812. The paternal grandfather, Jeremiah Reeves, was a soldier in the Revolutionary War. James Reeves, was a minister of the Baptist Church, and followed the occupation of farming for a living. A family of twelve children was born to himself and wife, only three are now living: James (a Baptist minister in Georgia), Eliza (Barzell, in Cleveland County), and Joseph A. (the immediate subject of this sketch). The latter was not named until sixteen years of age, then as his parents could not decide on a name he took the matter into his own hand and named himself while going from Atlanta to Covington, Ga. He remained in the State of Georgia until almost grown, receiving the most of his education there, and in 1855 went to Mississippi, and was engaged in clerking in a store until 1859, when he came to Camden, Ark., where he was making his home when the war broke out. On May 15, of that year, he joined the City Guards of Camden, but became a lieutenant in Company H, Sixth Arkansas Regiment, and was afterward promoted to captain. He commanded the company for two years and was a participant in all the engagements west of the Mississippi River. After the final surrender he returned to Camden and resumed merchandising, which occupation had received his attention before the war, being associated in business with D. W. Fellows, receiving one-third of the profits. By economy he managed to save considerable of this money, but after remaining a member of the firm until 1880, he withdrew and became associated in business with a Mr. Ross, their connection lasting three years. In 1886 the present firm was organized, and they are now doing an exceptionally paying business. Their stock of goods is valued at $12,000, and they do an annual business of $120,000. Mr. Reeves was married in 1866, to Miss Lizzie Parker, a native of Camden, and by her he has two sons and a daughter: Orlin C. (who is associated with his father), Edwin J. (a medical student in New Orleans), and Lizzie E. Mr. Reeves is a member of the K. of P., the R. A., the K. of H., and he is a stockholder in the Camden National Bank and the Camden Compress and Electric Light Company.

Source: *Biographical and Historical Memoirs of Southern Arkansas,* 1890.

Note: James Reeves, father of Joseph A. Reeves and subject of the previous sketch, is buried at Pleasant Grove Baptist Church near Villa Rica.

HARRY MAURRELLE REID

Col. H. M. Reid, attorney at law, Carrollton, Ga., was born in Blairsville, Union County, Ga., February 15, 1853. Simpson Reid, the father of the subject, was an attorney also by profession, a prominent man politically, and was State senator from the fourteenth district at the time of his death, which occurred May 10, 1864. He had also represented Union County in the State legislature two terms. His father, Jesse Reid, was a native and planter of Virginia, and lived to the ripe old age of ninety-six years.

Simpson Reid married Catherine M. Whiteside, of Asheville, Buncombe County, N. C., and a daughter of John Boen Whiteside. She bore her husband six children, of whom the subject of this sketch is the fourth. He received his literary education in Lexington (Ga.) Academy, and for one year attended Oglethorpe University, Atlanta, Ga. After finishing this course it was his intention to prepare for the Presbyterian ministry, to which he had given some attention, but at the age of eighteen he changed his professional inclination to that of the law. His preliminary reading was done with Marshall L. Smith, of Dawson County; he was admitted to the bar in September, 1873, and located in Palmetto, Ga., for practice. His legal abilities were soon recognized and he was elected, in 1880, solicitor-general of the Coweta circuit by the legislature, was re-elected in 1884, and is the present incumbent of that office. He is also a member of the board of trustees of the public schools of Carrollton. He was married in November, 1877, to Miss Gertrude Carlton, daughter of John Carlton, of Palmetto, Ga. To this happy marriage are born four children, viz.: Willie K. and Jesse S., who are twins, and Arthur M. and Carlton.

Col. Reid is a Master Mason, a Knight of Honor, and, with his wife, a consistent member of the Presbyterian Church.

Source: *Biographical Souvenir of the States of Georgia and Florida*, 1889.

HARRY MAURRELLE REID

Harry Maurrelle Reid, lawyer, Atlanta, Ga., was born in Blairsville, Union Co., Ga., Feb. 15, 1853, and lived there until he was seventeen years old, receiving his primary education at the schools at that place. In 1870 he entered Meson academy at Lexington, Ga., for the years 1870-71, and from there he went to Atlanta, studying one term at old Oglethorpe university, now extinct, and leaving in his junior year. Immediately afterward he commenced the study of law with a relation, Marshall L. Smith, at Dawsonville, Dawson Co., Ga., and was admitted to the bar in 1873. He located in Campbell county, Ga., and began to practice his profession in 1875, being six years later

HARRY MAURRELLE REID

elected by the state legislature solicitor-general of Coweta circuit for the term of four years. His term of office expiring he was re-elected for four years more, and soon afterward removed to Carrollton, Ga., a city in the same circuit. In January, 1889, he came to Atlanta and very soon entered into partnership with J. B. Stewart, with whom he was associated under the firm name of Reid & Stewart until April 1, 1894. Since that date he has practiced alone. In 1887 Mr. Reid was chairman of the board of commissioners of Palmetto, Ga., and while a resident of Carrollton he was a member of the board of school commissioners. Up to a late date he has always taken a very active interest in democratic politics. He is a master Mason and a member of the Presbyterian church. In 1877 he married Gertrude, daughter of John Carlton, of Campbell county, and they have two sons and two daughters: Willie Katherine and Jessie Cicely (twins), Arthur M., and Carlton. Mr. Reid's father was Simpson Reid, and was a native of North Carolina, and was serving as a member of the Georgia state senate from the Fortieth senatorial district at the time of his death in 1864. Simpson Reid was a lawyer by profession, the principal field of his practice being the old Blue Ridge circuit.

Source: *Memoirs of Georgia*, 1895. Volume 1.

HENRY W. REID

Henry W. Reid, farmer, Mandeville, Carroll Co., Ga., son of Robert and Lucinda (Chandler) Reid, was born in Carroll county in 1841. His paternal grandfather, Henry Reid, was a native of South Carolina, and migrated to Georgia about 1820. His father was born in South Carolina in 1806, and came with his parents to Georgia. They settled in Gwinnett county, and he remained with them until he was eighteen years of age, when he went to Franklin county, Ga. Subsequently he removed to Carroll county, settled in the woods and made his log cabin home where the subject of this sketch now lives. He was a soldier in the Florida Indian war. Mr. Reid's maternal grandparents, Wyatt and Mary B. (Liner) Chandler, were natives of North Carolina. Mr. Chandler was a soldier in the war of 1812, removed to Georgia and settled in the woods in Carroll county early in its history, his nearest neighbors being seven miles away. Mr. Reid was reared on the farm where he now lives, and was educated at the common schools of the county. In 1862 he enlisted in Company H (Capt. Parrish),

HENRY W. REID

Fifty-sixth Georgia regiment, but he remained only a short time – as his father was taken seriously sick, and he, being the only child, came home and remained with him until his recovery – sending a substitute to take his place in the army. In 1863 he enlisted in a state battalion, in which he served six months, and then re-entered the regular service, enlisting in Company E, Capt. Shuford, First Georgia cavalry, and served until the surrender. He joined the army at Resaca, under Gen. Johnston, and saw much very hard service between there and Atlanta. On one occasion a comrade near him was shot through the head and some of the blood and brains flew on him, leaving stains which remained until the clothing was worn out. A wife and two children and an old cavalry horse were the sum total of his possessions at the close of the war. But with a light heart and a strong will he went to work to regain lost ground, and now he has a well-improved farm of 500 acres and a comfortable home. Mr. Reid was married Dec. 20, 1860, to Miss Nancy C. – born in Meriwether county, Ga. – daughter of James G. and Sisley (Hammock) Davenport. Mr. and Mrs. Reid have had thirteen children born to them, of whom James R., Charles J., Henry M., Martha F., Sallie A., John T., Nancy I., George W., Amanda, Elijah, and Irene J. are living, and Lucinda and William R. are dead. Husband and wife are members of the Primitive Baptist church, and no citizens of the county are more highly esteemed than they.

Source: *Memoirs of Georgia*, 1895. Volume 1.

JAMES A. RHUDY

James A. Rhudy, merchant of Carrollton, Ga., was born in Chattooga County, Ga., November 2, 1848, and is a son of Alfred and Susan (Griffith) Rhudy. He located in Carrollton in 1875 and for several years clerked there. In 1882 he began business for himself in partnership with T. Spurlock, the style of the firm being, Rhudy & Spurlock. They deal in all kinds of general merchandise, dry goods, boots, shoes, groceries, etc., and have established a prosperous business.

In 1870 Mr. Rhudy married Miss Susie, daughter of T. Spurlock, and a native of Alabama. To their union have been born the following children, viz.: Chas. S., Mamie, Walter, Susie, Angie (dead), and Kathleen. Mr. Rhudy is a deacon in the Baptist Church, and was also elected financial agent of the same a few years ago.

Source: *Biographical Souvenir of the States of Georgia and Florida*, 1889.

WILLIAM T. ROBERTS

William T. Roberts, lawyer, Douglasville, Douglas Co., Ga., son of Mellville C. and Susan E. (Skeen) Roberts, was born in Campbell county, Ga., Dec. 26, 1858. His paternal great-grandfather, Josephus Roberts, was North Carolina born, of English parentage. His grandparents were Grant and Frances (Pass) Roberts – the grandfather born in Buncombe county, N. C., Nov. 14, 1804. He was a large farmer, a prominent and influential citizen, and accumulated a very large fortune. In 1815 he migrated to Georgia and settled in Clarke county, subsequently moving to Campbell county, where he died March 16, 1888. Mr. Roberts' father was born in Campbell county, Sept. 28, 1834, was reared a farmer, and received such education as the best country schools could give. Soon after the war between the states began he enlisted in Company C, Thirty-sixth Georgia regiment, and served in all Gen. Lee's campaigns in defense of Richmond until July 3, 1863, when he was killed at Gettysburg. His mother, daughter of Purnell H. and Adaline (Steed) Skeen, an old North Carolina family, was born in Coweta county, Ga., Feb. 12, 1836, and was educated at the La Grange Female college, at La Grange, Ga., from which she was graduated in 1854. She was married Feb. 25, 1858, and became the mother of three children: William T., the subject of this sketch; Mrs. Sarah E. Terrell, deceased, and John M. Mr. Roberts was raised on the farm and received his education at the near-by country schools. He began life for himself as a clerk in the store of his uncle in Whitesburg, Ga. After clerking a few years he studied law and in 1881 was admitted to the bar in Carrollton, at the October term of Carroll county superior court, and in April 1882, he located in Douglasville. He at once secured a good practice, which has increased in volume and value as the years rolled by. In 1884 he was elected mayor of Douglasville, and the following year was elected solicitor of the county court. In 1890 he was elected to represent Douglas county in the general assembly. In October, 1894, he was elected solicitor-general of the Tallapoosa circuit. Possessing fine talents and great energy, and being a close student, he has bright prospects before him.

Source: *Memoirs of Georgia,* 1895. Volume 1.

ALBERT C. ROBINSON

Albert C. Robinson, merchant and farmer, Carrollton, Carroll Co., Ga., son of John W. and Mary M. (Burrow) Robinson, was born in 1856. His grandfather, John Robinson, was a native of Virginia, whence he removed to North Carolina, and subsequently to Georgia and settled in the woods in Carroll county, near where the subject of this sketch now lives. Mr. Robinson's father was born in North Carolina in 1827 and came with his parents to Georgia when a small boy. His mother was a daughter of William and Eliza (Bradbury) Burrow, who were among the earliest settlers in that part of the state. His father enlisted in 1861 and remained in the service until the surrender. Mr. Robinson was reared on the farm and in consequence of the war, which was at its fiercest when he was of school age, his education was limited. But he was endowed with pluck and perseverance, and enterprise and energy, and was also possessed of a thorough-going disposition, which have told wonderfully on his prosperity. He first began business at Shiloh, but last year he removed his business to his farm near that place. When he was married he was not worth a dollar; now he has a fine, large farm, and is doing a large and increasing mercantile business. Mr. Robinson was married in 1879 to Miss Mary M. Arthur, daughter of Kabus and Ann (Barnes) Arthur, who were among the earliest settlers of Marion county, Ga. Mr. Arthur lost his life during the late war. Seven children have blessed this union: Emory C., William M., Zella V., Luther L., Verdie E., Lizzie M. and Minnie Pearl. Mr. and Mrs. Robinson are members of the M. E. church. He is one of the rising young men of Carroll county with a bright future.

Source: *Memoirs of Georgia*, 1895. Volume 1.

GEORGE W. ROOP

George W. Roop, merchant, Roopville, Carroll Co., Ga., son of Martin and Elizabeth Roop, was born on a farm where Roopville now stands, Sept. 25, 1858. He was educated at the common country schools, and after completing his education, he in 1880 engaged in a general merchandise business in Carrollton with profitable results. Two years later he went "down the river," where he remained two years, still prospering and then returned to his old home, Roopville, where he is in business to-day. He started on $200 given him by his father, which he has used with such superior judgment as to place him on the high road to fortune. He has now a large store-house and stock, a large and profitable trade and a fine home, his store and dwelling, the result of his own supervision and contributed labor. He stands high

GEORGE W. ROOP

as a business man of capacity and integrity and takes a great interest in all movements promotive of the advancement of his community, to which he gives liberal financial encouragement. Mr. Roop was married in 1880 to Miss Eliza Almon (born in Heard county, Ga.), daughter of Zachariah and Antoinette (Babb) Almon, by whom he has four children: Major C., Quanah Parker, William and Addie. Mr. and Mrs. Roop are members of the Baptist church, and Mr. Roop is a master Mason.

Source: *Memoirs of Georgia*, 1895. Volume 1.

JOHN K. ROOP

John K. Roop, leading merchant, Roopville, Carroll Co., Ga., was born in Union district, South Carolina, Oct. 20, 1839. He was reared on a farm, and what schooling he had was obtained at the common country schools of that period. When grown he taught school some himself. In 1861, when the civil war reached the fighting point, he enlisted for six months in Company D (Capt. J. R. Thomason), First Georgia regiment, and at the end of that time he enlisted in a cavalry company in Phillips' Legion, and remained in the service until the surrender. While in the service he did a great deal of scouting, notwithstanding which he participated in many of the hardest-fought battles of the war, among them: Sharpsburg, Chancellorsville, Gettysburg, Culpepper courthouse, Mine Run, etc. He was also a considerable time with Gen. Wade Hampton. As was the case with many thousands he came out of the war without anything but its sad experience, and entered upon the work of reconstruction in Carroll county. In 1880 he opened a store, building the first house on the spot; established a mill in 1874 and has succeeded in securing a large and profitable trade. Population increased, and a post-office being wanted one was established in 1881 and named "Roopville," for the founder of the embryo town. He served as justice of the peace at Roopville for eight years, and when the board of county commissioners was organized in 1886 he was elected a member and continued in office six years, until 1892. He has been solicited to become a candidate for the general assembly, but has always refused, as he craved no political honors. Mr. Roop was married in 1872 to Miss Eliza Moore (born inHenry county), daughter of W. H. and Sarah (Barnes) Moore, natives of Georgia. Her grandfather, Joshua Moore, was an early settler in

Henry county. Mr. and Mrs. Roop have had born to them five children: Nora L., wife of Dr. B. J. Veal; Henry A., Charles C., Bessie and Fannie. Mr. Roop was a prominent member of the Farmers' alliance and president of the Carroll county organization. He is a master Mason, and has been worshipful master of his lodge many years. He and wife are members of the Missionary Baptist church. Beginning with nothing at the close of the war, he has become the leading merchant in his part of the county; has acquired some two thousand acres of fine land, and is recognized as one of the most influential citizens of Carroll county.

Source: *Memoirs of Georgia*, 1895. Volume 1.

MARTIN ROOP

Martin Roop, deceased, one of the earliest settlers, and when living, a very prominent citizen of Carroll county, was the son of John and Phoebe (Pilcher) Roop, native South Carolinians, and was born in South Carolina in 1810. He attended and received his education at the old field school. In 1845 he migrated from South Carolina to Georgia (nine days on the road by wagon) and settled in Jackson county. At the end of a year he bought a piece of cleared land, on which he lived four years, and then removed to Coweta county, and cleared a part of the tract for a farm. When he made this change his wife rode nearly all the way on horseback. After remaining here four years he removed to Carroll county and settled where the flourishing town of Roopville, named in honor of his son, John K. Roop, now stands. There was not a stick amiss. To many it will sound odd to relate that when Mr. Roop settled in Carroll county, his family made use of the now unknown (and almost forgotten) pewter dishes, and that Mrs. Roop carded, spun and wove the cotton and wool into cloth, and then made the clothing for the family. During the war all the time that could be spared from household duties she employed in providing socks and clothing for the soldiers. Mr. Roop himself was exempt by law from going into the army. Mr. Roop was married in 1839 to Miss Elizabeth, daughter of Abraham and Lucy (Bradford) King, South Carolinians, by whom he had ten children: John K., William W., Robert H., Benjamin J., Thomas M., Henry O., James G., Sarah Elizabeth, Savannah and George W. Mr. Roop was made a master Mason during the war and himself and wife were members of the Missionary Baptist church. The family have been, and is yet, one of prominence and influence, and enjoy the confidence and esteem of the people.

Source: *Memoirs of Georgia*, 1895. Volume 1.

W. W. ROOP

Rev. W. W. Roop was born April 23rd, 1841, in Union District, South Carolina. In 1844 his parents came to Georgia, and made their home in Carroll county, which has ever since been the cherished *locale* of the family. Possessing but little property, the parents were unable to give all their children a collegiate education, and the subject of our sketch, being second of a large family, was necessarily called to aid in the regular round of labors requisite for their support on a farm. Of course his opportunities for culture were limited as to time, and the advantages only such as are afforded in the common schools of our country; but with all these hindrances, he had at the age of twenty, acquired a good practical education. In 1861, feeling that his country demanded his services in the civil war just commencing, he joined the Confederate army and remained in it until the close of the war, 1865. Returning to his home, he was tendered a situation as teacher in a country school and such was his success that he never afterward found any difficulty in securing a good position in the profession of his choice. For four years he devoted his time and talents to this work, receiving the support of the entire community.

During these years of labor and self-denial, by untiring application to business and study, his education was greatly improved. He was not satisfied with partial attainments and while teaching, continued to be a student himself, diligently searching for the treasures of knowledge. Through all this time, while devoted to literary pursuits, he made the Bible his daily companion.

In 1869 he was married to Miss M. J. Moore. He has three children. He prosecuted his profession, filling up spare moments with agricultural pursuits, until called to the position of principal of the Carroll Masonic Institute, located in Carrollton, of which, for two years, he faithfully discharged the duties, to the satisfaction of his patrons. Now, however, the time had arrived when this conscientious man of God was made to feel that these duties were more than he could properly and successfully discharge in addition to others still more sacred; and this leads us to speak of his religious life which began in his earlier years. When quite young he manifested deep interest in religious worship, and the Sabbath-school exercises were peculiarly dear to him. He loved the family altar, too; and as early as twelve years of age he gave evidence of being a Christian, but did not then unite with the church. He was baptized in 1860, when nineteen years of age, by Rev. W. H. Daniel, and united with the church at Bethesda, Carroll county, where his membership has remained ever since. In 1872 he was licensed, and the following year was ordained to the ministry and called to the care of the Yellow Dirt church, in Heard county. In 1874, New Lebanon and Bethesda desired his services, and to these three churches he gave his pastoral labors until 1878, when he resigned two of them, that he might accept the care of the church in Carrollton. To this and the Bethesda church he still devotes his labor as pastor, and has been blessed in witnessing the conversion of many.

His manners are quiet, and adorned with meekness, which gains for him the love of his people and the respect of the community. Though not remarkably eloquent, his style is earnest and persuasive and in contending for the truths and doctrines of the Gospel, firm and uncompromising. He is rather tall and slender in form. His face already bears the marks of much thought and study and toil. Kind in his deportment towards all, he seeks the happiness of his people, the prosperity of the church, and the glory of God.

Source: *History of the Baptist Denomination in Georgia*, 1881.

MOSES R. RUSSELL

Moses R. Russell, superintendent of county schools, Carrollton, Carroll Co., Ga., son of Harris and Leah (Steed) Russell, was born in Coweta county, Ga., in 1835. His grandparents, Gabriel and Patsy (Bell) Russell, planters, were born and lived and died in North Carolina. He was a soldier in the war of 1812, and died at the age of sixty-six years. His wife lived to be ninety-two years of age. Mr. Russell's parents were born in North Carolina, migrated to Georgia in a wagon in 1833, and settled in the woods in Coweta county; occupied a dirt floor log cabin which a brother who had come to Georgia built for them a year

MOSES R. RUSSELL

or two before. Mr. Russell's mother was the daughter of Sarah (Harris) Steed, born in North Carolina, whose ancestors were among the pioneers of that state. Mr. Russell was reared on the plantation and was educated in a dirt floor log cabin school-house, with its big fireplace and dirt and stick chimney, and its square holes cut through the logs to let the light in. he rather gleefully relates the following incident of his boyhood days: When fourteen years old a brother was married. Until then he had worn only the "regulation" copperas-colored clothes, but his mother, wishing him to make as impressive an appearance as possible on so important an occasion, bought some blue cottonade goods costing about seventy-five cents, and made him a suit which excited the admiration of the girls and the envy of his boy schoolmates. When eighteen years of age he left home and went to Alabama, where he remained for twelve years, then returned to Georgia and settled in Carroll county on the farm where he now lives. He taught school several years and then merchandised at Lineville, Ala.. about two years, after which he engaged in farming. In 1862 he enlisted in Company D, Capt. Hester, Seventeenth Alabama regiment, Col. Johnson, and was stationed at Mobile about eighteen months. Becoming disabled by sickness he returned home and sent a substitute. But in 1864 he enlisted in Company B, De Armand's battalion, with which he remained and helped to fire the last cannon of the war at Silver run, Talladega county, Ala., eight days after Gen. Lee's surrender, which killed thirteen Yankees. The Yankees afterward captured the gun and brought it to Georgia, and within a quarter of a mile of where Mr. Russell now lives they loaded it, then piled rails on it, which they set fire to, and when the cannon exploded it shot over the house in which he lives. He has been superintendent of county schools ten years, a member of the board of education seventeen years, of which he was president five years, and has been county commissioner eleven years; he has been on the executive committee of the State Agricultural society thirteen years, and one of the managers of the state fairs six years. In 1857 Mr. Russell was married to Miss Fannie Bell (born in Coweta county), daughter of Sylvanus and Betsey (Stripe) Bell. Her parents were descendants of some of the first Scotch emigrants to North Carolina. Six children were the offspring of this union: Elizabeth, George B., Josephine, Robert L., Marvin E. and Katie. This wife, who was a devout member of the Methodist church, died April 23, 1873.

Mr. Russell celebrated his second marriage, with Miss Elizabeth L. Brown, Oct. 7, 1873. Her parents, Franklin and Agnes (Stripe) Brown, were natives of North Carolina, but she was born in Coweta county. By this marriage he had seven children born to him: James H., Lula, Annie, Buena Vista, Frank, Hugh B. and Grover C. Mr. Russell is a member of the I. O. O. F. and in Masonry a royal and select master. Himself and wife are active and influential members of the Methodist church. The many important and responsible county and state agricultural offices Mr. Russell holds show in what estimation his fellow-citizens hold him, while in local social standing himself and family rank among the highest.

Source: *Memoirs of Georgia*, 1895. Volume 1.

HASTINGS C. SCOGGINS

Hastings C. Scoggins, educator and farmer, Dallas, Paulding Co., Ga., son of Gillim and Oretha (Chandler) Scoggins, was born in Carroll county, Ga., in 1844. His father was born in Virginia in 1780, where he grew to manhood and then came to Georgia and settled in Oglethorpe county – one of its earliest settlers. He afterward moved to Coweta county, and thence to Carroll county, where he died – about 1860. He was a commissioned officer in the war of 1812. His mother was born in Virginia in 1800, and was married to his father in 1836 – each being the other's second conjugal companion. To them three children were born: Mrs. Elizabeth Nixon, Seaborn S., and Hastings C., the subject of this sketch. She died in 1874. Mr. Scoggins was educated in the common schools of the county – meantime working on the farm, until he was eighteen years of age, when he began teaching. Alternately teaching and going to school, he finally acquired a good classical education and adopted the profession of a teacher. Having had the misfortune to be born with but one foot, he was exempt from military service. In 1867 he moved to Chattooga county, where he prospered; but in 1870 returned to Carroll county. Two years later he moved to his present home. In 1874 he was elected justice of the peace and served three years; in 1879 he was elected tax receiver and served one term; and in 1881 he was elected school commissioner, which office he held four years. In 1885 he was elected ordinary of the county and held the office eight years, during which time he superintended the erection of the new court house. Since 1880 he has been engaged in farming, in which he has been very successful. The public offices to which he has been successively and continuously elected, and each new office a promotion, shows that he is very popular and that his official faithfulness and ability have been appreciated. Mr. Scoggins was married Aug. 27, 1868, to Miss Sarah, daughter of Andrew and Katie (Woods) Millican, of Chattooga county, who has borne him seven children, all sons: Charles A., Gillim A., Jesse E., O'Connor, Claudius, Alphonso C., and Robert B. It may safely be assumed that Mr. Scoggins will be continued in the public service.

Source: *Memoirs of Georgia*, 1895. Volume 2.

B. A. SHARP

B. A. Sharp, cotton broker and guano dealer, Carrollton, Carroll Co., Ga., son of Andrew and Martha (Elliott) Sharp, was born in Alabama in 1840. His father, son of John Sharp, was born in the emerald isle, and came to the United States in 1818. he stopped in South Carolina a short time, and then, when about fifteen years of age, came to Georgia in an old-fashioned block-wheel cart, in which he afterward made many trips to South Carolina and back. He came as a teacher and followed that calling for many years. Mr. Sharp's mother, born in South Carolina, was a daughter of John Elliott, a soldier in the war of 1812, came from South Carolina to Georgia about 1835, lived in that state a few years, and then moved to Alabama, where her parents passed their lives. Mr. Sharp was reared on a farm in Alabama, and was educated in the historic log cabin school house. Thus equipped, he "opened school" himself, and was making a satisfactory record when the civil war broke out and he enlisted in 1861 in Company K (Capt. E. B. Smith), Thirteenth Alabama regiment (Maj. Marks, Col. B. D. Fry), which was assigned to the command of Gen. Raines. Among other engagements, he participated in the following important battles: Williamsburg, Seven Pines, and Richmond, and others in northern Virginia, was at Appomattox at the surrender, and walked all the way from there to Washington, Ga. He now began life in earnest, without a dollar, farming on shares. He was industrious, saving, successful, and now has a choice 365-acre farm in the county, and an interest in forty acres close to it – partly inside – the corporate limits of Carrollton. He is engaged also in buying cotton and selling guano. He served four years satisfactorily as county commissioner. Mr. Sharp was married in Alabama in 1866 to Aphra A., daughter of Asa W. and Eliza Roundtree. To them four children have been born: Emmett A., Belle, Leila, and Bertram. Mr. Sharp is a member of the Farmers' alliance, a Knight of Honor, a member of the I. O. O. F., and a Royal Arch Mason. Himself and wife are members of the Methodist church. No citizen is more esteemed than he for business capacity and integrity, and no family enjoys a more enviable social position than his.

Source: *Memoirs of Georgia*, 1895. Volume 1.

EDWIN R. SHARPE

Edwin R. Sharpe, editor and proprietor of the "Free Press," Carrollton, Carroll Co., Ga., son of William O. and Susannah (Harrell) Sharpe, was born in Chambers county, Ala., in 1841. His great-grandfather on his father's side, Rev. Thomas Reese, was a noted Presbyterian clergyman, and one of the signers of the Mecklenburg declaration. His paternal grandparents, Elam and Elizabeth (Miller) Sharpe, were natives of North Carolina, but moved to Pendleton, S. C., at an early age, where they lived and died. His father was born in South Carolina in 1819, and lived, in boyhood, in the same town with the great South Carolina statesman, Calhoun. When about seventeen years of age he left his South Carolina home and went to West Point, Ga., in Troup county, where he engaged as a clerk in a store, and later went into business with Dr. J. A. Cherry, in which he remained several years. After his marriage, his wife's father having given him a fine tract, 600 acres, of land in "Miller's Bend," he engaged in farming. He was an enthusiastic and active politician, but would never accept an office. His great-grandfather on his mother's side, Miller, was born in Wales, was exiled on account of some publication in London, and came to South Carolina and published the first newspaper issued in the state, the "Pendleton Messenger." Mr. Sharpe's maternal grandparents were Samuel and Susannah (Heath) Harrell, he being a native North Carolinian. Mr. Sharpe was reared in Chambers county, Ala., and received his early education in the common schools of the day. He then went to a college in Tennessee, to prepare for entering the state university of Virginia, but in about a year the war began, and he quit college and joined the state troops. Soon after he enlisted in the Fourth Georgia regiment, Gen. Dole's brigade, and served through the war, a long time as sergeant. He was in many hotly contested, fiercely fought battles, and was severely wounded in the battle of the Wilderness [and] on the skirmish line at Charlestown, W. Va., each time in the leg, the last time receiving three separate wounds, and was temporarily disabled for active service. After the war he went to West Point, Ga., where he taught school three years, when he and Judge Longley began the publication of the West Point "Shield," and continued it until 1871. Mr. Sharpe then came to Carrollton, where he established the "Carroll County Times," and published it until 1882, when he sold it. He then went to Texas, but soon returned, and in 1883 established the "Free Press," which he has continued to publish with financial success. In addition to the paper he has profitably conducted a farming interest. In 1888 he was elected to represent his senatorial district in the general assembly, and in 1890 he was elected to represent the county in the same body. That he served his constituency faithfully and well is evidenced by his election in 1894 to represent his senatorial district again. In 1868 Mr. Sharpe was married to Miss Annie E., daughter of H. H. and Eliza Greene, an old Georgia family of Greene county, said to be related to Gen. Nathaniel Greene. To them eight children have been born: Edwin, Annie, Robert L., Hamilton H., Lucy E., William O., Elam H., and Marcus L. He is a master Mason, and himself and wife are members of the Presbyterian church, in which he has been an elder since he was twenty-six years of age. He is progressive, "a man of affairs," and deservedly popular and influential.

Source: *Memoirs of Georgia*, 1895. Volume 1.

WILLIAM H. SHAW

William H. Shaw, of the firm of McCord & Shaw, dealers in general merchandise, Carrollton, Ga., was born in Troup County, Ga., October 1, 1863. His father, G. W. Shaw, M. D., is an experienced physician of Troup County. He was born in Jasper County, Ga., July 4,1837, and is a son of William Shaw. He married Mary L. McCord, born in Newton County, Ga., in 1840, and a daughter of William McCord, of Abbeville District, S. C.

WILLIAM H. SHAW

William H. Shaw is the only child born to the above marriage. He received his education in Emory College, graduating from that institution as A. B. in 1883. He then engaged in planting for one year, and then taught school for the same length of time. In the fall of 1885 he began business in partnership with Joseph A. McCord, and they now have one of the best establishments of the kind in Carrollton. Mr. Shaw is a member of the I. O. O. F., Carrollton lodge No. 96, the college fraternity, Alpha Tau Omega, and, with his wife, is a member of the Methodist Church, South.

Source: *Biographical Souvenir of the States of Georgia and Florida*, 1889.

THOMAS G. SHEATS

Thomas G. Sheats, M. D., Carrollton, Ga., is a son of W. H. and Susan F. (Autry) Sheats, both natives of Georgia. Thomas G. was born November 8, 1858, and is the fourth of nine living children born to his parents. He received his literary education in the common schools and then read medicine with Dr. J. T. Slaughter. In March, 1881, he graduated from the Atlanta Medical College, and for the following three years practiced his profession in Villa Rica, Carroll County. He then moved to Shady Grove, the same county, where he resided until 1887, since when he has practiced in Carrollton in all branches of his profession, making a specialty, however, of children's diseases.

December 22, 1887, he married Miss L. M. Kelly, daughter of J. M. B. Kelly, of Georgia. He is a member of the Missionary Baptist Church.

Source: *Biographical Souvenir of the States of Georgia and Florida*, 1889.

JOHN B. SHIELDS

John B. Shields, Probate Judge of Walker County, son of Dr. Milton and Priscilla J. (Bradson) Shields, was born at Marshall's Ferry, in Granger County, Tenn., August 25, 1840. He attended an old field school in that neighborhood until about fifteen years of age, when he went to Greeneville College, East Tennessee, and pursued his studies there for two years. He next studied medicine for two or three years, and upon the breaking out of the war became first lieutenant of Company I, Fifty-ninth Regiment Tennessee Confederate Infantry.

JOHN B. SHIELDS

This regiment was captured at the siege of Vicksburg, but was paroled at once, and thereafter mounted as cavalry under Gen. J. C. Vaughan (since the war a Congressman). His brigade made a campaign into Maryland in 1864, under Gen. Early. After the raid into Maryland they went into East Tennessee and Western Virginia. He then commanded the company as captain. He was engaged at the battle of Grand Gulf, siege of Vicksburg, Baker's Creek, Piedmont, Morristown, Bull's Gap, Monocacy Junction, Md., Winchester and many others. After Lee's surrender he went into North Carolina and joined Joseph E. Johnston's army, but surrendered at Athens, Ga.

After the war he went into mercantile business at Newnan, Ga., and remained there eighteen months. During this time he married and returned to his native place in East Tennessee in 1866. He found his home entirely desolate, and his first business was to rebuild the old house and re-establish the homestead. After accomplishing this he clerked two years at Morristown.

In 1868 he moved to Wolf Creek, then the terminus of the Cincinnati, Cumberland Gap & Charleston Railroad, as merchant and railroad station-agent. In 1871, he moved to Carroll County, Ga., to superintend the Georgia Paper Manufacturing Company. (His childhood had been largely spent in his father's paper-mill.) In 1873 he moved to Walker County, re-fitted Long's Mill, on Black Water Creek, and became a merchant and miller there. After three years he sold out that interest to B. M. Long, moved to South Lowell, and ran a steam saw and planning-mill, which he conducted individually for two years. He still owns an interest there as a member of the firm of Shields & Cartter.

His old homestead in Tennessee has been in the possession of his family for sixty years, and it has been very recently discovered that the place contains a ledge of solid marble of many different colors, beautifully variegated, and more than 300 feet thick.

The Judge's residence is properly at South Lowell, which was once a flourishing village (six miles from Jasper), but is now neglected and dead.

Judge Shields was elected to the Legislature in 1878 on the Greenback ticket, by a majority of twenty-eight votes, but was counted out. In 1884 he was again elected to the Legislature on an Independent ticket, and served in 1884 and 1885. In the year 1886 he was elected

Probate Judge of Walker County, and is still the incumbent of that office.

Judge Shields was married September 19, 1866, in Carrollton, Carroll County, Ga., to Miss Carrie E., youngest daughter of Judge John Long, who was a native of Tennessee, and served as judge, legislator, and in other offices, for more than twenty-five years. He settled in Carroll County in 1826, when the county was full of Indians, and reared a family of four sons and three daughters. One of these sons, B. M. Long, of Cordova, is one of the most prominent and influential men in Walker County, and pays more taxes than any other man in the county.

Five children have been born in Judge Shield's family, all of whom are girls. Their names are: Nannie P., Lily Lou (now dead), Carrie May, J. Maud, and Johnnie B. The Judge is a member of the Masonic fraternity, and of the Presbyterian Church. His wife is a Methodist.

Milton Shields, the Judge's father, was a son of James Shields, and of Irish descent. He was born in Greene County, Tenn., in 1804, and died in Sevier County, Tenn., December 20, 1866. He owned paper-mills at Marshall's Ferry and at Middlebrook, near Knoxville, and was interested in an iron furnace. He made the writing and printing paper that was used throughout this country fifty or sixty years ago, and shipped it here down the Tennessee River. This paper was at first made by hand, and one sheet moulded at a time.

Source: *Northern Alabama Historical and Biographical*, 1888.

F. FRANK SIKES

F. Frank Sikes, farmer, Villa Rica, Carroll Co., Ga., son of Darling and Sarah (Cochran) Sikes, was born in Baker county, Ga., in 1853. His parents were born in North Carolina, and migrated by wagon and on horseback to Georgia and settled in the woods in Baker county in 1851. There he had cleared a farm and had just got well settled when the "unpleasantness" was precipitated. In 1861 he enlisted in Capt. Kendricks' company, Fifty-first Georgia regiment, and was in the service nearly four years, and most of the time was "one of Stonewall Jackson's men," and was in the battle and under the command of that distinguished officer when he was killed. Mr. Sikes was a sharpshooter, and was killed at the battle of the Wilderness. He was always a farmer, and was a consistent member of the Baptist church. His mother was a daughter of Eli and Mary (Griffin) Cochran, also Carolinians, who came to Georgia and settled in Baker county about the time Mr. Sikes' family came. They, also, were members of the Baptist church. Mr. Sikes was reared in Baker county, received but little education, came to Carroll county when only sixteen years of age, and settled where he now lives. He had nothing but good health, pluck and self-reliance to start with, but was a live, wide-awake farmer, worked hard, and lived and managed closely, and now has a large enough farm, well-improved, a two-story dwelling, and a good substantial bran and out-buildings. Mr. Sikes was married in 1875 to Miss Virginia Green — born and reared in Carroll county — daughter of Alexander and Eliza (Chappell) Green, by whom he has had three children: Walter C., Anna B., and Lois G. Mr. and Mrs. Sikes are members of the Missionary Baptist church, and enjoy in the highest degree the respect and esteem of their friends and neighbors.

Source: *Memoirs of Georgia*, 1895. Volume 1.

ABNER A. SIMONTON

Abner A. Simonton, miller and cotton gin operator, Carrollton, Carroll Co., Ga., son of Albert and Mary (Reed) Simonton, was born in Alabama in 1849. His paternal grandparents, Abner and Nancy (Bailey) Simonton, were of Scotch-Irish ancestry and came to America before the revolutionary war. They first settled in Virginia, then moved to North Carolina, and finally, in 1805, came to Georgia in ox carts, and settled in the woods in Greene county — encountering and suffering all the dangers incident to pioneer life. His maternal grandparents, James and Rebecca (Duke) Reed, were also early settlers. Mr. Reed was a soldier in the war of 1812. Mr. Simonton's father was born in Greene county in 1809, and died in 1859. Mr. Simonton was partly educated in the "old field" log school house, common in that day, with its dirt floor, slab seats, great fireplace in a chimney built of sticksand stiff mud, and square holes cut through the sides to let in the light. He began life after the war without a dollar, but full of energy and enterprise, and went to work to make a living and a competency. In 1873 he had the courage to go heavily in debt for an outfit for a corn mill, cotton gin and saw mill. To the corn mill machinery were added mills for making flour. His energy and determination were exemplified by his working in his mills, sawing lumber, grinding and ginning, oftentimes far into the night. His financially independent circumstances to-day amply attest his success. Besides his beautiful home in the outskirts of Carrollton, surrounded by a fine tract of land, he has a large plantation on the river, with fine water power, where his mills are located. More than sixty years ago this power was utilized. In September, 1830, corn mill machinery was put in operation here, and ground corn for the Indians; and in 1848 machinery for grinding wheat was added. With the ravages of war these went down, but the energy and progressive spirit of Mr. Simonton have replaced them – the machinery improved and increased. In 1887 he had the misfortune to have his dwelling, tenement houses and out-houses – all except his mills, miller's house and smithy – destroyed by a cyclone; but they have all been restored, and he now rejoices in being in better condition than ever before, and proudly contemplates and enjoys the reward of his enterprise and labor. Mr. Simonton was married in 1878 to Miss Margaret Johnston, born in Catoosa county, Ga., in 1850, daughter of William H. and Susan (Adams) Johnston, who came to Georgia from North Carolina. Five children have blessed this union: Cora M., Susan R., Albert A., Margaret E., and William J. Mr. Johnston, Mrs. Simonton's father, came to Catoosa county in October, 1846, as a pioneer Presbyterian minister, having consecrated himself to the Master's cause. Mr. Simonton is a master Mason and himself and wife are members of the Presbyterian church.

Source: *Memoirs of Georgia*, 1895. Volume 1.

WILLIAM T. SIMPSON

William T. Simpson, farmer, Rockmart, Polk Co., Ga., son of Rev. W. W. and Allie (York) Simpson, was born in Polk county, Aug. 17, 1849. His father was born in North Carolina, and while a young man came to Georgia and settled at Van Wert, Polk Co., where for many years he carried on a general merchandise business. He was a zealous Methodist, of which church he was a local preacher. His mother was a native of Tennessee. Mr. Simpson was raised in Van Wert, Polk Co., but the war intervening he was deprived of the education which,

WILLIAM T. SIMPSON

but for that, he would have received. He started in life with but little, but has so managed as to place himself in easy and comfortable circumstances. During a part of his life he has profitably engaged in mercantile business, but for some years past has devoted himself to agriculture. He is now a well-to-do, prosperous farmer, highly esteemed by a wide circle of friends and by all who know him. Mr. Simpson has been twice married, first April 8, 1869, to Miss Ophelia, daughter of Judge W. C. and Sarah Barber, of Polk county, who died leaving no issue. His second marriage was Feb. 2, 1875, to Miss Elna E., daughter of Judge W. D. and Marguerite Heslap, of Polk county. Four children have blessed this union: Maggie, Nannie, Cornelia and William Wyley. He is a prominent member of the Methodist church.

Source: *Memoirs of Georgia*, 1895. Volume 2.

Note: Ophelia Ann Barber was a child of Wiley C. Barber by his first marriage. His third marriage was in September 1861 in Carroll County, Georgia to Emily Gresham.

WILLIAM M. SPENCE

William M. Spence, farmer, Carrollton, Carroll Co., Ga., son of Hiram and Angeline (Cheney) Spence, was born in Morgan county, Ga., in 1845. His paternal grandparents, George and Mary (Knight) Spence, were born in Maryland, came to Georgia in ox-carts in 1798 and settled in the woods in what is now Morgan county. He was a delegate to the secession convention, served many years as a justice of the peace and lived to be a very old man. Mr. Spence's parents were born in Morgan county, his father in 1821, and removed to Carroll county in 1847, settling in the woods and clearing for a farm the place where Mr. Spence now lives. He was a justice of the peace many years. During the war he served in the state militia and participated in the defense of Atlanta. Both parents were members of the Primitive Baptist church and were much esteemed by their neighbors. The parents of his mother, Thomas and Lucy Cheney, were born in Maryland and came to Georgia in 1798. They ranked among the best people in every respect. Mr. Spence was reared on the farm where he now lives, and taught by his mother, he learned his A B C's out of the old family bible. Then he attended school in a log cabin in the woods, with dirt floor, seats made of slabs and the chimney of sticks and mud, with square holes cut through the sides for windows. In March, 1864, he enlisted in Company K, Second Georgia regiment, known as state line troops, and after the Confederate army entered Georgia, served under Gens. Johnston and Hood. After the war he resumed farming, at which he has prospered and placed himself in comfortable circumstances. Mr. Spence was married in 1868 to Miss Delphia McPhearson (born in Carroll county), daughter of Elijah and Sarah McPhearson, who migrated from Tennessee to Georgia and were among the early settlers of the county. To him nine children have been born: Leon, Ella, Ida, Cora, William, Newton, Albert, Mary and Ivey. Mr. Spence is regarded as one of the county's most substantial and reliable citizens, and is highly respected by all who know him. Mrs. Spence is a member of the Primitive Baptist church.

Source: *Memoirs of Georgia*, 1895. Volume 1.

ANDREW J. STEWART

Andrew J. Stewart, farmer, Buchanan, Haralson Co., Ga., son of Walter and Nancy (Calloway) Stewart, was born in Monroe county, Ga., in 1816. His paternal grandfather, Jarret Stewart, was a native of Scotland, and one of the early settlers of Georgia. Mr. Stewart's father was born and grew to manhood in what is now Henry county, in Georgia. He was a very good English scholar for the times, and his surroundings, and was a soldier in the last war with Great Britain. In 1837 he moved from Henry to Carroll county, Ga., settling and clearing a farm in the woods, undergoing all the privations and hardships incident to frontier life. He lived on this farm until 1863, when he came to the home of his son, Andrew, where he lived until he died. He was a very pious man, and strictly observed all the ordinances of his church. Mr. Stewart's mother was a daughter of Obadiah and Elizabeth Calloway, who were natives of Maryland, and came to Georgia in this century. Mr. Stewart grew to manhood on the farm, and was entirely deprived of educational advantages. But he was a hard worker, economical and a good manager, as may be inferred when it is stated that when he settled where he now lives, his only worldly possessions were a wife and child and fifteen cents in money; but now he owns 900 acres of good land, and very considerable property in Buchanan. Mr. Stewart has been married four times. His first wife was Miss Nancy, daughter of Elijah and Rachel Brooks, whom he married in 1837, and by whom he had six children – four living: John, Mary J., Nancy A., and Calloway B. The mother was Georgia-born, a member of the Baptist church, and died in February, 1856. In November of that year he married Miss Jane, daughter of Jerman Burton, who died early in 1858. October following he married Miss Emily, daughter of Martin and Sarah Ayers, who died April 1, 1882. In September, 1888, he married Melinda, daughter of John K. Holcombe. Himself and wife are members of the Baptist church.

Source: *Memoirs of Georgia*, 1895. Volume 1.

J. S. STIDHAM

J. S. Stidham, physician and surgeon of Floyd, Hunt county, Texas, is a native of Georgia, born in Polk county, November 12, 1850. He was reared in Polk and adjoining counties of Georgia, and received a fair literary education in the private and high schools of the several localities where he lived. He graduated from the Atlanta Medical College, in Atlanta, Georgia, in 1881. Practiced medicine two years in Cobb county, Georgia, and came to Texas in 1883, locating at Floyd, Hunt county, where he has since lived and given his time exclusively to the practice of his profession.

April 22, 1879, Dr. Stidham married Annie, daughter of T. C. Moore, of Bartow county, Georgia, of which Mrs. Stidham is also a native.

Dr. Stidham's father, Elihu Stidham, was eldest son of Martin and Hannah Stidham. He was born in South Carolina in 1818, and reared in northwest Georgia, near Stilesboro. He died in Collin county in December, 1884, in his sixty-sixth year, having engaged in farming throughout his life. Dr. Stidham's mother was Elizabeth, daughter of Tyrey Reeves, of Meriwether county, Georgia, was born and reared in Meriwether county, and is still living. Dr. Stidham is the third of six children born to his parents, but has only one brother and one sister now living – C. Martin Stidham, a farmer of Collin county, Texas, and Lizzie, wife of J. M. V. Mathews, now living in Paulding county, Georgia.

Source: *Biographical Souvenir of the State of Texas*, 1889.

Note: Elihu Stidham married Sarah Elizabeth Reeves in Meriwether County, Georgia December 15, 1844. In 1850 they were residing in District 848 in Paulding County, Georgia and in 1860 they were residing in the Sixth District (P.O. Hickory Level) in Carroll County, Georgia.

HENRY H. STRICKLAND

Henry H. Strickland, farmer, Carrollton, Carroll Co., Ga., son of John M. and Sarah (Knight) Strickland, was born in Coweta county in 1842. His father was born in Butts county, Ga., in 1811, and his mother was a daughter of John Knight. Mr. Strickland was reared on the farm and received a good common-school education. In 1861 he enlisted in Company B (Capt., afterward Col. Ector) Thirteenth Georgia regiment, and was first in Gen. Lawton's brigade, then in Gen. J. B. Gordon's and lastly in Gen. Clement A. Evans'. He was with Gen Evans when the following incident occurred: Gen. Evans received an order from Gen. Lee to assault and capture a certain position, but afterward, believing it too hazardous, Gen. Lee countermanded the order. When Gen. Evans received the first order he made the assault and received the counter order in the captured position. Mr. Strickland was in the battles at Cotton hill, Martinsburg, Winchester, Cedar run, the seven days' fight, Spottsylvania court house, Sharpsburg and second Manassas, and in innumerable skirmishes in the valley, at one thirty days of almost continuous fighting. He was wounded three times – at Sharpsburg, Cedar run and second Manassas – one wound disabling him for nearly three months, but he escaped capture. After the war he attended Bowdon college two years and a half, afterward taught school three years and then engaged in farming, at which he has prospered, owns a fine landed estate, including a farm and property in Bowdon. Mr. Strickland was married in 1871 to Miss Mary E. Camp, born in Coweta county, daughter of G. W. and Mary A. (Colbert) Camp, and to them ten children have been born: Maud, George, Henry, John, Sallie, Lillian, Colbert, Lee, Warner and Katie. Mr. and Mrs. Strickland and all of their children save Sallie are members of the Methodist Episcopal church south, and Mr. Strickland is a Master Mason. He has honestly obtained the high estimation in which he is held.

Source: *Memoirs of Georgia*, 1895. Volume 1.

JAMES R. THOMASON

James R. Thomason, physician and surgeon, Mabry, Carroll Co., Ga., son of Bartlett and Mary (Thomason) Thomason, was born in Newton county, Ga., in 1826. His great-grandfather, William Thomason, was born in Ireland and came to America before the revolutionary war and was a soldier in the patriot army. His grandfather, William Thomason, was born in Virginia, whence he emigrated to South Carolina. His grandfather was a soldier in the war of 1812. His parents were born in Abbeville district, South Carolina, and came to Georgia and settled in the woods in what is now Walton county, in 1816. They came in a borrowed ox-cart, and when they reached their destination their "goods and chattels" were disposed under a large tree and their friend took his departure. He and his wife then cleared an "opening" and began to farm, their principal food being corn and wild game. After enjoying this luxurious life a few years they moved into what is now Newton county, where his father bought his first land and cleared a farm. In addition to farming he practiced as a botanic doctor in the neighborhood for a number of years. He also "exercised" as a Methodist exhorter, and on many occasions in his early life he went to his "appointments" on foot and barefooted stood and delivered his message. When he was married it was in a home-spun and wove home-made suit of white cotton cloth; it knew no dye pot. Dr. Thomason's grandfather on his mother's side, John Thomason, was a native of South Carolina and settled in what is now Newton county, early in the century. Dr. Thomason was reared on his father's farm and received his education in the primitive, oft described dirt-floor log school-house, with its puncheon seats and mud and stick chimney. In 1844 he determined to be a doctor and began to study, he at the time being a clerk in a store where a doctor had an office, who gave him the privilege of using his books. In 1848 he went to his brother's in Coweta county, who became his preceptor. In 1849-50 he attended the medical college of Georgia at Augusta, and in 1850 located in Carroll county, remaining three years; then removed to where he now lives. In 1860 he attended the Atlanta medical college, and graduating just as the war begun, tendered his services to the Confederate army, which were rejected. He next made up a company and went to the army, but was sent home, not participating in a single battle. He managed, however, to serve awhile at one time during the war as captain of a militia company. After the war he resumed his practice, which he has continued since. In 1870 he was elected to represent his county in the general assembly and was re-elected in 1872, serving two terms. Dr. Thomason was married May 2, 1852, to Miss Maria L., born in Hancock county, Ga., in 1832, daughter of Thomas and Elizabeth (Harris) Colbert, who moved to Coweta county in 1838. Her father was a Methodist preacher, born in Georgia in 1796, and was a son of John and Elizabeth Colbert. Mrs. Thomason's mother, born in South Carolina, in 1806, was a daughter of Thomas and Martha Harris. To Dr. and Mrs. Thomason six children have been born: James H., Francis G., Walter C., Benjamin B., John M. and Joseph R. Dr. Thomason is a member of the I. O. O. F. and has been a Master Mason since 1850. Himself and wife are members of the Methodist church, and he has been an ordained preacher since 1854. He is a popular and useful citizen and is very much liked by the community in which he lives.

Source: *Memoirs of Georgia*, 1895. Volume 1.

BENSON F. TIGNER

Benson F. Tigner, a successful farmer of this county [Meriwether], belongs to a family of considerable prominence in the state during the last century. His grandfather, William Tigner, of Scotch nativity, was a pioneer of Elbert county; his son, Hope H. Tigner, married Miss Eliza Glenn, and was the first settler of Meriwether county, where he built the first frame house ever erected in that county, which was for many years noted through an extensive region of country as the Tigner homestead. Mr. Tigner was a man of large influence and greatly liked, and he organized a company to serve in the Indian war, but his health broke down and he died before the time came to go. His wife was the daughter of William and Elizabeth (Crawford) Glenn, early settlers of Monroe county, Ga. Mrs. Glenn was a sister of Hon. William H. Crawford, so long distinguished among the eminent citizens of the state, and this gentleman took charge of the education of the niece, Mrs. Tigner, which under such direction was of unusual excellence. Benson F., the son of Hope H. and Eliza (Glenn) Tigner, was born in Meriwether county in 1833, and in that sparsely settled community enjoyed but limited educational opportunities. He enlisted in 1862 in the company commanded by Capt. Bragg, and was in the battle of Atlanta, and was present at the surrender at Savannah. Mr.

BENSON F. TIGNER

Tigner began life for himself with little means, but with a character combining energy and perseverance, and by resolute endeavor and arduous work has accumulated a large property, has a beautiful home, and over a thousand acres of choice land in a fine state of cultivation, and enjoys the high esteem of all who know him. In 1858 Mr. Tigner married Miss Martha Stinson, a daughter of Dr. J. W. and Martha (Jackson) Stinson, the former for many years a leading physician of this section, with a widely extended and very lucrative practice, and a man of wealth and influence and great liberality. Mrs. Tigner was born in Meriwether county in 1836, and her union with Mr. Tigner has been blessed with seven children: Frank C., Mattie G., George S., Edward A., James H., Carrie O. and Julia B. Mr. and Mrs. Tigner are both members of the Methodist Episcopal church south, in the work of which they are very active. Mr. Tigner is a member of the board of trustees of the church and also of the school, and bears the same responsibility in relation to the camp ground, a beautiful tract of land in Meriwether county which for sixty-four years has been held for religious purposes. It was chartered by the legislature in 1832.

Source: *Memoirs of Georgia*, 1895. Volume 2.

Note: Benson F. Tigner was an ancestor of Carrollton businessman and artist C. P. Tigner.

HOPE TIGNER

Hope Tigner, a valued citizen and prosperous farmer of Meriwether county, of which he is a native, is of Scotch ancestry, his great-grandfather, William Tigner, with two brothers, having come from Scotland during the last century. They were the ancestors of the Tigner families in this country. William Tigner settled in Elbert county, where his son Hope was born, who married Miss Eliza Glenn, and many years ago settled in Meriwether county, and erected the first frame house built in the county. Their son, W. S., born in Monroe county, married Miss Mary J. Baldwin, a daughter of James and Mary (Scott) Baldwin, natives of Virginia, who settled in Hancock county in 1824, and later moved to Upson county. Mr. Baldwin, who commanded a regiment in the war of 1812, was the son of George and Rachel Baldwin, of Virginia, the former a soldier during the revolutionary war. Hope Tigner, the son of W. S. and Mary J. (Baldwin)

Tigner, was born in 1852, and passed his early years upon the farm. He attended the school at White Sulphur Springs, and also enjoyed and profited by a year at Bowdon college. Mr. Tigner's chosen vocation is the tillage of the soil, and this he has pursued with the ardor and determination which compels success. His country home is a most delightful one, in the midst of his large and beautiful plantation. He has given considerable attention to horticulture, and has four and a half acres devoted to the culture of grapes, which are in fine condition. Mr. Tigner is a man of estimable character, and truly respected by all. In 1876 Mr. Tigner married Miss Carrie Pitts, whose parents, Lewis and Martha (Marshall) Pitts, Georgians by birth, afterward removed to Alabama. Mrs. Tigner was born in Russell county, Ala., in 1854. Both Mr. Tigner and his wife are members of the Methodist Episcopal church south. They have two children: W. S. and Mary A.

Source: *Memoirs of Georgia*, 1895. Volume 2.

Note: This sketch included because Hope Tigner attended Bowdon College and also because of his relationship to Mr. C. P. Tigner, Carrollton businessman and artist.

D. N. TILLMAN

D. N. Tillman, farmer, Carrollton, Carroll Co., Ga., son of Asa and Marinda (Sparks) Tillman, was born in Fayette county, Ga., in 1835. His father was born in South Carolina, and while yet a youth ran away from home. He went into the army during the war of 1812 as a substitute for a man named Felix Simonton and served through the war. In after life he drew a pension for this service. Mr. Tillman's maternal grandparents, John and Elizabeth (Small) Sparks, were natives of Ireland, who came to Georgia early in this century and were among the pioneer settlers in Newton county. Mr. Tillman was reared on a farm in Carroll county and went to school in all his life only six days. In 1861 he enlisted in Company F (Capt. Curtis), Nineteenth Georgia regiment, which was first assigned to Gen. Hampton's command, afterward to that of Gen. J. J. Archer and finally to Gen Colquitt's brigade, in which he remained until the surrender. He participated in quite a number of battles, some of them the most important fought during the war. He was at Seven Pines, May 30 and June 1, 1862, and in the seven days' fight around Richmond, commencing June 26, 1862, and was wounded in the right breast by a ball near Gaines' Mill, June 27, 1862. He was at Antietam, Sept. 17, 1862; at Mecklenburg, Dec. 13, 1862, where he was wounded in the left hand; Chancellorsville, May 1, 1863; Kingston, N. C.; siege of Charleston, Morris Island; Olustee, Fla., Feb. 20, 1864, where he was wounded across right arm; Bentonville, N. C., and the siege of Petersburg, June 18, 1864, where he was wounded in the right leg by a piece of shell. He was in every battle in which his command was engaged except when temporarily disabled by wounds. He rendered good and faithful service in the ranks throughout the war. The war being over he returned to Carroll county and engaged in farming, and although he had to start on nothing but good health, a strong will and a determined spirit, he has a good, well-improved farm and comfortable home. Except serving eight years as justice of the peace, he has devoted all his time and energies to his farm, which he manages on the progressive principles of the day. Mr. Tillman was married in 1865 to Miss Mary A. McPherson, born and reared in Carroll county, daughter of Elijah and Sarah McPherson, early settlers of Carroll county, coming in 1829. To them five children were born: Amanda, Charles N., Henry, Dora and Daniel. Mrs. Tillman, who was a member of the Primitive Baptist church, died in 1885. Oct. 20, 1885, Mr. Tillman contracted a second marriage with Miss Nancy J. Adams, born in Carroll county, daughter of Robert and Martha A. (Jones) Adams, early settlers of Coweta county. This marriage has been blessed with three children: Samuel, Robert W. and John. Mr. and Mrs. Tillman are members of the Primitive Baptist church, and their unostentatious worth commands the general respect and esteem of all who know them.

Source: *Memoirs of Georgia*, 1895. Volume 1.

J. THOMAS TOLBERT

J. Thomas Tolbert, farmer and retired stock-trader, Villa Rica, Carroll Co., Ga., son of Roland A. and Elizabeth (Tolbert) Tolbert, was born in Villa Rica in 1836. His paternal great-grandparents, Thomas and Judia (Reeves) Tolbert, were natives of Ireland, came to America in the last half of the last century and settled in North Carolina. He cleared and cultivated a farm, and also engaged in gold-digging. He was a consistent member of the Methodist church. Mr. Tolbert's father

J. THOMAS TOLBERT

was born in North Carolina, July 3, 1799, and is now alive and in good health at the home of the subject of this sketch. His educational advantages were meager, as he had to work hard and long and late on the farm. He came to Georgia and settled in Madison county in 1827; but in 1832 came to Villa Rica to work the gold mines. He continued this until 1853, when he engaged in farming and followed it until 1872, when he went to live with his son. When he came to Carroll the country and the mines were rough, whisky was freely drank and free fights of the fists and skull, rough-and-tumble sort, were common. Mr. Tolbert was usually "at home" for all comers, though he sought no conflict. He was a member of the military force which escorted the Indians to their new homes, and draws a pension now for that service. He was the eldest of eight children, and is the only one now living. He is a devout and exemplary member of the Methodist church. Mr. Tolbert's maternal grandparents were Josiah and Bersheba (Cranford) Tolbert. He was born in North Carolina, and she was of English parentage; was born in 1795 and died in March 25, 1872. She was a strict member of the Methodist church from childhood, and was the mother of six children, who all grew to maturity, and two of whom are now living — a daughter and the subject of this sketch. J. Thomas Tolbert was reared on the farm, and work was such an imperative necessity that he attended school but little. In 1862, he enlisted in Company A, Ninth Georgia battalion artillery, Maj. Austin Leyden, with which he served until July, 1863, when he was transferred to Company E, First Georgia cavalry. On one occasion he and five others were sent out on a scout and suddenly came upon a company of guerrillas, who chased them five miles, shooting at them all the time; but they finally escaped. He was in many hard fights, but never wounded. At the siege of Knoxville — 1864 — he was captured by the same men, an interesting coincidence, who chased him when scouting. He was held until after the surrender — sometimes, he alleges, on starvation rations. After his release he went to Cincinnati, where he remained about seventeen months, and then returned to his old home in Carroll county. Mr. Tolbert was married Dec. 19, 1866, to Miss Elizabeth W., daughter of Valentine Mc. and Elizabeth (Rice) Hodgson, of English descent. Six children have blessed their marriage — Thomas W., Elizabeth H., wife of Lyman Stutts; Minnie R., and Elba, living, and Abby Estelle and Montra May, deceased. After marriage Mr. Tolbert went to farming, supplementing it with trading in stock, prospering beyond his most sanguine expectations. He is now one of the most substantial and ranks among

J. THOMAS TOLBERT

the best citizens in Carroll county. Mr. Tolbert's success illustrates the great possibilities of life in Georgia when pluck and perseverance are coupled with energy and fair business judgment. Financially and socially himself and family occupy first-class positions. Himself and wife are members of the Presbyterian church.

Source: *Memoirs of Georgia*, 1895. Volume 1.

BENJAMIN HILL TOMPKINS

Benjamin Hill Tompkins, planter, Franklin, Heard Co., Ga., son of Nicholas and Lucinda T. (Springer) Tompkins, was born on the plantation on which he now lives, in 1860. (For sketch of his parents, see that of his brother, Humphrey A. Tompkins, elsewhere in this work.) Mr. Tompkins was left fatherless when an infant, was raised on the family homestead, and educated at the common schools of the county. His surroundings compelled him, while very young, to assume the duties and responsibilities of mature manhood. But following the example, and inspired by the spirit and courage of his brother Humphrey, he set manfully to work to solve the great problem of life and success. He, like his brother, determined to know no such word as fail – and like him, he has worked out a splendid success. He owns several thousand acres of fine land, including the original family homestead, improved by his father more than sixty years ago – of which he is justly proud – and is otherwise supplied with an abundance of the good things of this life – and is, therefore, happily situated. Mr. Tompkins was married Sept. 1, 1880, to Miss Montie, daughter of Joseph and Mary (Pendergrass) Holliday. To them the following children have been born: Nicholas, Joseph B., John, Berd Berry, Mary Baxter, and Levi Ridley.

Source: *Memoirs of Georgia*, 1895. Volume 1.

Note: Benjamin Hill Tompkins' mother was a daughter of William Green Springer.

HUMPHREY A. TOMPKINS

Humphrey A. Tompkins, farmer, Franklin, Heard Co., son of Nicholas and Lucinda T. (Springer) Tompkins, was born in Heard county March 9, 1851. His paternal grandfather, Giles Tompkins, was a soldier in the patriot army during the revolutionary war, and migrated part of the last century. Mr. Tompkins' father was born in Oglethorpe county in 1798, received such education as could be obtained at the country schools of the locality at the time, and when grown, entered upon farming as a life pursuit. Later, he moved to Putnam county, Ga., and thence to Troup county about 1830, and settled on land now within the bounds of Heard county. He served during the Seminole war, holding a commission as major. He also served as a soldier in the war with Mexico. At the close of that war he returned to his farm. Such were his skill as a planter and his business sagacity and management that he became the owner of 175 slaves and the largest land-owner in Heard county. He died Aug. 12, 1860. He was married twice; his second wife being the mother of the subject of this sketch. She was a daughter of William G. and Mary (Baxter) Springer. Mr. Springer was for many years an Indian agent. By this marriage he had five children: William G., John T., Humphrey A., Benjamin Hill, and Eliza Baxter. Mr. Tompkins was raised on the family plantation, and received as good an education as was obtainable, considering the locality, and the fact that his boyhood was passed during "war times." When only fourteen years old he assumed control of his father's extensive plantation, which had suffered immensely from the ravages of war, and entered upon the management of the property. With wonderfully good judgment, a perseverance and a spirit of determination, that quailed not at any obstacle, he succeeded in preserving intact and rehabilitating the large and valuable estate, which to-day stands as a monument to his unwearying industry and tireless energy. Notwithstanding the apparently stern and inflexible will needed to accomplish such results, he is one of the most genial and whole-souled gentlemen to be found in any community. In 1890 he was elected treasurer over an opponent, who had held the office fourteen years, and was regarded as invincible, which speaks volumes for the estimation in which he is held, and the good will entertained toward him by his fellow-citizens. Mr. Tompkins was happily married in 1882 to Miss Viola L., daughter of Matthew and Louisiana (Yates) Monk – a union which has been blessed with four children: John S., Effie Lou, Eliza Baxter, and Florence C. He is an ardent member of the Masonic fraternity, and prominent and influential member of the Methodist church.

Source: *Memoirs of Georgia*, 1895. Volume 1.

Note: Humphrey A. Tompkins' mother was a daughter of William Green Springer.

CHESTER L. TUMLIN

Chester L. Tumlin, of Cuthbert, Ga., was born in Cartersville, Ga., November 25, 1848, and is the son of George W. and Laura (Wade) Tumlin (see sketch of Wm. L. Tumlin for ancestry). He is the youngest of a family of eight children born to his parents, and was reared in Bartow County and received his education at Bowdon College in Carroll County, Ga. When quite young he engaged in the stock business in Bartow County. In 1864 he removed to Cuthbert and carried on the mercantile business until 1871, when he contracted on the railroad for one year. In 1872 he commenced the livery business in Cuthbert and is now recognized as one of Cuthbert;s substantial men. He is also carrying on farming on a large scale.

May 10, 1870, he was married to Miss Mattie McDonald, daughter of Edwin and Eliza H. (Ross) McDonald, of Cuthbert. They have two children: Lilla and Mary.

Source: *Biographical Souvenir of the States of Georgia and Florida*, 1889.

GEORGE S. TUMLIN

Rev. George S. Tumlin was born in Bartow (originally Cass) county, Georgia, December 16th, 1852. His father, George W. Tumlin, was a prosperous farmer on the Etowah river, and a Baptist minister of considerable influence and usefulness. His mother, whose maiden name was Laura J. Terhune, was a daughter of Judge Cornelius D. Terhune, a highly esteemed gentleman, resident in Cass county at the time of his death in 1854. The home of the family was transferred in 1860 to Bowdon, Carroll county, partly for the health of the mother, partly for the advantages offered at that place for the education of the children.

As the only child of his father's second marriage, he was, from the earliest period of his life, the subject of great care on the part of his parents, with regard to both intellectual and moral education. Their efforts were successful, for he always shunned evil associations, never drank, never used tobacco, and from boyhood had a reverence alike for the house of God and for the religion of the Bible. He lost his father at the age of fourteen, and was called to walk "the slippery paths of youth" without his wise counsel. But he was blessed with a well-educated, well-principled mother, whose piety was of the highest type, and who was practical and judicious in business affairs. Many a

fervent prayer did this mother offer for the conversion of her only son, and she was permitted to live until the answer came, rich in blessing beyond the measure of the supplication. She saw him not only brought to Christ, but licensed to preach Him; and then, having finished her work, God took her to Himself.

He graduated in the spring of 1870, at Bowdon College, and in the fall of that year, at the Bryant & Stratton Commercial School, Baltimore. Selecting the legal profession, he completed his course of preparation at the Lumpkin Law School, Athens, and in 1872, at the request of his uncle, Lewis Tumlin, who had been to him as a father, he located in Cartersville. During his first two years at that place, while laying the foundation for a law practice, he utilized his commercial education by keeping books for the City Bank.

The year of his removal to Cartersville was also the year of his conversion and of his baptism by Rev. R. B. Headden, the pastor of the church there. He was married, June, 1874, to Miss Alice Gilreath, of Cartersville. In the early part of 1877, he was appointed Solicitor for the Criminal Court of Bartow county. But that year was to be marked by events of greater moment and of higher dignity. He was licensed to preach in February, and in the fall was ordained to the ministry. During 1878 he served three churches in the county — Kingston, Stegall Station and Rowland Springs — as pastor, with more than ordinary success, fifty-four members having been added to these churches, and their spiritual growth furthered. In September, 1879, though his legal practice was remunerative, he abandoned it, actuated by the conviction that he could do a better work for Zion and her King if his life were devoted entirely to the preaching of the gospel.

By virtue of his training at the bar, his style is argumentative and logical, forcible and earnest. As a pastor, he is much beloved by his people, mingles freely with them, and speaks words of encouragement to the weak, of comfort to the sorrowing, of advice to the erring, and of warning to the stout-hearted. In looks a boy, he is every inch a man; modest and unobtrusive in spirit, gentle and easy in manners, and abounding in love and good works.

Source: *History of the Baptist Denomination in Georgia*, 1881.

GEORGE W. TUMLIN

William Tumlin, a farmer and a "Primitive" Baptist, came from South Carolina and settled in Gwinnett county, Georgia, where his son, George W. Tumlin, was born, April 1st, 1815. While the son was yet a mere boy, the home of the family was changed to Cass (now Bartow) county; and there, at the age of nineteen, he married Miss R. Wade, who became the mother of eight children, including Hon. N. J. Tumlin of Polk county, and W. M. Tumlin of Cuthbert.

He possessed very limited early educational advantages, but these were not suffered to pass without improvement. When called to labor in the vineyard of the Lord, he did not draw back on the plea that he was "slow of speech" and that some one of more thorough culture should be sent in his stead, but took up the cross at once and showed that he was no stranger to the self-development which does a better work without the schools than the schools can do without it. He was ordained to the ministry in 1848, about ten years after his conversion, at Mount Zion church, Cass county, and preached to the close of his life with a zeal and ardor that knew no abatement. As a speaker he was earnest and forcible, having an attractive and commanding manner, which enchained the attention of his hearers. He was a most successful and beloved pastor, and it was his privilege to constitute several churches, to which he rendered liberal pecuniary assistance. A man of energy and excellent business capacity, he accumulated a large estate, the proceeds of which he was always willing to share with the needy. In 1860 he was attracted to Bowdon, Carroll county, as the site of a college and as furnishing admirable facilities for the education of his children. He soon established a Baptist church in that place, where previously there had been only a Methodist church. He preached also to the Carrollton church, and to churches in the country around, up to the time of his death, which occurred suddenly, of heart disease, at his home in Bowdon, July 17th, 1867. He was found with his armor on. In his death the community mourned the loss of a true citizen, the church of a faithful and efficient pastor, the wife of a tender and confiding husband, the children of a kind and devoted father.

His second marriage was to Miss Laura Terhune of Cass county, a woman of rare endowments of head and heart, and a great help to her husband as a co-worker for the Saviour. She lived to see her son, George S. Tumlin, then a small child, licensed as a minister to wear the mantle of his father.

Source: *History of the Baptist Denomination in Georgia,* 1881.

WILLIAM M. TUMLIN

Hon. William M. Tumlin, of Cuthbert, Ga., is a native of Gwinnett County, Ga., and was born November 25, 1836. His father, George W. Tumlin, born in the same county in about 1813, was a farmer and a Baptist minister, and a man very highly esteemed for his many Christian virtues. He died in 1855 in what is now Bartow County. His wife, Laura (Wade) Tumlin, also a native of Gwinnett County, Ga., was born in about 1815, and died in 1846.

Hon. William M. Tumlin, the subject of this sketch, lived in the territory now known as Bartow County when young and received his education from the common schools. In 1861 he joined the Confederate army as second lieutenant of company R, Nineteenth Georgia volunteers, and served with that command until 1862, when he was commissioned to raise a cavalry company, which he did, and was made captain of the company, which joined the First Georgia cavalry as company H (Col. J. J. Morrison commanding regiment). Late in 1865 he moved to Cuthbert and engaged in the mercantile business and farming, and continued the mercantile business until 1875. He has since been farming, trading and buying cotton. In 1868 he was elected to the legislature from Randolph County and served through the reconstruction of the State, and in 1871 was re-elected to the legislature and served in the session of 1871-72. August 13, 1868, he introduced a resolution in the legislature to expel all colored members of the body, and succeeded in getting the resolution passed. In 1858 he was married to Miss Amanda B. Morgan, daughter of Benjamin F. and Minerva (Young) Morgan, of Polk County, Ga. To this marriage were born four children, viz.: William B., George W., Alice F., and Ella. Mr. Tumlin is a Royal Arch Mason and a member of the Baptist Church.

Source: *Biographical Souvenir of the States of Georgia and Florida*, 1889.

W. S. TWEEDELL

Rev. W. S., son of Jeremiah Tweedell, was born in Athens, Georgia, on the 9th of April, 1806. To his mother, who was a Miss Mitchell, and his grandmother, Jane Mitchell, he feels that he is indebted, under God, for his conversion: for they led him to the house of God, and with earnest prayers besought the Lord to make him one of His children. In answer to the prayers of these "holy women," he

W. S. TWEEDELL

was brought to the feet of Jesus an humble penitent in 1826, and in August of that year he was baptized in the Appalachee river. It was not long before he felt it his duty to preach Jesus to the people, but he struggled against his impressions and made strong efforts to suppress them. Grace, however, subdued this rebelliousness; he yielded, and spent a portion of 1827 and 1828 in traveling and preaching in western Georgia, eastern Alabama and western Florida. He married the daughter of William Anderson about that date, and in 1840 moved to Marietta to educate his children and benefit his feeble health.

The Marietta church called for his ordination, which was performed by Revs. D. G. Daniell, James Davis and Henry Collins. He then went through the Cherokee country, at that time in a measure destitute of the Gospel, preaching Christ and organizing churches. The Lord greatly blessed his labors, and not a few, under his ministry, were added to the churches.

In 1860 he left Marietta, moved to Alabama and settled on the Tallapoosa river. Here his services were called for by Providence, Indian Creek, Eden and Bowdon churches. During the war his ministerial labors were so incessant and severe that his health failed. His voice became so feeble that he could not be heard, and he was forced to abandon all pulpit work. Though he could not speak "in the great congregation," his heart was still in his Saviour's work. He acted as superintendent of the Sunday-school at his church, and still manifests a most lively interest in everything that tends to the prosperity of Zion.

He raised and educated five children. His oldest son went to Brazil in 1867 as civil engineer. On his return home he died at Panama, and sleeps in the land of strangers. The other children are living near their parents, and are members of Bowdon church with them.

Never was a man more scrupulously faithful to all his obligations, and no man ever had more entirely the confidence of all who knew him. He is a faithful friend, ever ready to open his hand to the poor and to impart comfort to those in distress.

Source: *History of the Baptist Denomination in Georgia*, 1881.

W. L. WATERS

W. L. Waters, merchant of Alexander City, is a son of John and Mary E. (Russell) Waters, the former of whom was a native of Coweta county, Ga., and when quite a boy came to Alabama with a gentleman named Ballard, who reared him, his parents having died when he was a young boy. John Waters was married in 1860, ten miles south of Alexander City, and had two children:W. L., and Tilla, now the wife of C. C. Evans, a framer of Tallapoosa county. The father of these children served in the Fourteenth Alabama infantry, and served until the surrender, in the army of northern Virginia. W. L. Waters was born March 13, 1861, and lost his father in 1867, whose death was caused by his service in the war. His mother married again to a Mr. Picthford, and is still living. W. L. Waters had a hard time when a boy. He was compelled to work very hard, but with the assistance of his mother he was enabled to secure some little education. At the age of nineteen he moved to Alexander City and accepted a clerkship with Renfrow & Lancaster, and at the expiration of about eighteen months he went to Lexington, Ky., and there took a course of study in the business department of the university of Kentucky. In the fall of 1882, he went into business for himself on a small scale, in Alexander City, and continued on until 1885, when he formed his present partnership with B. F. Russell, under the firm name of Waters & Russell. At first he was in a small building, but after some time he erected a fine two-story stone building, at a cost of about $4,000. The firm keep a general stock, valued at about $12,000. In 1891, they erected a large warehouse, and in connection with that building they deal in mules, horses and fertilizers. In 1883, a young men's ticket was gotten up in order to give the young men representation in the council, and Mr. Waters was elected a member of the council, though only twenty-two years of age. He served one term at that time, and in 1891 he was elected and also in 1892. He was elected by the council, in 1891, city clerk, and still retains that office. He was married at Wilsonville, Shelby county, in 1882, to Lela H. Henderson, daughter of Milton and Matilda Henderson; this family came originally from Georgia, relatives of the family living at the present time in Atlanta. By his marriage to Miss Henderson he had two children, William, died in infancy, and Benjamin, died when seven years old. Politically, Mr. Waters is a democrat. He is a member of the Knights of Pythias and of the Knights of Honor, and is vice dictator of his lodge. He is a member of the Baptist church, and is a very active worker in the Sunday school. He is a member of the Alexander City rifles, organized in 1887, and containing about forty members. He was at first sergeant of his company, and is now quartermaster-sergeant. Mr. Waters has been remarkably successful in his business and is a very popular man.

Source: *Memorial Record of Alabama*, 1893. Volume 2.

Note: John Waters' sister, Eliza, was residing in Carroll County, Georgia in 1850.

WILLIAM M. WHISENHUNT

William M. Whisenhunt was born in Georgia, July 5, 1847, was taken at the age of three to Arkansas by his parents, and in 1860 brought to Texas. His father, Noah Whisenhunt, was born in Tennessee, was a blacksmith by trade, was also a farmer, and while in Arkansas was for six years a justice of the peace. He married Miss Eliza Ballard, daughter of John Ballard, of Georgia. Eleven children were born to this union, named – James M., Adam L., John B., William M., Mary S., Barbara J., Louisa M., Martha F., George W., Thomas J. and Noah L. The father, Noah Whisenhunt, died in Texas in 1871, at the age of fifty-three years.

W. M. Whisenhunt, in 1868, married Minerva J. Batten, daughter of William H. Batten, a native of Tennessee, who moved to Missouri, then lived in Texas, and Arkansas a few years, after which he returned to Missouri, where he is now in the hardware business. While in Arkansas he was judge of Madison county court for a term of years, and was also a justice of the peace. Before the war he was in the dry-goods business in Polk county, Missouri; while in the army he was wounded and remained at home thereafter. To the union of William M. and Minerva Whisenhunt have been born thirteen children – Millege M., Eliza M., Noah H., Alice C., Sanora, Ira F., Eula A., Cleveland M. and Iva M., all of whom are deceased, the living four being –Marshall, Margaret, French and Myrtle.

The year 1869 Mr. Whisenhunt passed in Arkansas and then returned to his farm in Texas, where he still follows the pursuit of agriculture, although he is a natural mechanic and can do blacksmithing, carpentering or bricklaying. During the late war he served in Captain Morris's company, Bolan's regiment. He is a member of the Methodist Episcopal church South, and is highly respected by his neighbors. He is also a fruit and stock raiser, and dealer in both.

WILLIAM M. WHISENHUNT

Source: *Biographical Souvenir of the State of Texas*, 1889.

Note: Noah Whisenhunt and Eliza Ann Ballard were married in Carroll County, Georgia September 13, 1840.

THOMAS PORTER WHITBY

Thomas Porter Whitby, D. D. S., a leading practitioner of dental surgery of the state of Alabama, was born at Fayetteville, Fayette county, Ga., February 24, 1845. His father, Rev. Thomas H. Whitby, was a native of South Carolina, in which state he was reared, educated and married. His wife, E. M. Porter, was born in South Carolina, and died in Georgia in 1856. She was the mother of six children, and after her death, Rev. Mr. Whitby removed to Alabama, where he married, for a second wife, a Mrs. E. M. Gunn, by whom he had one child. While he was a farmer by occupation throughout life, he is also a minister of the Methodist Episcopal church, south. In this church he was well known as an able minister and a devout, pious man. He remained in connection with the Alabama conference of the Methodist Episcopal church, south, until his death, which occurred in October, 1870, when fifty-nine years of age. Dr, Thomas P. Whitby was raised in Auburn, Ala., and was educated in the East Alabama Male college, and was in attendance there when the Civil war came on. In January, 1862, he enlisted as a private soldier in company D, Thirty-seventh Alabama infantry, with which regiment he remained as a private soldier until the end of the war, surrendering with Gen. Joseph E. Johnston, at Greensboro, in 1865. In every skirmish or battle in which his command was engaged, Dr. Whitby participated. He was in the battles of Iuka, Corinth, Hatchet Creek, Vicksburg, in January, 1863; Fort Pemberton, siege of Vicksburg, Lookout Mountain, Missionary Ridge, Dalton, Rocky Face Ridge, the other battles down to Atlanta; and so on down to the last great battle, at Bentonville, N. C. He was three times wounded, but never disabled. After the war Dr. Whitby again attended the East Alabama Male college, at Auburn, for one year, and then began the study of dental surgery under a private preceptor, who was then a practitioner at Auburn. In 1887 he was located at Wetumpka, Elmore county, engaged in the practice of his chosen profession. He remained here until January, 1888, when he located at Selma, Ala., and has since then been located at that place. While at Wetumpka he

THOMAS PORTER WHITBY

acquired the reputation of being a first-class dentist, and became prominent in the state, and became a member of the Alabama state board of dental examiners, of which he is still a member, and is its secretary at the present time. He is a member of the Alabama State Dental association, and has been its president. On February 24, 1870, he married Miss Eliza J. Campbell, of Wetumpka, where she was born and reared, being educated at the Female college at Tuskegee. Dr. and Mrs. Whitby have eight children. Mrs. Whitby is a member of the Presbyterian church, while Dr. Whitby is a member of the Methodist Episcopal church, south. He is a royal arch Mason, has filled the most important offices in his lodge, and is now past master. He is also a member of the Odd Fellows and has passed all the chairs. His practice in dentistry is such that he may be safely considered a leading practitioner. Dr. Whitby sustains the reputation of being a perfect gentleman, a respectable citizen, and a faithful Christian.

Source: *Memorial Record of Alabama*, 1893. Volume 1.

Note: In 1850 Thomas H. Whitby was a Methodist clergyman residing in Carroll County, Georgia. See 1850 Census.

HENRY M. WILLIAMS

Henry M. Williams, physician and surgeon, Bowdon, Carroll Co., Ga., son of John B. and Mary (Strother) Williams, was born in Meriwether county, Ga., Aug. 5, 1834. His great-grandfather was a native of Ireland and came to America about the middle of the last century and settled in Virginia. His grandparents, Samuel and Susan Williams, were born in Virginia, migrated thence to South Carolina, and from there they removed, in 1805, to Georgia and settled in Jones county – moving, as was the fashion and the necessity in those days, in ox-carts. Dr. Williams' father was born in 1800 in Edgefield district, S. C., and came with the family to Georgia in 1805. When growing up he only received six months' schooling, but learned a great deal at home by studying by the light of a pine-knot firelight at night. His lifetime pursuit was that of a farmer, and from choice and necessity he was his own blacksmith, wood-worker, and shoemaker. He removed to and settled in Meriwether county in 1825, where he made himself a good farm and a comfortable home. He was a Primitive Baptist in religion, and in forty years' preaching gained an enviable local reputation. It was his custom on preaching day to carry his shoes in his hand and go bare-footed until he crossed the last branch, when he would wash his feet, put on his shoes, and go to the church and preach. Returning, he would remove his shoes and walk home bare-footed. Dr. Williams' maternal grandfather, John Strother, was a native Georgian. Dr. Williams was reared and attended school at Rocky Mount, in Meriwether county. The school was of the "regulation" order of architecture of the period – log house, dirt floor, split-log seats, stick and mud chimney, and square apertures cut through the sides for windows. In 1858 he began the study of medicine, Dr. M. H. Westbrook being his preceptor, and in 1859 he entered the medical college at Nashville, Tenn., attended one course, and commenced the practice. In 1861 he enlisted in Company F (Capt. I. Curtis), Nineteenth Georgia regiment (Col. W. W. Boyd), Colquitt's brigade. He was in many battles, notably Seven Pines and the seven days' fight around Richmond. At the last-named fight he was wounded on the first day and was off duty for ninety days, but immediately on his recovery he returned to his command and participated in the battles at Bunker Hill and Chancellorsville and was afterward with Gen. Colquitt in Florida in the battle of Olustee, where he was again wounded, this time in the left leg, and disabled for active service. He, however, entered the state militia, with which he remained until the surrender. After that he went to Alabama, where he remained a year, and then came to Bowdon and located and established himself in his profession – under a license. In 1874 he attended a course of lectures at the Georgia Medical college, Augusta, and in 1875 he was graduated from Atlanta Medical college. He has continued in the practice at Bowdon, where he has established a fine reputation and secured a large and remunerative practice. He is the leading physician and the highest medical authority in that locality. Dr. Williams was happily married in 1869 to Miss Cora Hight – born and reared in Carroll county – daughter of William B. and Mary (Tolbert) Hight. Mr. Hight was a pioneer, a farmer, and a leading merchant. This union has been blessed with eight children: Anna, Nora, Paul, Ernest, Ida, Jonnie, Willie and Manzie. Dr. Williams is a royal arch Mason, and himself and wife are members of the Baptist church. Anna, Nora and Ernest are members of the Baptist church.

Source: *Memoirs of Georgia*, 1895. Volume 1.

WILLIAM M. WILLIAMS

William M. Williams, farmer, Buchanan, Haralson Co., Ga., son of Wyatt and Nancy (Wood) Williams, was born in Paulding county, Ga., in 1836. His father was the son of Hezekiah Williams, and was born in Tennessee, came to Georgia after reaching manhood, and was a member of the guard which accompanied the Indians from Georgia. He came to the state a poor man, but before he died – Jan. 15, 1885 – he had acquired an excellent tract of land and a competency. His mother was born in Buncombe county, N. C., and when a child came with her father, Lawrence Wood, to Carroll county, Ga., where she was raised. Husband and wife were members of the Missionary Baptist church. Mr. Williams was raised on the farm, and with no educational advantages. After he was married he attended school for a time and obtained a pretty fair education, on whose foundation he has since built. March 13, 1862, he enlisted under Capt. Alexander Merchanson, Fortieth Georgia regiment, Col. Ab. Johnson, and went to the front. With his command he participated in the battle at Fairsville, Tenn., after which he was taken sick, and never sufficiently recovered to return to the army. During the war all his personal property was destroyed, and his farm left a devastated waste. By untiring application and good management he has improved and added to the value of his property, is regarded as one of the solidest of the county's citizens, and stands as high as any in the estimation of the people. Not being ambitious to hold office, he has never aspired to, or held, any political position. Mr. Williams was married in 1858 to Miss Annie E., daughter of Walton and Sarah (Ellender) Berry. Her parents were from Massachusetts, but came to Georgia and settled in Putnam county, Ga., where she was reared. Three children have blessed this union: Nancy Ellen, Mary Frances, and James B. Mr. Williams' family are members of the Missionary Baptist church.

Source: *Memoirs of Georgia*, 1895. Volume 1.

JASPER J. WILLIAMSON

Jasper J. Williamson, a wealthy and prominent citizen of Carrollton, Carroll Co., Ga., son of Robert and Matilda (Goggens) Williamson, was born in South Carolina in 1838. His grandfather, John Williamson, was born in South Carolina in 1791 and was a soldier in the war of 1812-14. His maternal grandfather, James Goggens, was also a South Carolinian. His father came from South Carolina to Georgia in 1850, bringing all he had in a four-horse wagon and a one-horse cart, laid his claim and settled in Coweta county. In 1854 he removed to Carroll county and settled four miles west of Carrollton. Mr. Williamson was twelve years old when his father came to Georgia, and received such an education as could be imparted by a plain teacher in a dirt-floor log cabin, with openings cut in the logs to let the light in and furnished with puncheon seats. He walked three miles to school and attended only in the intervals between working the crops. After his graduation he taught school himself a while. In 1861 he enlisted in Company K (Capt. J. D. Calhoun), Eighteenth Alabama regiment (Col. Bullock), and was assigned to Gen. Gladden's command. He was in several hard-fought battles, among them Shiloh and Chickamauga, where he was wounded. He was captured at Marietta, Ga., and sent to Camp Douglas, Ill., and held a prisoner until after the surrender. After the war he returned to Alabama, where he lived and farmed for three years, when he moved to Carroll county and conducted his plantation until 1886; then he removed to Carrollton to enjoy his ample income and the social advantages of town life. He has a fine plantation and two large brick business houses in Carrollton. In 1866 Mr. Williamson was married to Miss Julia A., daughter of Louis and Nancy (Brown) Walker, by whom he has had one child – Nancy E. Mrs. Williamson is a member of the Methodist church. Mr. Williamson is a master Mason.

Source: *Memoirs of Georgia*, 1895. Volume 1.

WILLIAM J. WOOD

William J. Wood is a son of Jordan Wood, whose father, a Baptist minister, was by birth a South Carolinian. Early left an orphan he came to Georgia in 1811, and cleared up a small farm in the woods. After a time he sold this and moved to Flat Rock, Ala., where he spent the remainder of his life. His son Jordan was born in Georgia, Monroe county, Nov. 7, 1821; he was reared upon the farm and received a good common school education, after which he taught three or four years. By his own energy and perseverance he made his way in the world and acquired quite a fortune. During the war he was in the state militia, and carried on a blacksmith shop, doing all work without charge. His wife, Miss Emily Clegg, was born in Coweta county, and is of an

WILLIAM J. WOOD

old pioneer family. Their son, William J. Wood, was born in Alabama, in 1854, and reared upon the farm with very limited educational privileges. When he reached manhood his father gave him $125, and with this he engaged in an evaporator; little by little he has accumulated until he is now worth a considerable property. He has one of the best farms in the county, is also engaged in mercantile business in Sharpsburg, and is a stockholder in the Sharpsburg ginnery. He is a member of the Masonic fraternity and one of Coweta's most respected citizens. His wife bore the maiden name of Lovida F. Neeley, is a daughter of D. C. and Amanda (Carpenter) Neeley, and was born in Carroll county, Ga., July 4, 1859. Mr. and Mrs. Wood are both members of the Methodist Episcopal church. Their union has been blessed with nine children: Ola B., born Aug. 13, 1877; Thomas H., born Jan. 21, 1879; Leonard E., born Sept. 27, 1881; Erma May, born March 26, 1883; Robert A., born Dec. 23, 1884; Ina R., born Dec. 30, 1886; William J., Jr., born April 15, 1889; Hubert G., born Feb. 17, 1892; Love, born March 1, 1894.

Source: *Memoirs of Georgia*, 1895. Volume 1.

JOHN H. WORD

John H. Word, merchant, Bowdon, Carroll Co., Ga., son of John Bryson and Amelia (Sparks) Word, was born in Carroll county in 1836. His great-grandfather, Charles Word, was a revolutionary soldier and was killed in the battle of King's Mountain. His grandparents, William and Elizabeth (Bryson) Word were North Carolinians, and he was a soldier in the revolutionary army. His father was born in Surry county, N. C., Jan. 1, 1796, and his mother in Franklin county, Ga., June 15, 1803. He came to Georgia when a young man and settled in Franklin as a school-teacher and taught there for many years, many of the scholars coming as many as seven miles to school. Himself and wife were married July 22, 1819. In 1836 he removed to Carroll county, where he soon rose to considerable prominence and was elected a justice of the inferior court, and for many years was a justice of the peace. On one occasion he married a couple and a short time afterward they called on him to "un-marry" them. For many years he was a deacon of the Baptist church. Mr. Word's mother was a daughter of Elijah and Amelia Sparks, early settlers in the country near Atlanta.

Mr. Word was reared on the farm, which he made his home until he married. He received a good common-school education and taught school a short time. In 1861 he enlisted in Company B (Capt. Charles A. McDaniel), Cobb's legion, and participated in many hard-fought battles – among them Dam No. 1, Yorktown, seven days' fight around Richmond, concluding with Malvern Hill, etc. He went to Maryland, but was too late for the Second Manassas. He was at the battle of South Mountain, Sept. 14, 1862, where he lost his left leg and was taken prisoner. Only four of his company escaped death or wounds. A month elapsed before his leg was amputated; after it was done he took the smallpox, was struck by lightning, and then he had to submit to a second amputation. In 1863 he was elected clerk of the superior court and served two years, and was made a notary public and filled the office six years at Bowdon. In the meantime he began a general merchandise business at Bowdon, and although he had but very small capital he has been eminently successful. He made his first start in business before the war closed, but some Federal troops passed that way, took everything he had and broke him up. In 1884 he was elected to represent the county in the general assembly and served one term. In 1893 he was elected county commissioner of Carroll county and took an active and prominent part in building the new court house. In1866 Mr. Word was married to Miss Virginia, daughter of William and Ann (Stringer) Colquitt, South Carolinian born. Mr. Colquitt was a soldier in the Confederate army during the war, and a part of the time was a guard at the Andersonville prison. When he was married he and his wife began housekeeping with only a frying-pan and two old chairs, but they are better, and more comfortably, if not luxuriously, "fixed" now. Himself and wife are members of the Missionary Baptist church. He ias a liberal contributor to all worthy enterprises.

Source: *Memoirs of Georgia,* 1895. Volume 1.

WILLIAM JASPER WORLEY

William Jasper Worley, ex-editor and farmer, Dahlonega, Lumpkin Co., Ga., son of James H. and Millie (Donelson) Worley, was born in Dahlonega, May 29, 1837. His paternal grandfather, William Worley, of English extraction, was a native of Rockingham county, Va., married a Miss Eaton, and migrated to Georgia and died

WILLIAM JASPER WORLEY

in Cherokee county, where, also, two of his brothers, Thomas and Pleasant, died. Capt. Worley's father was born in Spartanburg, S. C., Sept. 10, 1807, where he received his education and grew to manhood, and in 1828 came to Georgia and settled in what is now Lumpkin county near where Dahlonega stands. He was the first justice of the peace in Dahlonega, was sheriff of Lumpkin county two terms and clerk of the superior court of the county fourteen years. He served a year as first lieutenant of his company in the Seminole war. His maternal grandfather, William Donelson, was of Scotch descent. Capt. Worley's parents raised six children: Martin V.; William Jasper, the subject of this sketch; Columbus W.; Timothy H.; Roxanna E., and James H. He died April 1, 1869, and his wife, born in Pickens district, S. C., Oct. 14, 1812, died Aug. 29, 1880. Capt. Worley grew to manhood in Dahlonega, where he received an academical education, and then engaged in farming, which he followed until the occurrence of the war between the states, when he enlisted as a private in Company D, First Georgia regiment state line. A month later he was promoted to a lieutenancy, and soon afterward commissioned as a captain of the company and served through the war. His regiment was assigned to Stovall's brigade, Stewart's division, Johnston's corps, and was first ordered to Savannah. Afterward it was ordered to Chickamauga, and participated in the battles at Dalton, Resaca, Cass Station, New Hope Church and Kennesaw Mountain, and that of July 22, 1864, and the defense of Atlanta during the siege. His regiment then proceeded to Savannah, via Jonesboro, and during a part of the time on the way he commanded the left wing of the regiment. From Savannah his command was ordered to Augusta, where he was granted a thirty days' furlough to visit his sick wife, during which Gens. Lee and Johnston surrendered. After four years' arduous, faithful service, to which he had given the prime of his manhood, he returned to the peaceful pursuit of agriculture. During his service he had many thrilling experiences. On one occasion when the regiment was waiting in reserve in front of the enemy's trenches, expecting every moment to be ordered into battle, he was sitting on a log when a shell struck the ground in the rear, and passing under the log and coming out in front, upheaved the log and earth and threw him several yards away burying him under a huge mass of earth. He was soon extracted by the soldiers, and about the time he regained his feet Maj. Brown (brother of the late lamented ex-governor) rushed up and asked: "Captain, are you hurt?" "No, I think not," he replied. "Thank the Lord; sit down on this log," said the major. "No, thank you," the captain replied, "I prefer standing; I was sitting on that log when that ugly shell came along hunting for me." In the great battle near Atlanta, July 22, 1864, while his command was advancing on the enemy's works, two color-bearers were shot down in succession causing the soldiers to falter, perceiving which Capt. Worley, following the intrepid example of his illustrious namesake, William Jasper, of revolutionary fame, grasped the flag, and followed by his command, triumphantly planted it on the earthworks of the enemy. One night after a day of hard skirmish fighting, when the company was marching through rain and mud, a voice called out, "Close up, Company D." Col. Galt riding by at the time asked, "Who is in command of Company D?" "Capt. Worley," one of the soldiers replied. "That can't be," said the colonel, I had Capt. Worley buried this afternoon in the rear of my quarters." "There is something wrong about that," said the captain, advancing, "I am glad to say I am still on duty." The colonel rode up to the captain and threw his arms around him, and the two officers wept like children. After the war Capt. Worley moved to Cherokee county, but two years later returned to Dahlonega, and in 1868 was elected clerk of the superior court, and being successively re-elected, held the office eight years. In 1878 he became senior editor of the Dahlonega "Signal" newspaper, continuing for some years, and during this period read law under the preceptorship of Hon. Wier Boyd, of Dahlonega. In 1881 he was admitted to the bar in Lumpkin superior court, Judge J. B. Estes presiding. Later, he was elected justice of the peace, and held the office eight years, when he was appointed notary public and ex-officio justice of the peace. In 1888 he prospected extensively for gold and other mineral products, and became largely interested in mining properties. In 1889 he purchased the Buford (Gwinnett county) "Gazette," and placing his son, Claude H., then only in his fourteenth year in charge of its local department, conducted it as a mining and agricultural journal. This enterprise was suddenly and sadly terminated by the death of his son by a railway accident Aug. 7, 1891, he having been his main reliance in conducting the paper. This event preyed upon Capt. Worley's mind to such an extent that he sold his interest in the paper and returned to Dahlonega. He is a citizen of high character and excellent standing, as may be inferred by his fellow-citizens electing him continuously to office; and as one would say he deserved to be, when it is stated that

WILLIAM JASPER WORLEY

he never drank intoxicating liquors and never played cards. Capt. Worley was married at Blairsville, Union Co., Ga., in 1859, to Miss Georgia Victoria, daughter of Thomas Goodram, by whom he has had seven children: Thomas Jefferson, died Aug. 24, 1862; Mildred Caroline, wife of E. S. Copeland, Nelson, Pickens county, Ga.; James Edward, Atlanta, was manager of the Anniston Lime & Coal Co., of Atlanta; (sometime since he left that company and is now bookkeeper for the Blue Ridge Marble company, at Nelson); William F., timekeeper for the Blue Ridge Marble company, at Nelson, Ga.; Lee Anna, teacher, Dahlonega; Claude Howard, deceased, and Victoria Maude, at home. He is a charter member of the North Georgia Agricultural college, and for seventeen years has been secretary of the board of trustees. He is a royal arch Mason and past high priest, and has been an exemplary member of the Methodist church nearly half a century, his parents being among the members who organized the church in Dahlonega.

Source: *Memoirs of Georgia*, 1895. Volume 2.

Note: Two of William Jasper Worley's brothers, Columbus and Martin, were residents of Carroll County after the Civil War. Columbus is buried in the Carrollton City Cemetery.

W. C. WRIGHT

W. C. Wright, attorney, Newnan, Ga., is a son of B. H. and Emily E. (Tompkins) Wright, and was born in January, 1866. His father is a native of Georgia and quite a prominent planter of that State. He has been State senator from the Carroll County district, and was a member of the convention that seceded.

W. C., after receiving a common school education, read law with Judge L. H. Featherston and W. Y. Atkinson, and was admitted to the bar in September, 1886. He then formed a partnership with P. S. Willcoxon, style of the firm, Willcoxon & Wright, and is in a fair way to build up a large and lucrative practice. He is a member of the Baptist Church, and in politics is a Democrat.

Source: *Biographical Souvenir of the States of Georgia and Florida*, 1889.

Note: B. H. Wright represented Carroll County at the Georgia Secession Convention in 1861.

JAMES W. YATES

Judge James W. Yates. It is now thirty-one years since Mr. Yates first came to Miller County, Ark., and took up his residence, and during this time he has proven a most desirable citizen, as well as an upright and conscientious gentleman. He was born in Spartanburg District, S. C., on March 27, 1839, and is the son of William H. and Sarah (Cooper) Yates, natives also of Spartanburg District; he was born on January 6, 1814, and she on July 6, 1814. Their marriage was consummated in their native State on November 26, 1835, and in 1840 they moved to Campbell County, Ga., where, on the 7th of the following October, the mother passed from life, after bearing four children, two of whom only grew to maturity and are now living: James W. (our subject) and Tabitha E. (unmarried, and living with her brother, James W.). After her death the father married Miss Eleanor D. Smith, of Campbell County, Ga., whose birth occurred in Spartanburg, S. C., on June 27, 1814. Together they came to Arkansas in 1859, and located near where our subject now lives, and here the father resumed his former occupation (farming), in connection with tanning. He was a stanch Democrat, politically, and before the organization of Miller, served as justice of the peace of Lafayette County. While in Georgia he was very successful as a farmer, and was considered one of the leading agriculturalists in his county, and his good fortune followed him to Arkansas, where he was highly esteemed as a prominent and enterprising citizen, as well as an upright and honorable man. His death occurred in Miller County, Ark., on January 6, 1880, and was followed six years later by that of his wife, who passed away on August 19, 1886. For many years he was a deacon in the Missionary Baptist Church, to which denomination he and both his first and second wife belonged, and he always took great interest in church matters, attending as delegate all associations. He never talked much, but acted, and had but few enemies. He was a Royal Arch Mason, and was buried with all the honor and ceremony of that order. The fruits of his last marriage were eight children, of whom four are still living. James W. Yates' school days were spent in Campbell, Carroll and Polk Counties, Ga. At the age of nineteen years he left school, and turned his attention to farming. In 1858 he came to what is now Miller County, and located on a farm now owned by Allen & Smith, and has resided in this neighborhood ever since, with the exception of his term of service in the late war. He is the owner of a well improved farm, two miles south

JAMES W. YATES

of Bright Star, a good portion of which is under cultivation. In 1860 he went to Mississippi, and in April, 1862, enlisted from that State in the Thirty-fifth Mississippi Confederate Infantry, in which he served until the close of the war. His command was at the siege of Vicksburg, and he was once captured and paroled at Yazoo City, and in 1866 returned to his home in Arkansas. While in Mississippi in 1860, he met Miss Mary F. E. Richardson, daughter of Hon. W. R. Richardson, of Winston County, Miss., and on December 13, of the same year, their marriage was consummated. Their married life has been blessed with thirteen children, ten of whom are still living: James T. (a farmer of this township); Sarah E. wife of Joseph A. Stanley, a farmer also of this township), Mattie J., Mary E., Robbins P., Landrun C., Henry Erwin, Virginia F., Nicholas P., and Jasper F., at home, and William H., John C. and Frances E., deceased. The two former died in their sixth and seventh years, and the latter in infancy. Mr. Yates has been a deacon and secretary in the Missionary Baptist Church for eighteen years, and both he and his wife are worthy members of that body. He has been honored by his constituents with several offices of responsibility. In 1889 he served as president of the County Alliance. From 1874 to 1876 he served as justice of the peace, of Sulphur Township, and in the spring of 1888 was elected county and probate judge of Miller County, the duties of which office he is now discharging to the satisfaction of all. He has also served as treasurer and moderator of the Zion Missionary Baptist Association. He is a Council Mason, and in politics, a stanch Democrat. When a young man he learned the shoemaking trade, at which, in connection with saddlery, he worked in Bright Star for some time; but he now devotes his attention exclusively to cultivating his valuable farm.

Source: *Biographical and Historical memoirs of Southern Arkansas,* 1890.

Note: James W. Yates' grandfather, James Yates, was residing in Carroll County, Georgia in 1850 and 1860. See 1850 and 1860 Census. James W. Yates' father and his father's second wife were residents of Carroll County, Georgia in 1850. See 1850 Census.

JAMES YOUNG

James Young, Young's, Polk Co., Ga., son of Augustus and Katharine Young, was born in De Kalb county, Ga., Dec. 22, 1832. His father was a son of Robert and Celia (Strickland) Young, of what is now De Kalb county, a farmer, and was a member of the escort or guard which accompanied the Indians when they were removed from Georgia. Late in life his parents moved to and settled a farm in Polk county. Mr. Young received a very limited education, only such as could be afforded at that time and locality. He enlisted in 1862 in the First Georgia cavalry under Col. James Morrison, but after eight months' service he was discharged. Subsequently he enlisted and was commissioned a lieutenant in Yeiser's legion, state troops, and served to the end of the war. Since the war he has given his time and attention principally to his farm, though for some years at one period he conducted a general merchandise store at Young's. He started in life with some property, which by his superior management he has largely increased, until now he has a magnificent estate. He is regarded as one of the richest men and one of the best financiers in Polk county. He is popular and wields a wide and powerful influence. Mr. Young was married Aug. 3, 1854, to Miss Emiline, daughter of Jesse and Adeline Ammons, of Polk county, a union which has been blessed with six children: Sterling, Ida, Katie, Mollie, Augustus and Lucy.

Source: *Memoirs of Georgia*, 1895. Volume 2.

Note: Kerney Young of Carroll County was James Young's uncle.

M. L. YOUNG

M. L. Young, for a long time a well-known farmer and stock-raiser of Shaw Township, is a native of Georgia, and was born in Carroll County, that State, on June 4, 1833, being the second in a family of four children born to John J. and Jane (McDawell) Young, natives of South Carolina and Georgia. John J. Young was a millwright, and for years was engaged as a contractor, building mills in Georgia and Alabama. For eight years prior to his death, which occurred in 1840, he resided in Calhoun County, Ala., his estimable wife surviving him until 1852. Her death took place in the Choccolocco Valley, Ala. They were both members of the Methodist Episcopal Church. Mrs. Young belonged to an old family of McDawells in Georgia, whose names are very familiar to readers of Georgia history, they having been prominent and influential people. Of the four children born to them only two are now living: J. J. Young, (a farmer in Alabama) and M. L. (the subject of this sketch). He was reared on a farm, and received

M. L. YOUNG

his education in the common schools of Alabama and Georgia, but when quite a young man was thrown upon his own resources by the death of his mother. Beginning work as a farm hand, the first year his salary was $8 per month, the next $16 and the third year $20. He improved every advantage that presented itself for schooling, and the fourth year after his mother's death attended the high-school at Gadsden, Ala. After completing his studies here he again resumed agricultural labor, this time renting land in Gadsden, farming in the summer and working at his trade (carriage making) in the winter. In 1857 Mr. Young was married to Miss Sarah E. Christopher, a daughter of William and Eliza (Hardy) Christopher, natives of North Carolina and Georgia. Mrs. Young was born in Georgia, February 1, 1838. To this union have been given the following children: Frances Ida (born April 11, 1858, and the wife of Leonidas Brumbelow, a farmer of Grant County, Ark.), Genora A. B. (born December 11, 1859, and wife of N. B. Manning, of Saline County), J. C. (born December 4, 1860, married and resides in Saline County), Alter C. (born April 15, 1864, died September 28, 1885, as the wife of James Martin, of Saline County), D. A. M. (born October 15, 1866, and a brakeman on the St. Louis & Iron Mountain Railroad), John R. (born September 26, 1868, a farmer, in Saline County), Joseph L. (born October 24, 1870, died August 21, 1874), Margaret A. (born May 26, 1872, died October 15, 1888), Bessie E. (born April 16, 1874), Susan O. E. (born May 1, 1876) and O. L. (born July 2, 1879). After his marriage Mr. Young lived in Alabama until 1860, when he came to Bradley County, Ark., where he enlisted in Weaver's company, Nineteenth Arkansas Infantry, and remained till the close of the war. He participated in the battles of Shiloh, Corinth and Fort Pillow, and can say, what but very few can, that he was never wounded or taken prisoner during his entire service. After the battle of Corinth he became ill, and was sent home where he remained for one year. He rejoined the army at Shreveport, La., in 1864, and was paroled at the same place in 1865. In 1863 Mr. Young's family moved to Claiborne Parish, La., where Mr. Young joined them after the war. They remained there until 1867, when they moved to Ouachita County, Ark., one year later locating in Saline County. In 1871 he homesteaded eighty acres, and after a short time added eighty acres more, until he owned eighty acres in a fine state of cultivation, the rich soil of which yields excellent crops of cotton, corn, oats and potatoes. Mr. Young's opinion is that a farmer should make his land produce what he lives on, and he certainly does, for his crops have long been the admiration of the surrounding country. He votes with the Democratic party, but is not a political enthusiast. Huey Lodge No. 95, A. F. & A. M., counts him as a member, and he is also a Wheeler. Mr. Young and family are members of the Methodist Episcopal Church, and he lends his hearty support to all enterprises, educational and otherwise. While at Shreveport with the army he was engaged in the engineer department, doing carpenter work, and had charge of the ponton [sic.] and railroad trestle department. He has recently emigrated to the northwest portion of Texas to make it his home.

Source: *Biographical and Historical Memoirs of Pulaski, Jefferson, Lonoke, Faulkner, Grant, Saline, Perry, Garland and Hot Spring Counties, Arkansas,* 1889.

INDEX

Alphabetical Index of Biographical Sketches; Titles in *italics* include an illustration.

INDEX